"Why Won't You Just Tell Us the Answer?"

Teaching Historical Thinking in Grades 7–12

Bruce A. Lesh

Foreword by
Edward L. Ayers

Stenhouse Publishers
Portland, Maine

Stenhouse Publishers
www.stenhouse.com

Library of Congress Cataloging-in-Publication Data
Lesh, Bruce A.
    "Why won't you just tell us the answer?" : teaching historical thinking in grades 7–12 / Bruce A. Lesh ; foreword by Ed Ayres.
        p. cm.
    Reinventing my classroom : making historical thinking reality—Introducing historical thinking : Nat Turner's Rebellion of 1831—Text, subtext, and context : evaluating evidence and exploring President Theodore Roosevelt and the Panama Canal—Using the Rail Strike of 1877 to teach chronological thinking and causality—"Revolution in the air" : Using the Bonus March of 1932 to teach multiple perspectives—Continuity and change over time : Custer's last stand or the Battle of the greasy grass?—Long or short? : using the civil rights movement to teach historical significance—Trying on the shoes of historical actors : using the Truman-MacArthur Debate to teach historical empathy—How am I supposed to do this every day? : historical investigations versus sleep—Overcoming the barrier to change.
    Includes bibliographical references and index.
    ISBN 978-1-57110-812-8 (pbk. : alk. paper)—ISBN 978-1-57110-906-4 (e-book)
    1. United States—History—Study and teaching (Secondary). I. Title.
    E175.8.L48 2011
    973.071—dc22

                                                                        2010050306

Cover design, interior design, and typesetting by Martha Drury

Manufactured in the United States of America
PRINTED ON 30% PCW
    RECYCLED PAPER

17 16 15 14 13 12 11   9 8 7 6 5 4 3 2

For my parents

Contents

Foreword

History is the subject that American students take most often in school and appreciate the least. From the time they cut out turkeys around the shape of their small hands to commemorate the Pilgrims and Indians at Thanksgiving to the time they sweat through Standards of Learning exams, American students are continually exposed to the American past. The teaching of U.S. history is a huge business, with publishers of textbooks vying for the contracts of entire states, and the number of Web sites, videos, and enrichment activities constantly escalates. Despite these investments and innovations, pundits and politicians regularly declare themselves shocked to discover that our kids do not know the basic facts of history. Conflicts about the teaching and interpretation of history routinely erupt on the public stage.

Why is this? Why is a subject that is intrinsically accessible and interesting so problematic? Everyone has his or her favorite culprit, whether it is too great a reliance on textbooks and the dry facts they relate or too little reliance on standardized materials and hard facts. The left blames the right, and vice versa. Caught in the middle are the teachers who must navigate this minefield every day, every class period. Bearing the burdens of building citizenship along with critical thinking skills, of covering the entire span of our ever-lengthening history for ever more detailed tests, teachers of history might despair.

Faced with these challenges, all teachers of history would do well to read Bruce Lesh's book. The product of nearly twenty years of teaching and thinking about teaching, these pages are full of patience, wisdom, and humor. They are also full of determination that history be taught in ways that forever change the students who learn it. Lesh does not himself talk in such dramatic language, for he is refreshingly modest, but it is clear that he is not satisfied if the young people leaving his classroom do not see the world differently as a result of his teaching. Reading the fascinating stories and examples Lesh offers here, it is clear that many students are broadened and deepened and made more curious by their time in his class. All of us who teach history should have the same determination.

Lesh's techniques are built on the lessons of hard experience. He admits that he has tried things that have not worked, that he sometimes has tried too hard to include too much. He admits that fifteen-year-olds are not always focused on the matter at hand. He admits that controlling a class is a requirement for learning, and that standardized tests wait at the end of even the most innovative course of study. The advice he offers, in other words, is the most useful kind: borne of personal success and failure, of small triumphs and the certain knowledge that the class can be taught better next time.

As devoted as he is to the secondary school history classroom, Lesh also draws inspiration from his fellow teachers down the hall, in math and chemistry and English classes. He takes the best that academic historians have to offer without getting bogged down in their debates and details. Lesh has been an important leader at the local, state, and national levels, especially in his work with the National Council for History Education. In that work, where I have seen his passion and skill firsthand, Lesh is a powerful voice for the classroom teacher.

Bruce Lesh believes that students learn history best by discovering its patterns and secrets for themselves. He provides guidance and examples here, sharing useful frameworks and sources. But he also provides the one ingredient that is too often missing in our history classrooms: trust in the individual teacher. He knows that we all bring our own energies, experiences, and hopes to our teaching, and he leaves room for those elements to work. In short, Bruce Lesh has given a wonderful gift to everyone who teaches history.

Edward L. Ayers
President and Professor of History
University of Richmond
Winner of the Bancroft Prize and named National Professor of the Year by the
Carnegie Foundation for the Advancement of Teaching

Acknowledgments

The first book I ever wrote was titled *Paul the Ant and the Invasion from Space*. Not a best seller, it was still my inspiration to write. For that encouragement I have two loving parents to thank. The opportunity to write this book is one that has pushed me intellectually and emotionally, but I would not have even tried had you two not stapled paper together and encouraged me to write about the exploits of Paul and his insect pals. Thanks for all the time, love, guidance, and especially patience over the course of my life.

Sarah Drake Brown, Noralee Franklel, Tina Nelson, John Billingslea, Wendy Schanberger, Brigette Sheckells, and Mike Walsh graciously provided their time and abilities to read and comment on portions of this manuscript. Other colleagues, Catherine Holden, Rex Shepard, Phil Nicolosi, Jim Percoco, Carol Berkin, Mark Stout, Bruce VanSledright, and Fritz Fischer read the entire manuscript. This book would be less effective without their cogent comments, and I am grateful for their time, candor, and support.

I often tell my students that the true measure of a person is how they make those around them better. If that is true, then Carol Berkin's abilities are immeasurable. Her support for K–12 classroom teachers of history has empowered not only me but also numerous others to seek out opportunities to grow professionally. She is one of the few academic historians I have worked with who truly understands the demands that K–12 teachers face, yet manages to bridge the gap between the two worlds and help everyone understand the commonalities between teaching history to high school students and those in college. Her support and encouragement gave me the courage to take bigger and bigger professional risks. Thanks, Carol!

Jim Percoco facilitated my relationship with William Varner and Stenhouse. Jim's dedication to the profession of teaching and the importance of history in a child's education has been inspirational. Without his guidance and matchmaking the ideas found in this book would never have seen the light of day.

In the late 1990s I had the good fortune to help establish the Center for History Education at the University of Maryland, Baltimore County. Twelve years, seven Teaching American History Grants, and hundreds of teacher participants later we are still going strong! My gratitude goes out to Rachel Brubaker, John Jeffries, and Dan Ritschel for seeing the inherent benefits in providing history teachers with high-quality professional development. Many of the ideas within these pages bear the mark of our work together. Thanks for taking the plunge and starting what has been the singular institution in the state of Maryland for growing K–12 history teachers.

Collectively the teachers with whom I have had the pleasure of teaching deserve recognition. The efforts of you dedicated professionals who put countless hours into designing and implementing instruction that inspires students and who teach the lessons well beyond the scope of the curriculum do not go unnoticed. Geri Hastings, Don Everett, Jeff Fischer, Pam Nevel, Ralph Doyle, Bev Hickman, Ted Heun, and Rex Shepard have shared their wisdom with me over the years, and I am eternally grateful to each of you. My department at Franklin High School reminds me every day that teachers do work hard, do make a difference in the lives of students, and in no way embody the negative stereotypes that have become all-too-common descriptors of educators. Thanks so much for being not only fantastic colleagues but good friends as well.

Hundreds of students have passed through my classrooms. Without you this book could never have happened. Your willingness, on most days, to engage with me in an examination of the past has enabled me to test-drive the many ideas found within these pages. You have tolerated my madness, completed the volumes of work assigned, studied, argued, and generally enabled me to present the arguments posited in this book. I hope I broke some stereotypes about history teachers. If not, many of you still broke the stereotypes assigned to students today. A special thanks to Joni Agronin. Your assistance in taking notes during group sessions, transcribing my notes, and reflecting on your experiences in history class were extremely helpful. Thanks, and good luck as you embark on the next phase of your life.

My editor at Stenhouse, Bill Varner, has been gracious with fielding my every question and quelling my worries. His sage advice made this book better than I ever thought it could be.

To my wife, Christine, and my son, Ryan, words truly cannot express my thanks. Your love, support, humor, patience, and tolerance make me a better person. I love you both. This book is for you.

Introduction

In history courses I took in school we read about history, talked about history, and wrote about history; we never actually did history. If I had learned basketball in this way, I would have spent years reading interpretations and viewpoints of great players, watching them play games, and analyzing the results of various techniques and strategies.

—Anecdote from a teacher in Stéphane Lévesque's *Thinking Historically*

Irecall sitting with my father one day when I was a junior in college. It was time for me to decide what to make of my college education. Just like George Constanza of *Seinfeld* fame announced to Jerry, I said to my father, "Well, I like history." "That's nice," he said, "but what are you going to do for a living?"

In my youth, history was not dead; it was all around and incubated my fascination. From trips through the Virginia countryside hearing stories of Stonewall Jackson's Valley Campaign from my grandfather, to my parents' exhaustive genealogical research, to the white Civil Defense helmet in my other grandparents' basement, I was always interested in what had happened before rather than what might happen in the future. Sitting with my father, I figured that the chance to breathe life into the past for young people might be my passion. The conversation ended with me dedicating myself to teaching students about history—a decision I have yet to regret.

After that conversation my first opportunity to return to a high school classroom came as part of an undergraduate winter-semester education course. Making my way through the hallways for the first time as an adult rather than as a student, I considered a recent paper I had written that asked me to describe the traits of my best and worst teachers. What stuck with me while composing that paper was that my best teachers were passionate about their subject matter and sought approaches that directly involved students in examining, discussing, and applying the material. Entering the classroom, assigned to observe a university-selected social studies teacher and record my thoughts about his instructional practices, I hoped to witness instruction that was passionate, engaging, and reminiscent of that which had carried me to teaching.

The teacher initiated the class by turning on the overhead projector and informing students that they should take notes on World War I and that, when they were finished, they could watch CNN's broadcast of the Gulf War. Students copied an outline that laid out the events that precipitated the start of the Great War. Under the outline were several vocabulary words with definitions. Every four to five minutes, the teacher placed a new overhead sheet on the projector. After about twenty minutes of furious copying, students closed their notebooks and the teacher turned the television to CNN's coverage of the war.

Okay, I thought. The Gulf War had just started; maybe this was the instructor's way of connecting a past war to one in the present. Sixty minutes later, the teacher emerged from his office in the back of the room and prepared for his next class, where he proceeded to implement the same "lesson plan." For four straight weeks, instruction was essentially the same:

notes, CNN, an occasional quiz, and, on numerous occasions, structured reading and questions from the textbook. I left my first experience disheartened. I wondered: Is this what teaching history is all about, or could it take another form?

Since those first thought-provoking classroom observations during my junior year in college, I have defined, applied, and refined my methods for teaching history. This book explores the process and results of my attempts to transform my instruction from history as memory to an approach that is based on a melding of historical content with the disciplinary skills more reminiscent of what historians actually do when they practice their craft (Lévesque 2008). It is on the middle ground—between those who claim that fact-laden history courses destroy student interest and those who argue that process has destroyed substantive historical study—that I hope to stake claim for an investigatory approach to developing an understanding about history.

This book captures the journey I undertook to engage my students in a deeper understanding of history as a discipline. My goal was to generate not only what Virginia high school teacher Jim Percoco calls "a passion for the past," but to stimulate my students to develop greater facility with Sam Wineburg's unnatural act of thinking historically (Percoco 1998; Wineburg 2001). Wineburg's research indicates that historians and students approach historical evidence differently, but that when taught, students can understand how to assess evidence and apply that information to the development of a response to a deep historical question. *"Why Won't You Just Tell Us the Answer?"* outlines my arrival at an approach to teaching history in hopes of promoting discussion and prompting classroom teachers to reconsider how they teach the past. Preservice teachers, classroom teachers looking to revise their instructional approach, and policy makers can find within these pages food for thought on teaching and learning history in the classroom.

For a course in history to be a useful and thought-provoking learning experience, it must engage students in the application of evidence to make reasoned arguments about the past. Facts unto themselves are useless, but I hope to illustrate that when evidence is applied to deep historical questions, history becomes something students can "do" while learning the required material. We must temper our love affair with lecture and textbooks and history as a litany of facts and instead complement these traditional tools with what we know about cognition, brain-based instruction, and the growing research base on history education. For students to think of history not simply as memorization, but instead as the construction and evaluation of evidence-based arguments, they must do the following:

- See history as a discipline driven by questions
- Understand the nature of historical evidence and be able to analyze a variety of sources and apply them to historical questions
- Develop and defend evidence-based interpretations of the past

Central to the re-envisioned approach to school history is the idea of the history lab, or historical investigation process. Used synonymously, these experiences find students unleashed on historical sources to generate interpretations of historical questions that frame the organization of the overall course. History does not pivot on the provability of theories. Instead, history is about the debate between competing interpretations of events, individuals, and ideas of the past based on the utilization of historical evidence. So, the investigatory work conducted in the lab-centered history class is exactly that: interrogating historical sources to develop and defend a source-based historical interpretation that responds to a question about the past. What I have discovered, and hope to illuminate, is that students—when taught, reminded, and provided with numerous opportunities to practice—can interrogate historical sources and generate answers to historical questions.

Most of my students go on to college. Some pursue Ivy League educations, others attend state schools or community colleges. A few head to the military or the world of work, and some leave with no direction whatsoever. Few know exactly what it is they are going to do with their lives. This book is not the story of an Advanced Placement, International Baccalaureate, or gifted and talented U.S. history course. Instead, it is about what happened when I attempted to reinvent my approach to teaching history with average to above-average students.

The three high schools in which I have taught were each unique in terms of racial, ethnic, religious, and socioeconomic diversity. Each school had unique personalities, memorable positives, and sleep-depriving challenges. There are no "ideal" teaching situations—only the realities of the one in which you find yourself—so I firmly believe that some degree of the approach outlined in the following pages can be implemented in any teaching situation. Students can learn, utilize, and retain the thinking processes of historians and gain important knowledge of the American and global pasts.

My intention is not to fully undermine the manner in which history has been taught; this is not a case of throwing the baby out with the bathwater. Textbooks, vocabulary, reading, tests, videos, and other trappings of memory-history are still part of my instructional repertoire. There is a place within my proposed framework for the methodologies that have defined our craft for centuries. To help foster discussion and ease the transition to a more investigatory approach, I provide a road map for anyone interested in altering how they promote an understanding about the past to students. By adjusting the definition of historical knowledge to include the cognitive and metacognitive disciplinary skills that historians themselves employ in the investigation and representation of the past, teachers provide students with a deeper, more rigorous learning experience and establish within those students a set of lifelong skills easily transferable to the world of work.

Anecdotal examples from my perspective and the perspective of my students populate each of the investigations highlighted in *"Why Won't You Just Tell Us the Answer?"* The book's goal is to open the door to my classroom and shine light on an approach to reinventing history instruction that has paid great dividends for my own professional growth and my students' interest in studying the past. My approach reflects both a deep reading of the research and the realities of trial and error—a lot of trial and, thankfully, decreasing amounts of error!

The lessons discussed are exemplars of how to generate historical thinking with students. The skills and processes presented can and should be infused throughout the study of the American past. The key historical thinking skills—causality, chronology, multiple perspectives, contingency, empathy, change and continuity over time, influence/significance/impact, contrasting interpretations, intent/motivation, and source work—unify my approach to teaching history. The classroom lessons narrated within the book are connected by their use of these specific thinking skills. By presenting these exemplars, my hope is that teachers will be able to adapt their curricula and approach to teaching history so that they accommodate the needs of their students and the demands of their districts.

I do not teach students to think historically just to do it. Instead, this process generates more enthusiasm, interest, involvement, and retention of the stuff of the past, while simultaneously developing a skill set that will greatly benefit students as they continue their education and enter the workplace of the twenty-first century. I see historical thinking skills as a methodology that can better facilitate students' comprehension of the past. Adding historical thinking to the curriculum deepens students' understanding of specific historical content while simultaneously reinforcing the thinking skills necessary for them to compete in the modern world. Instead of the almost career-deadening experience I conveyed at the outset of this introduction, history education can be engaging and thought-provoking; it can promote a set of transferable thinking skills; and, yes, it can be fun to learn!

CHAPTER 1

Reinventing My Classroom

Making Historical Thinking Reality

I haven't always been the biggest fan of social studies because I'm much more math oriented in my thinking. . . . I liked this year because of all of the discussions! Debating and arguing over controversial topics in our country's history was very exciting.

One thing I liked about the class was when you taught us the material; you left it up to us to decide whether an event was right or wrong; justified or unjustified.

—Former students' observations provided in end-of-course evaluations

Natalie, an eleventh grader, came to my class assuming that history would be taught as it has always been. The "textbook" would serve as the core instrument for delivering the catechism, "lecture" would break up text reading, and she would again "memorize" and then regurgitate the content dictated by the curricula. Her understanding of historical thinking as a methodology was one defined by the consumption of facts that were communicated by an authority—textbook or teacher—and processed in order to replicate an approved narrative about the nation's past. She left my class nine months later stating that she liked the "idea of debating the past . . . and looking at different types of sources to understand the past." Natalie's definition of thinking historically now encompassed notions of evidence, investigation, and interpretation. Her cognitive understanding of the past was now more parallel to the discipline of history than it was to the traditional parameters of historical instruction in the United States. In addition, she actually enjoyed studying the past. Natalie's testimony that history is about evidence and debate, and not—as she had originally envisioned—about authoritative texts delivering a linear narrative, is core to my belief about classroom instruction. But to fully understand the transition of how she understood the study of the past, one must first understand my evolution as a teacher.

Mr. Lesh's History Class 1.0

I still remember my first day as a teacher. I was nervous beyond belief. Was I prepared? Were the students willing? These and numerous other queries flooded my mind. Having concluded graduate school and taken my first teaching position, it was now my turn to unlock the past for my students. Naïvely, I figured that the mental architecture put in place by my formal education would allow me to simply go into the classroom and teach history differently and effectively. As the bell rang on my first day as a teacher in the fall of 1993, reality arrived—in the form of a teenager.

Despite my best efforts, the initial experience teaching history to high school students was frustrating. I love the past and find its study useful for understanding human behavior and current events, and for refining skills that can be used in a number of contexts. In addition, I have always perceived history as a dialogue and debate. What I found in the classroom was that my students generally did not share the same feelings about the utility of the past, nor did they sense a connection between the course and their goals for the future. For my students in 1993, just as for Natalie in 2009, history was an exercise in memorization and something akin to a rite of passage necessary to proceed to the next grade. The order of the presidents, the names of state capitals and treaties—these and other facts constituted the whole of history for my students. "Just tell me what I need to know for the test" was a refrain I heard frequently during my first year of teaching. Considering my own educational experience, it was not hard to see why this was my students' perception.

[handwritten margin note: not an option!]

Fact retention has been the goal of history education since its inception. My observations that winter semester were the partial result of a discipline that measures its effect through student acquisition of a body of information. Traditionally, teachers move students to this end through lecture, questions at the end of textbook sections, movies, true-false assessments, and even crossword puzzles. These methodologies have been the dominant modes of delivering the stories of the past and have not changed in light of the standards movement (van Hover, Hicks, and Irwin 2007; van Hover and Heinecke 2005; Grant 2003).

In addition to dealing with students' preconceived notions of what it means to study history, I confronted my own instincts of what constituted good instruction. When faced with the responsibility for the education of a teenager, most teachers—no matter what they learned in their methods courses or the structure of their student teaching experience—consider how they were taught in the past and then mirror it in their own classrooms. This "apprenticeship of observation phenomenon" occurred with me as well (Grossman 1991; Lortie 1975). I considered my history and social studies teachers from middle and high school as well as the professors I had encountered as an undergraduate and graduate. What worked? What did I like? What didn't I like? Much of this consideration occurred in the midst of trying to survive my first year of teaching—neither the time nor the context for the most thoughtful reflections. Nonetheless, I tried to teach in a manner that communicated that history was an engaging topic for study. I also realized that I needed to change students' perceptions about the past and what it means to learn history.

Looking to Other Subjects for Help

I quickly realized that, if I truly wanted to alter the way my students perceived their study of the past and generate their proficiency at thinking historically, I could not start my course with the first event to be covered in the curriculum. Instead, I needed to teach students how to think historically.

Although some colleagues thought this was simply replacing content with process—and I initially shared their concerns—I decided to gain a broader perspective by considering how other subjects in a student's course load were taught, organized, and approached.

You Mean Not Everyone Gets Math Anxiety?

Doing math is not about having the teacher give students an answer, require them to memorize it, and then regurgitate the answer on an assessment. In math classes, students are taught whole, prime, positive, and negative numbers. Most important (or frustrating, depending on how you felt about math class), they are taught to "show their work." Math is about understanding general principles that guide the behavior of numbers and then applying these principles in a variety of scenarios to generate mathematical solutions to problems. To reach this end, students learn the tools, mind-set, and habits of thinking mathematically so that they can then apply those skills to problems. For example, when teaching students to solve a geometric problem, math teachers introduce the concept, define the theorem, model examples, and then set students loose to apply their skills to solving problems where the variables change. What I learned from exploring math classrooms and picking the brains of my colleagues in the math department was that history as it was currently taught had nothing to do with teaching a set of thinking skills, applying information, or using newly acquired content. Math had a lot to offer my investigation of how to better interest my students in the past.

Weird Science

As a student, I enjoyed science class up to the point that I had to substantiate theories with mathematical proof. Despite my reticence to apply math to science, my explorations into instruction revealed that my colleagues in biology, chemistry, and physics had a number of lessons to offer those of us in the history classroom. In science, teachers outline the scientific method and how to accurately document work in a lab report. Science teachers excel at using demonstration labs to introduce a concept. They also rely heavily on student-run labs so students can draw conclusions about concepts being explored in class. Process and content are well balanced in most effective science classrooms. My colleagues in white coats have more experience with teaching students not only the content of their discipline but also the tools used by chemists, biologists, and physicists.

Sometimes a Tree Is Just a Tree!

At first I was shocked at the dramatic differences I found between history and social studies teachers and our colleagues in English. Then I became intrigued by the parallels between our approaches. Students in English classes learn tone, personification, allegory, onomatopoeia, and a multitude of other literary devices. These techniques are not learned in isolation; they are immediately put to use in analyzing written works. Then students utilize the skills by incorporating them into their own writing. In English, students aggressively question the text, make connections between an author's biography and his or her work, and place novels or short stories within their historical context so that the work can be understood as a product of a particular place and time.

Conclusions

What I discovered from talking with colleagues from other subject areas is that history and social studies are the only disciplines in which students are not explicitly taught the tools necessary to understand how knowledge is created. What history educators do is look for ways to make the content to be memorized relevant, interesting, or fun to learn. This instructional pattern, if employed in the math classroom, would be akin to a math teacher giving students the answer to a question and asking them to simply memorize and recite it. This was exactly what we were trained to do in social studies instruction and is precisely why students are neither engaged with nor remember history (National Center for Education Statistics 2002, 2006; Rosenweig and Thelen 1998; Bracey 1991, 1997; Schick 1991; Whittington 1991; Goodland 1984; Cuban 1982, 1984, 1991; Shaver, Davis, and Helburn 1979; Weiss 1978). My revealing, albeit cursory, examination of the instructional methods used in effective classrooms from other disciplines recharged my belief that history instruction could evolve. Instead of making the study of history's tools, vocabulary, and processes apparent to students, we present our discipline as one whose sole goal is to provide volumes of information. The information I gathered generated questions about whether the dichotomy between content and process was real, where I stood on the debate, and what kind of effect my response would have on my approach to history instruction.

Content Versus Process

Before progressing any further in my journey, it was important to ensure that I was not simply replacing content with process. This dilemma is at the heart of the transition I was trying to engender in my own instruction. Too much process, and you can be the "fun" teacher who has lots of projects, dresses up like historical figures, shows feature-length films, and spends inordinate amounts of time having students make posters, castles, and dioramas. Understanding is sacrificed at the altar of fun. Too much content, on the other hand, can lead to the label of the "boring" teacher who drones on about stuff dead people did that has no relevance. The lists of facts, dates, and endless questions at the end of a textbook chapter quickly replace the fun of process with the litany of content. In history this can be a particularly deadly conundrum because of the simple fact that you cannot teach it all and thus must make hard decisions about what content to leave out of a course. Often teachers and curriculum writers leave process on the cutting-room floor so that they can squeeze in one more unit, or give more attention to the history of technology or to the contributions of various ethnic groups.

The discipline of history is especially prone to the false dichotomy between content and process because much of the content covered is tied to the heritage of the American experience. Holidays, wars, heroes, villains, accomplishments, and the overcoming of national failures often populate the progressive narrative that has dominated the telling of American history (Lowenthal 1996; VanSledright 2011). The movement to state standards has simply exacerbated this phenomenon. States, pressured by the false crisis raised by the 1983 report from the National Commission on Excellence in Education called *A Nation at Risk*, have spent millions of dollars designing standards documents that define the study of the past as a collection of names, dates, and facts. Standards documents are subject to review and criticism by numerous political groups to ensure that the "correct" names and events are present. The result has been a series of documents that are a mile wide and an inch deep and do not promote effective instruction in history. They simply reinforce the same techniques that have generated a hundred years of dismal scores in knowledge of the past.

Assessing my own personal beliefs about the false division between content and process, I quickly realized that content is important, but not as an end in itself. Knowledge that is not used, and used frequently, is lost. Just providing reams of information is pointless. There needs to be a use for that content. I was particularly struck by the words of Stephen J. Thornton who argues that "a common barrier to the improvement of method seems to be the suspicion that attention to process comes at the expense of significant content and vice versa. To the contrary, the most effective learning of content stems from engaging methods" (2005, 82). How to strike the balance between content and process was the problem.

What stuck with me was a course I took in computer programming when I was a high school senior. (Okay, it's time to date myself: the course was in Basic on an Apple Classic!) The content I learned had an immediate application. Learn to write a certain type of program, and then you can apply it. Science was similar. Learn a concept, test it in the lab. What I wanted was for my history students to have the content but also a venue in which they could then apply and use the information. Phil Nicolosi and Mike Walsh at West Morris High School in New Jersey have titled this approach a "history laboratory." This model envisions students engaging in the same types of thought processes in history as they do in a laboratory science course. In the history lab, students would confront information (conduct experiments), draw conclusions (analyze data), and defend their hypothesis (do lab write-ups). This model has been called a historical investigation, or history lab, and structures much of what I do in the classroom.

Skills

Thus, the challenge was set. My job was to design and implement a course that struck a balance between the historical content and the skills particular to the investigation of the past (and still grade papers, coach football, serve on committees, pay attention to my family, and get home before sunset).

Has Anyone Else Asked These Questions Before?

Teaching is often correctly referred to as a profession executed on an island. Teachers, sequestered in their classrooms or learning cottages (trailers), often lose sight of the successes and challenges their colleagues face. In addition, the island of teaching can remove teachers from the academic world where issues are being researched and written about and new content is being developed. Frustrated by this isolation and desirous of finding new ways to reach my students, I took the summer after my second year of teaching to search out and read any academic literature that might be available on teaching history. Despite having a BA and an MA in history, I was never exposed to the research on history education that was initiated in mid-1970s England. I was quite surprised to find how much had been written, how relevant it was to my classroom experiences, and how applicable it was to my instructional program.

The research on history education revolves around two major issues: 1) how historians create and represent the knowledge that comes to be known as history, and 2) whether students can replicate these procedures in the classroom. In a nutshell, the answer to the second question generated by the research seems to be a hedged yes. Students can be taught to think historically. How to teach students to embrace this way of thinking lies at the intersection of questions, evidence, and interpretation.

Historians Ask Questions

When people discover that I teach history for a living, they generally respond in one of two ways. The most common reaction is to say something along the lines of "I never liked history—too many names and dates." The alternative response is something like "In what state was General Lee born?" Trivia—whether they're distracted by it or obsessing over a discrete chunk—is what most people seem to associate with the study of history. Of course, one can hardly blame people—the constancy of testing nuggets of historical information and the subsequent turnoff generated by history classes is well documented. Interpreting these responses has led me to realize that I am being overtly warned by former consumers of K–12 history about what not to do when teaching the past. If history, my questioners seem to argue, is nothing more than preparation for a game of Trivial Pursuit, then they, and I, are not interested. History is about posing questions that drive the study of the past and then using information to answer those questions. Key to the enterprise are the queries.

The proposition that history is about questions often generates the refrain, "How can students think critically until they know something to think about?" If this were the case, then no one could ever think critically until they reached the upper levels of graduate school. The refrain is an excuse. "The notion that students must be given facts and then at some distant time in the future they will 'think about them,'" argued University of California at Berkeley historian Charles Sellers, "is both a cover-up and a perversion of pedagogy. . . . One does not collect facts he does not need, hang onto them, and them stumble across some propitious moment to use them. One is first perplexed by a problem and then makes use of facts to achieve a solution" (1969, 511). Investigating the past by considering a series of historical questions alters the traditional role of the history teacher, but ultimately it does not reduce his or her importance. In fact, it actually elevates the teacher's importance, because students need to understand the context of the time they are exploring and to gain familiarity and—ultimately—mastery of the skills necessary to think historically. The teacher has an essential role in providing context and guiding students from being novices to being masters in the art of thinking historically.

By organizing student learning around questions, the overall history classroom experience can be more engaging. The best instruction focuses on "essential questions" that are deliberately formulated and thought-provoking (Wiggins and McTighe 2005). The centrality of questions to both teaching and learning history allows "teachers [to] introduce a sense of mystery into the most ordinary and standard lessons by raising thought-provoking questions, ones that demand answers supported by reasons, by evidence" (Gerwin and Zevin 2003, 8). From the perspective of students, it is not learning the litany of information about any subject that inspires interest. It is instead the utilization of information to address complicated and thought-provoking questions (Branson 1971; Sipress 2008; Linden 1972).

To frame successful classroom investigations of the past, the questions must be worth discussing, not have a simple or single answer, and be linked to significant historical evidence (Bain and Mirel 1982; Sipress 2008; Levstik and Barton 2001). Questions, not a list of answers or content-based state standards documents, drive engaging instruction and draw students into exploring the past. Thus, questions are central to the job of historians, and it is therefore logical that they also serve as the central focus of history instruction.

This conclusion raises the next issue: What constitutes a question that effectively promotes student interest in a historical subject and provides the scaffolding for an approach that incorporates consistent historical thinking?

Formulating and Articulating Questions

If questions are important to historical inquiry, where do classroom teachers find significant questions to guide their instruction? In seeking the key questions, I approached a number of documents and realized that the best ones were those that drove the discipline of history (Lattimer 2008).

Discipline-Specific Questions

The National Standards for History, published in 1996, contain a useful source of discipline-centered questions. Organized under the title of "Historical Thinking Skills," the standards present what historians engaged in the creation of the document believe best represents the thought processes that define the study of history. Arranged in a relative hierarchy from least to most complex, the Historical Thinking Skills (Figure 1.1) represent the types of questions historians ask. These skills parallel much of what can happen in a history classroom.

My exposure to these skills brought light to the process that was implicit in my training as an undergraduate and graduate student but was infrequently made explicit. I realized that classroom discussions about the causes of the Civil War contained the thought processes surrounding multiple causality. Within classroom analysis of sources related to the American Revolution lie the skills of historical perspectives. The Standards in Historical Thinking laid bare what actually made history into a set of skills, not a discipline defined solely by memorization. Concomitant with this discovery was the challenge of how to narrow this extensive list so that it was suited to students. The list needed to be one that students could acquire, practice, and incorporate into the mental framework they used when studying the past. Part of this narrowing required me to determine what from the list best lent itself to the curriculum I teach, the developmental needs of my students, the time I had to dedicate to their study, and, most important, the issues I could actually feel comfortable with in the classroom.

In *Thinking Like a Historian: Rethinking History Instruction*, Nikki Mandell and Bobbie Malone (2007) narrow the disciplinary questions found in the Voluntary National History Standards to five "Historical Categories of Inquiry." By having students organize their focus questions around "cause and effect, change and continuity, turning points, using the past, and through their eyes," Mandell and Malone argue that students' approach to studying the past can be "spiraled and sequenced throughout the curriculum" and build a common language to structure students' examination of the past (2007, 16). This common language enables them to approach the study of history with a purpose other than simply memorizing the requisite names and dates.

Historical questions that center on the thinking skills laid out in the Historical Analysis and Interpretation section of the National Standards are most applicable not only to the curriculum I teach but also to almost all U.S. and world history courses. Questions about causality, multiple perspectives, historical contingency, empathy, change and continuity over time, influence/significance/impact, contrasting interpretations of the past, and intent/motivation occupy the research and writing of historians and are easily mined for historical investigation with students. They are a fabulous location from which to begin historical inquiry in the classroom, and I have used them to structure the approach outlined in the chapters that follow.

Figure 1.1 Historical Thinking Skills—National Standards for History

Chronological Thinking

- Distinguish between past, present, and future time.
- Identify the temporal structure of a historical narrative or story.
- Establish temporal order in constructing historical narratives of their own.
- Measure and calculate calendar time.
- Interpret data presented in time lines.
- Reconstruct patterns of historical succession and duration.
- Compare alternative models for periodization.

Historical Comprehension

- Reconstruct the literal meaning of a historical passage.
- Identify the central question(s) the historical narrative addresses.
- Read historical narratives imaginatively.
- Evidence historical perspectives.
- Draw upon data in historical maps.
- Use visual and mathematical data presented in charts, tables, pie and bar graphs, flow charts, Venn diagrams, and other graphic organizers.
- Draw upon visual, literary, and musical sources.

Historical Analysis and Interpretation

- Identify the author or source of the historical document or narrative.
- Compare and contrast differing sets of ideas, values, personalities, behaviors, and institutions.
- Differentiate between historical facts and historical interpretations.
- Consider multiple perspectives.
- Analyze cause-and-effect relationships and multiple causation, including the importance of the individual, the influence of ideas, and the role of chance.
- Challenge arguments of historical inevitability.
- Compare competing historical narratives.
- Hold interpretations of history as tentative.
- Evaluate major debates among historians.
- Hypothesize the influence of the past.

Historical Research Capabilities

- Formulate historical questions.
- Obtain historical data.
- Interrogate historical data.
- Identify the gaps in the available records, marshal contextual knowledge and perspectives of the time and place, and construct a sound historical interpretation.

Source: National Center for History in the Schools (1996).

Unto themselves, these disciplinary questions are not enough to generate student interest, generate the dissonance to promote cognitive change, or immerse students in the content that they are studying and upon which they will be assessed. Instead, they serve as the organizing concepts by which students investigate questions posed about past events, actors, or ideas. To be effective, disciplinary questions such as those about change

and continuity over time or causality must be married to content that facilitates their investigation. Here again, content and process are married.
Examining a question about why an event or person is historically significant
is pointless without deep historical content to undergird the investigation.

What then is the structure of effective questions that generate authen-
tic classroom instruction focused on the learning, application, and measurement of not only historical content but also historical thinking skills?
Here are seven criteria for effective questions to guide historical inquiry:

- Does the question represent an important issue to historical and
  contemporary times?
- Is the question debatable?
- Does the question represent a reasonable amount of content?
- Will the question hold the sustained interest of middle or high
  school students?
- Is the question appropriate given the materials available?
- Is the question challenging for the students you are teaching?
- What organizing historical concepts will be emphasized? (Change
  over time, continuity, causality, context, or contingency?)

By developing focused questions, teachers place their students in a position
to be successful in interrogating the residue of the past to develop an evidence-based response to the query (Caron 2005).

Since questions—rather than answers—drive instruction, how then
does classroom instruction in history reflect this change? The body of
research on history education indicates that to achieve this instructional
approach, history teachers should emulate their peers in other disciplines
by engaging students in an investigatory process to determine the answers
to questions about the past. To reach this goal, students must apply a range
of thinking skills to the analysis of historical sources.

Historians Gather a Variety of Sources and Ask Questions of Those Sources

In a memorable *Saturday Night Live* sketch, comedian Jerry Seinfeld paro-
dies the teaching of a high school history class. Faced with students played
by Adam Sandler, David Spade, and Chris Farley, teacher Seinfeld asks
students to "think history." He then proceeds to ask a series of recall ques-

tions about World War II. Frustrated with his students' one-word, pedantic answers (and their foremost desire to know whether the content will appear on the test) Seinfeld throws in the towel and asks his students to sit quietly. This comedic image reminds us that most history teachers conflate historical thinking with the knowledge of discrete facts about the past. Despite the teacher's encouragement to "think history," what Seinfeld wanted was simple recall of facts to support the argument he was making about the arsenal of democracy. This is not what historians do. Instead, "in the initial investigative phases of their work," Bruce VanSledright reminds us, historians "occupy themselves with reading and digesting the residues of the past left behind by our ancestors. Much of this residue remains in the form of documents or sources. Source work then," he argues, "becomes the staple in the investigative lives of these experts" (2004, 230). This source work is done to generate tenable interpretations to questions about events, personalities, and ideas about the past.

The next step in the transition of the history classroom is to develop within students an awareness of variety and pitfalls of historical sources. In addition, students must develop and refine the skills necessary to interrogate these sources and use the information to address historical questions. Had the Seinfeld sketch desired to teach in addition to mock, it would have had students examining a series of sources to determine what they thought were the causes of World War II instead of simply generating responses to their teacher's questions.

Facilitating the use of historical sources in the classroom has been an ongoing process for me. In order for students to effectively and consistently replicate the questions and mind-sets that historians employ when examining sources, they need some sort of tool to evaluate historical evidence. The tool I use calls on students to ask three questions of any historical source they use (see Figure 1.2). By analyzing the text, context, and subtext of any source, students can quickly engage in a truncated version of the source work that occupies much of historians' time.

Empowering students to dissect historical sources with a cognitive tool leads to greater levels of literacy and promotes a consistency of approach. My students attack all historical sources by analyzing the text, placing each source in its historical context, and drawing conclusions about how the authorship, audience, and intention of the source's creator affect the information provided by the source. Aggregating the information derived from historical sources, students can then compare, contrast, and apply it to the discussion of the investigatory question. Armed with information from a variety of historical sources, they can engage in historical interpretation.

Figure 1.2 Learning to Think Historically: A Tool for Attacking Historical Sources

> **Text**
> - What is visible/readable, i.e., what information is provided by the source?
>
> **Context**
> - What was going on during the time period? What background information do you have that helps explain the information found in the source?
>
> **Subtext**
> - What is between the lines? Ask questions about the following:
>   - Author: Who created the source, and what do we know about that person?
>   - Audience: For whom was the source created?
>   - Reason: Why was this source produced when it was?

Historians Develop, Defend, and Revise Interpretations

History is always debatable, which my family has learned the hard way. After my grandfather passed away in the mid-1990s, we learned that he had actually never graduated from college. Instead, he left campus three credits short of his diploma. The culprit was the Civil War. In his last semester, as my grandmother remembers it, he took a course on the Civil War taught by a professor from Alabama. His final paper examined the causes of the war. Raised in Scranton, Pennsylvania, my grandfather made an argument focused much more on Southern culpability than his Southern-born-and-bred professor could endure. The professor failed my grandfather, who could not afford to return for another semester because his football scholarship had expired. He left college three credits short of his degree. Although now part of the family legend, this incident is instructive for the classroom. What my grandfather's professor wanted was an interpretation of the past; unfortunately for my grandfather, this professor supported only one "correct" interpretation.

History, however, is never about one right answer. Yes, generally the facts (who, what, when, where) are not debatable, but questions of why and how, and the effect of choices, are perpetually open to reinterpretation as new documents and fresh questions are applied to the past. History is much more complicated and challenging than simply memorizing facts. This can be frightening to some, according to Linda Levstik and Keith Barton:

> *Sometimes people characterize alternatives to traditional approaches to history as throwing open the gates to the barbarians. They fear that where there are multiple "right" answers there are no "wrong" ones, that history becomes a complete fiction or simply chronological arrangement of ungrounded opinions arrived at by group consensus . . . historical thinking is fundamentally about judgment—about building and evaluating warranted or grounded interpretations. History, then, is not just opinion: It is interpretation grounded in evidence.* (2001, 191)

But history is alive; its interpretations change, emphasis is altered from political to social to economic perspectives, new sources are discovered, and old sources are read with different eyes. All this equates to a dynamic field defined by debate and interpretation of historical evidence (Husbands 1996).

Thus, to fully promote a study of the past, students must be taught and provided the occasions to engage in the development, defense, and revision of evidence-based historical interpretations. It is only with the happy marriage of content and process that teachers can fully engage students in a comprehensive study of the past.

"I Know You Think That, but Where in the Evidence Can You Find Support for Your Theory?"

For a course in history to be a useful and thought-provoking learning experience, it must engage students in the application of evidence to make reasoned arguments about the past (Spoehr and Spoehr 1994). The quote in the heading is one I have uttered countless times over the past decade. For students to think of history not simply as memorization but instead as the construction and evaluation of evidence-based arguments, they must see it as a discipline driven by questions, understand the nature of historical evidence and be able to analyze a variety of sources and apply them to historical questions, and develop and defend evidence-based interpretations of the past.

To meet these ends I have adopted and modified the concept of a historical investigation based on the work of Bruce VanSledright, the California

History Project, Elizabeth Yeager, and Stuart Foster, and reflective of the work of Keith Barton, Bob Bain, Linda Levstik, Peter Sexias, Sam Wineburg, and other researchers in history education. This model, when implemented in the classroom, facilitates a change in how students and teachers can approach the teaching and learning of the past. Instead of seeing the discipline as driven by the memorization of facts, it allows students to approach the discipline as its practitioners do: facts become important as they are applied to a historical question. The model in Figure 1.3 promotes the active investigation of the past in a manner parallel to that employed by historians.

Central to the envisioned approach to school history is the history lab or historical investigation process. These experiences unleash students on historical sources to generate interpretations of historical questions that frame the organization of the overall course. History does not pivot on the provability of theories. Instead, history is about the debate between competing interpretations of events, individuals, and ideas of the past based on the utilization of historical evidence. The investigatory work conducted in the lab-centered history class is exactly that: interrogating historical sources to develop and defend a source-based historical interpretation that responds to a question about the past.

Armed with the research and a series of useful tools for students, and buoyed by my own optimism (or naïveté), I felt more confident that I could revise the structure of my history courses. Upon initiating these changes, one final issue arose for consideration: textbooks.

"We Spend a Lot of Money on Textbooks!"

In education circles textbooks are often presented as the origin of all that is wrong with history education. From promoting the lies told by our former teachers to generating a tangible form of political correctness, textbooks bear the burden of promoting stereotypes, denying full representation of various minority groups, and promoting a progressive narrative about the American story (Baxter, Ferrell, and Wiltz 1965; Shaver, Davis, and Helburn 1979; FitzGerald 1980; Hertzberg 1985; Loewen 1995, 2009; Moreau 2003). Although all of these criticisms are accurate, they are not what bother me the most about textbooks. My issue with textbooks is that their use in the classroom limits the ability of the teacher to approach history in a manner parallel with historians.

Any source used to investigate the past, be it a diary, cartoons, textbooks, historical lectures, or a PBS documentary, possesses an overt or

Figure 1.3 Conducting a Historical Investigation

I. Establish a focus question to guide students' investigation.

- Question should be provocative and encourage investigation and discussion.
- Question should be central to the curriculum needs of the teacher.
- Question should help deepen students' understanding of history as an interpretive discipline.
- Focus questions should emphasize disciplinary concepts such as the following:
  - Causality
  - Chronology
  - Multiple perspectives
  - Contingency
  - Empathy
  - Change and continuity over time
  - Influence/significance/effect
  - Contrasting interpretations
  - Intent/motivation

II. Initiate the investigation.

- Access prior knowledge by reading from a narrative, poem, or journal entry, or by examining a map, broadside, political cartoon, or other historical source.
- Hook students' attention and set the context for the event or person being investigated.

III. Conduct the investigation.

Teacher: Collect relevant and conflicting historical sources that allow students to investigate all aspects of the event or person being investigated. Be sure to identify relevant vocabulary and edit for readability.

- Analyze one document individually. Instruct students to take notes on the information they can glean from their source in addition to determining the "who, what, when, where, and why" information they extract from it.
- Determine the answers about context and subtext and how these answers affect the central question.
- Group individual students so that all documents are represented in a group, and have them generate an interpretation of the documents based on the focus question.
  1. As students share their interpretations, they must cite information from documents as evidence.
  2. Multiple interpretations can emerge and may or may not be accepted by everyone, but that is okay at this point.

IV. Report interpretations and class discussion.

- Share group interpretations and discuss the sources that most influenced their decisions and why.
- Discuss the various interpretations presented, looking for commonalities and differences.

V. Debrief student investigations.

- Have a teacher-driven discussion of the event or person being investigated. The teacher should solidify the basic historical facts and clarify the reasons for varying interpretations.

IV. Assess student comprehension of the content of the past and historical thinking.

- Assess students' understanding of the historical content and the process used by historians.

Adapted and modified from Bruce VanSledright (2002), Stuart J. Foster (2001), and the University of California, Davis, History Project (2006).

covert perspective. To isolate textbooks as the sole bearer of a bias is to simply ignore the panoply of sources used to tell the story of the past.

During my first year as a classroom teacher I decided to simply place the textbook off to the side and teach without it. My decision to set aside this expensive and comprehensive device generated two major issues. First, the lack of textbook-driven instruction both intrigued and confused my students. By and large, most of my eleventh graders were trained to see the textbook as the tool by which they gained an understanding of the past. In-class readings, examinations of supplementary materials that complemented the text, and answering the textbook questions had served as the basis for much of their historical instruction. Removing the textbook was liberating to some students. The sheer instructional variety inspired by the absence of it as a resource generated an increase in students' interest in the course and its content. By the same token, the absence of an old friend made many students unsure of what they were to do. Students in this category would often say, "Can't we just read the book?" The idea of needing to investigate a variety of sources frustrated them because it meant more intellectual work than that inspired by the reading of the text. For students reading below grade level, second language learners, and those with documented educational deficits, the loss of the textbook as a key pedagogical tool was serious.

The second response to my decision to forgo intensive classroom use of the textbook came from school- and system-based decision makers. I was quickly reminded that principals, superintendents, and school boards spend millions of dollars to secure textbooks for students and teachers. As I have discovered from meeting and working with teachers across the nation, the pressure to use textbooks is intense. Educators who have core texts are pressured to make use of them because of the costs incurred by their purchase, whereas teachers who do not have a core text campaign loudly to receive an ample number of books. Textbook producers reinforce the relationship between history instruction and core texts by ensuring that their books and the multitude of supplementary materials that accompany them are consistent with the content objectives that structure the state's assessment and accountability programs. Setting the textbook aside could have placed me in direct conflict with the instructional approach delineated by my district.

My ultimate decision has been to use the textbook as a tool for home learning and as one of several sources that informs the process of thinking historically. Pragmatically, this means I have the luxury of being able to assign my students a take-home textbook that remains at home. In addition, it requires them to be responsible for keeping track of their reading. This is not the norm, and in many districts is nearly impossible to pull off. Yet, as I have learned from traveling the country and working with numerous teachers, many educators know how to adapt, be flexible, and make do with the supplies they are provided. Even if the textbook must remain central to the classroom experience because of district demands or supervisory preference, it is not an insurmountable limitation to the idea of historical thinking. Textbooks can be used to spur the investigation of a key historical question or to provide context before an investigation (Bain 2006; Martin and Monte-Sano 2008; Martin 2008; Schur 2007; Mayer 1999). Whatever decisions teachers ultimately make about the relationship of the textbook to historical investigations and historical thinking, the two are not diametrically opposed. Treat the textbook as just another piece of historical evidence and move on.

Mr. Lesh's History Class 2.0

"What I don't understand," argued Terrell, "is why you think Frick [Henry Clay Frick of Carnegie Steel] is responsible. The only evidence pointing to his guilt is the statement by Carnegie [Andrew Carnegie] that it was Frick's responsibility and songs sung by the workers. The songs obviously are going to reflect what the workers knew at the time and not the full picture." Within Terrell's argument exist the by-products of a course focused on having students interrogate historical sources and apply the information derived to a question of historical significance. Terrell's discussion of historical sources occurred as he and his classmates were evaluating a speech given by Andrew Carnegie in which he placed the responsibility for the events of the Homestead Strike squarely on the shoulders of his assistant Henry Clay Frick. Just as Natalie at the outset of this chapter mentioned that the "idea of debating the past . . . and looking at different types of sources to understand the past" had become central to her understanding of history, the same mechanisms also infected Terrell's mind.

The creation of an instructional program capable of facilitating the changes in Natalie and Terrell's cognitive understanding of history as a discipline cannot be done overnight. But, with the exemplar lessons I share in the next seven chapters, I intend to outline how history educators can grow their students' abilities to think historically. It is through Nat Turner that I begin to cover the conceptual bones of historical investigations with the clothes of historical content.

Introducing Historical Thinking

Nat Turner's Rebellion of 1831

So what is the answer?

—Student question during lesson on Nat Turner

In August 1831, Nat Turner, an enslaved man in Southampton, Virginia, led a brutal rebellion against his owner and more than fifty other whites in the area. Professing a series of visions he interpreted as God's will, Turner organized and executed the largest slave rebellion in United States history. Eventually tried, hanged, and skinned, Turner became a catalyst for changes within the American system of slavery. Emancipation, a newly broached topic in the Virginia legislature, was summarily dropped as fears about rebellion trumped potential humanitarian concerns. Abolition, just beginning to move into the broader public consciousness with the publication of William Lloyd Garrison's antislavery newspaper *Liberator*, gained greater attention from both those in support of and in opposition to its message. Turner's attempted but ultimately failed rebellion frightened many Americans. For many the specter of Haiti, site of the 1791 rebellion that resulted in former slaves controlling the nation that previously considered them property, became all too real in light of Turner's rebellion.

Nat Turner revolted against the institution that had sold him three times and left him legally owned by a ten-year-old boy. Fervent in his faith, persuasive among his peers, and a martyr to the cause of freedom, Turner and his actions elicit deep debate about the role of faith in history and the efficacy of violence as a tool for social, political, or economic change. Turner is fertile ground for planting new ideas in students' minds about history (Baker 1998; Greenberg 2003; French 2004). In Nat Turner and his actions on that August day in 1831, I found my inspiration for motivating students to alter their perceptions about history. The Southampton slave revolt and its leader are ripe for generating student learning about thinking historically and serve as the focal point of the lesson I teach on the third and fourth days of school.

My goal in this chapter is to formalize, through discussion of the design, implementation, and evaluation of this lesson in my classroom, the skills necessary to shift the focus of history instruction away from simply memory and toward engaging the past in a manner more consistent with that of historians.

Why Nat Turner?

Nat Turner is an intriguing figure in American history. Partially, my attentiveness stems from the fact that Turner—like many other nontraditional characters—did not exist in the American story I was told in school. The bravery of Alice Paul in the jails outside of Washington, D.C., the determination of Walter W. Waters and the Bonus Marchers of 1932, the diligence of Eugene Debs, the audacity of Phyllis Schlafly, and the nobility of Chief Joseph, as well as the courage of Nat Turner, did not populate the history of my youth. Although the traditional diplomatic, political, and military historical narrative conveyed in my precollegiate education was filled with fascinating characters and important events, it did not fully represent the panoply of issues generated by the efforts of enslaved people, immigrants, women, and other aspects of the social history to which I was introduced as an undergraduate.

In addition, again unlike many of the events and personalities that populated the school history of my youth, Turner was not victorious. Skinned, dismembered, and vilified by many, Turner allows students to see that much about the American story can be learned not just from those who were on the winning side, but those who were considered criminals, dissidents, and troublemakers. Within the traditional triumphant progressive narrative that still dominates most school districts' United States history curricula, I always try to look for alternative ways to approach key events in the American past so that those outside the traditional narrative can find a home. Nat Turner fits that bill perfectly.

It was not until I encountered Stephen Oates's *Fires of Jubilee* in a used-book store that I was introduced to Turner's Southampton, Virginia, rebellion as more than a three-sentence paragraph in a textbook. Several years later, while researching a lesson I was writing for a series on using primary sources to teach the Jacksonian Era (Lesh 2004), published by the Center for History Education, I came across a lithograph depicting Nat Turner holding a Bible in one hand and a sword in another (Figure 2.1).

Jarred by the juxtaposition of the two objects and the calm yet serious manner in which Turner was depicted, I was persuaded to search out other visual represen-

Figure 2.1

tations of him and his rebellion. It became apparent as I collected these images that Nat Turner has been represented in a number of ways over the years. From the bloodthirsty murderer of women and children in a contemporary woodcut to the leader of men in a current graphic novel, Turner becomes more of a shape-shifter than a well-understood actor on history's stage. It was this alternating depiction of Turner, mirrored in text sources as well, that pushed me to consider using the events of August 1831 as the forum in which to teach students how historians think and how they read historical sources, as well as to challenge their notions about what history is and how it is best studied.

praise

Turner's Rebellion and Historical Thinking

The focal point of my initial unit on thinking historically is a lesson that aims to expose students to the skills historians use when they approach a historical issue: essentially, how to think as a historian. Nat Turner's rebellion serves as the content focus, and text, subtext, and context structure the skills to be acquired. These skills, as found in the historical investigations model in outlined in Chapter 1, are derived from the work of Bruce VanSledright, Sam Wineburg, Linda Levstik, Keith Barton, Peter Sexias, Sarah Drake Brown, Bob Bain, the National Standards for History, and other research on history education. Approaching this lesson at the beginning of every school year can appear daunting to both teachers and students. Especially, as longtime high school teacher Bob Bain reminds us, because

> *. . . students learning history do not yet share the assumptions of historians. They think differently about text, sources, argument, and the structure of historical knowledge . . . students may reject the transplanted activity . . . Engaging students in some legitimate disciplinary activity without restructuring the social interaction or challenging students' presuppositions may yield only ritualistic understanding. (Bain 2000, 335)*

Students must be shaken out of their history comfort zone before they can legitimately undertake a course focused on a disciplinary approach to studying the past. Nat Turner becomes the forum by which I ask my students to drink the history Kool-Aid in a different way. This lesson is taught early in the year to ensure that students gain exposure to three major concepts unique to thinking historically. First, I want students to leave the two-day lesson with an understanding that history is a discipline centered on questions and the application of information to generate interpretations about how those questions could be answered.

Changing how students perceive the study of history is very important. Much of the current research on history education points to the exact opposite conclusion. Instead of conceptualizing the discipline as based on questions, students discuss it as one based on answers, with the belief that proficient students of history are those who know, and can remember, the answers (Gabella 1994; Sandwell 2005; Shemilt 1980). Next, I need my students to understand that history is a discipline requiring its practitioners to question their sources. In doing so, students should be able to define and use the ideas of text, subtext, and context. Finally, the notion that history is alive, debatable, and connected to the present affords my students the opportunity to realize that although the key figures and events of the past are gone, their influence lingers today and defines many of the political, social, and economic characteristics of the modern world. All that in a two-day lesson—a daunting task, but as you will see, definitely not one that is unobtainable.

Implementing the Lesson

The lesson begins with students confronting a series of images of Nat Turner (two examples are shown in Figures 2.2 and 2.3). These images range from contemporary depictions to representations in graphic novels of the twenty-first century. Each image provides a distinct artistic perspective on the protagonist, yet they share similarities. As each image is displayed, students are asked to describe how Nat Turner and his actions are depicted by each artist. In addition, they are prompted to speculate about how Turner's personality and emotional state are portrayed.

Students are generally drawn to the images just as I was during their initial collection. At this point in the lesson, they

Figure 2.2

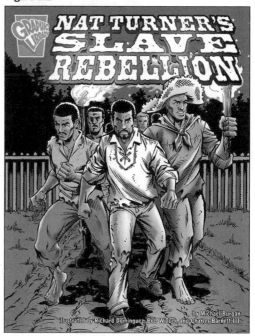

By Michael Burgan
illustrated by Richard Dominguez, Bob Wiacek, and Charles Barnett III

what is history

Figure 2.3

Discovery of Nat Turner.

rarely know it is Turner in each of the images unless they make a connection to the homework reading they completed. The differences between how Turner is depicted, and the tools the artists used, form the basis of student evaluation of the images. Height, skin coloration, facial features, clothing, and Turner's relationship to others in the image all provide students with insight into the artist's depiction of Nat Turner and his rebellion.

After looking at five or six of the images, students begin to realize that the various depictions are of the same person. After I confirm that each one depicts the same man, I ask students to consider why they would get such different views of him. Though these skills have not yet been introduced, students are now thinking about text, context, and subtext. With class discussion usually centering on the beliefs, intentions, and motivations of the artists creating the images, the students have moved from the basic interpretation of Turner to a more nuanced one.

I am always amazed at how visual images, be they photographic, hand drawn, painted, or sculpted, stimulate conversation among my students. It is a testament to the much discussed visual generation, of which they are a part. Inundated with images on television and online, combined with the decline of newspapers and print reading, this generation is more inclined to gather information from visual elements or sparse narratives. The predisposition for the visual over the written, particularly complicated text, is also indicative of the fact that students have been trained to see the study of history as one that involves textual sources, whose authority is to be unquestioned, to the exclusion of other types of historical sources (Sexias 1993). Textbooks, worksheets, and even certain genres of historical sources are text heavy. The chance to examine historical sources that are visual is often a welcome antidote to text. This provides numerous opportunities for teachers of history to use visual sources in the classroom. It also places on the shoulders of the history teacher the responsibility to ensure that text sources are used in conjunction with visual elements so that students can develop the skills necessary to analyze multiple types of historical evidence. The Turner images allow me to obey both masters: student predilection for the visual and my preference for a balance between text and image.

Student discussion of the various Turner images often gravitates to either impugning the artist's intentions or a question about when or why the source was created. I see this course of conversation as positive. By asking out loud who created the images and why, my students' potential to think about historical sources as historians emerges. In fact, one of the most common questions they ask as they reanalyze the sources is "Where did they come from?" Right then I know that kids are capable of restructuring the way in which they consider history.

Next, I direct the class conversation toward why the answers to these questions matter. Since from our discussion of the homework we know Nat Turner led a slave rebellion and that ultimately he was executed for his efforts, why does source authorship matter? Since we already know the answer to the inevitable multiple-choice question on Nat Turner, why ask about the author? At this point I have them hooked and can introduce the assessment focus of the lesson and the central question driving their ensuing investigation.

The conclusion of the lesson requires students to develop the narrative for a historical marker that would appear at the site of Turner's 1831 rebellion. In addition to the narrative for the marker, the students must assess their own thinking and describe how the sources with which they were presented influenced their interpretation of the past. The central question serving as the architecture of the activity is how we remember the actions of an enslaved man who led an ultimately unsuccessful rebellion of slaves. This is a question that parallels those asked by public historians in a number of settings. From the ill-fated display of the *Enola Gay* at the Smithsonian to the recent debates over the narrative conveyed at the Gettysburg Battlefield, historians are often asked to mediate the fine line between memory and history (Curry 2002; Nash, Crabtree, and Dunn 1997; Linenthal and Engelhardt 1996). Now, with a purpose for studying the past, students have a need to question the visual sources they examined at the lesson's outset. By communicating at the birth of the lesson that students are examining the past with the intention of answering a historical question, I am consciously attempting to alter their perspective from one in which history is a collection of facts to one based on making arguments based on these facts.

With the central purpose of the lesson established, students can compare and contrast the arguments made by other sources with those presented by the visual elements: a series of carefully selected quotes form the body of the investigation; editorials from the *Richmond Whig*; and interpretations from historians Herbert Aptheker, Stephen Oates, William S. Drewry, and John Cromwell, and the author of *The Confessions of Nat Turner*, Thomas R. Gray. Each source satisfies two main criteria. First, the quotes directly reflect the author's view either of Nat Turner the individual or of the rebellion. Knowledge of the authors' backgrounds, and not a quote divorced from its creator, is essential for students to begin to approach historical sources as a historian might. Since, in my class, this lesson is the first time that students are introduced to the concept of "thinking historically," it is important that the author's presence be overt. Too much digging by students to find evidence of the author in the excerpts would introduce frustration at the same time as the concepts: not a good idea.

The second criterion for selecting the documents for this activity has to do with the relationship among the documents. The sources must contrast enough for students to be able to plainly ascertain that historical interpretations change over time. Students approach the study of history as a set of fixed events whose causality, effect, and importance are universally agreed upon. Rarely are students exposed to the reality that causality, importance, and effect are debated and that interpretations change over time.

The idea that historical interpretations are the lifeblood of the discipline is an important intellectual Rubicon for students to cross. If they do not realize that history is debated, and that there are tools historians employ to develop and promulgate their interpretations, they will not be amenable to reconsidering their understanding of history. The quotes I use for the lesson do not reflect the full range of either contemporary reactions to Turner's rebellion or the full historiographical record; this is simply because smaller groups work best and six is usually, at least for me, the optimal group size. More quotes could be used. There are some fabulous sources missing from my collection—most notably William Styron—but the format for their delivery and discussion would need to change to best increase the amount of on-task behavior among students.

Armed with yet another version of Turner and his rebellion, my students are ready to move farther away from their history comfort level and enter the realm of Clio's apprentices. After students examine their source and identify the author's main argument about Turner and phrases or adjectives used to promote this viewpoint, they are organized so that each group has one student who read each of the six sources. Using their best group work behaviors (I hope) students are asked to share and converse about the sources. They must take notes about how each source depicts Turner and his actions (Figure 2.4).

After groups have completed this phase of the activity, I instruct them to discuss for two to three minutes (ages in teenage terms!) how Nat Turner should be remembered. Drawing students back to the product of the lesson can often provide more focus to the ensuing discussion. Next, I open the dialogue to the entire class. Preliminary discussion finds students gravitating to terms such as *heroic, brutal, villainous, fanatic, religious,* and *manipulative* to describe Turner and his actions.

Interestingly, since the September 11, 2001, terrorist attacks, some students have bandied about the term *terrorist* to describe Turner. This is a fascinating intrusion of the contemporary world into the analysis of a historical figure. What attracts students as they form their initial arguments about how to depict Turner are certain words or phrases in the quotes. Students take a statement such as "What strikes us as the most remarkable thing in this matter is the horrible ferocity of these monsters. They remind one of a parcel of blood-thirsty wolves rushing down from the Alps," which appears in an 1831 *Richmond Enquirer* editorial, and interpret it as a literal description of the events and participants. At this juncture they do not question the authorship of the source. Participants in the class discussion present well-reasoned arguments based solely on the words of the sources—just as we have trained them to simply spit back what the textbook says. I have my students right where I need them if they are to be challenged. The class believes they have given me exactly what I wanted: a right answer. Instead, I can now show them the sources of their "right"

Figure 2.4

Nat Turner's Rebellion: Evaluating Historical Opinions

Use the following worksheet to record information from the various primary and secondary sources. When deciding the term that best describes the document's position regarding Nat Turner, consider *hero, villian, fanatic, religious, insane, leader, manipulative, brave*, etc.

SOURCE 1: John W. Cromwell— **"The Aftermath of Nat Turner's Insurrection"**	**SOURCE 4: *The Richmond Whig***
Adjectives	Adjectives
Quote	Quote
Term	Term
SOURCE 2: Herbert Aptheker— ***American Negro Slave Revolts***	**SOURCE 5: *The Richmond Enquirer***
Adjectives	Adjectives
Quote	Quote
Term	Term
SOURCE 3: William S. Drewry— ***The Southampton Insurrection***	**SOURCE 6: Thomas R. Gray—** ***The Confessions of Nat Turner***
Adjectives	Adjectives
Quote	Quote
Term	Term

answers and introduce two of the most important historical skills they will need to develop: the interpretive nature of history and the process for attacking historical evidence. At this point I share with the class information about each of the six sources that formed the architecture of their examination (Figure 2.5).

Figure 2.5 Sources and Descriptions for Nat Turner Investigation

The Richmond Enquirer and Richmond Whig, 1831

Both newspapers were published in a Southern city and were read widely by planters throughout the region. They tended to promote the political views of the upper-class planters who paid to subscribe to the paper.

Thomas R. Gray, The Confessions of Nat Turner, 1831

After his capture and arrest on October 30, 1831, Nat Turner was imprisoned in the Southampton County jail, where he was interviewed by Thomas R. Gray, a Southern physician, failed planter, and slave owner. Gray said that only Turner's words were recorded, but in several instances Gray's words appear in the *Confessions*.

William S. Drewry, Slave Insurrections in Virginia, 1900

A white Virginian who grew up near the area of the rebellion and descended from a family of planters and slave owners Drewry researched Nat Turner for his dissertation at Johns Hopkins. Drewry read lots of primary sources and interviewed whites and blacks who knew people who were alive in 1831. He believed that slavery was a good thing, that slaves were happy, and that they rarely rebelled.

John W. Cromwell, "The Aftermath of Nat Turner's Insurrection," The Journal of Negro History, 1920

Born a slave in Portsmouth, Virginia, Cromwell was sent to a private school in Philadelphia after his father purchased the family's freedom. Cromwell became a teacher, writer, and political activist. He was one of the first to write in the academic field of African American history.

Herbert Aptheker, American Negro Slave Revolts, 1943

Aptheker hated segregation and racial stereotypes, and believed that slavery was exploitive and slave rebellions occurred frequently. He was a member of the Communist Party of the United States and in 1950 was blacklisted for his political beliefs. A committed labor unionist, Aptheker believed that tensions between social classes were important to understanding the past.

Learning to Read Between the Lines

I draw attention to the authors by asking students what sources informed their interpretation of Turner. As a student identifies a source and explains its influence, I reveal via PowerPoint slide or overhead projector the background information on the source. Many students respond with "Well, you didn't tell us that." "Yay," I think; they realize it matters! Through a series of questions students are asked to explain how or whether the new information they have learned about their authors affects their thinking. I link the opinions that have served as the basis of their interpretations of Nat Turner to authors who possess motivations. For the first time students are confronted with the fact that the information they have utilized in the investigation has an author and the author must be questioned.

Students are not accustomed to questioning the authority of text, and thus identifying issues of authorship is the crossroads of the Nat Turner lesson. Much of their past instruction in history/social studies has taught them, passively or actively, that the information they confront in their textbooks or other printed material is correct and that doing well in history is simply a reflection of how much of the information from these sources they can remember. When I pull back the curtain and show students how the subtext of the source informs the text, I have jostled them out of their history comfort zone. For some students this is empowering, whereas for others it is extremely disconcerting. Addressing these feelings becomes the challenge of the lesson, and in some ways, of the entire transition in history instruction I am outlining.

After I have intentionally injected a bit of confusion into the class's analysis of Nat Turner, students are introduced to the three concepts they will be asked to use throughout the year. These concepts, discussed in greater depth in the next chapter, serve as part of the historian's skill set that I teach my students. I provide a photocopy of the information in Figure 2.6 for each of my students. Printed on garishly colored paper and replicated on a classroom bulletin board, this information is referred to throughout the remainder of the Nat Turner lesson and the duration of the year.

When the students are finally confronted with having to put pen to paper and write the text of their historical marker (Figure 2.7) and then provide metacognitive insights, I am often met with many variations of the question, "So what is the answer, Mr. Lesh?" Once posited by an African American girl in my class, this query, and other variations, indicates that students are modeling the results of their former training in thinking historically and simultaneously considering the implications of the type of

Figure 2.6 Learning to Think Historically: A Tool for Attacking Historical Sources

Text
- What is visible/readable, i.e., what information is provided by the source?

Context
- What was going on during the time period? What background information do you have that helps explain the information found in the source?

Subtext
- What is between the lines? Ask questions about the following:
  - Author: Who created the source, and what do we know about that person?
  - Audience: For whom was the source created?
  - Reason: Why was this source produced when it was?

thinking I am attempting to foster. Malia, the student posing the question framing this chapter and giving birth to the book's title, went on to argue that Nat Turner was a deeply religious prophet who believed he was doing God's work. Her justification was an amalgam of information from the documents and her own religious background.

Although Malia sought out the "actual answer," she came to an interpretation not unlike that posed by the PBS series *Africans in America*. In the third episode of the four-part series, the narrative describes Nat Turner as a religious hero doing God's work. Unbeknownst to her, Malia had examined a selective spectrum of documents and come to an interpretation that parallels that of trained historians. If students can overcome this perception that there is a "right answer" and gain confidence in their abilities to interpret historical sources, address the commonalities and disparities among those sources, and formulate and defend an interpretation, then they will be well on their way to gaining proficiency in thinking historically.

Wrestling with Interpreting the Past

Students' responses to the assessment vary. Some have difficulty reconciling the varying viewpoints generated by the historians, newspapers, and other sources confronted and are unsure how to handle the questions raised by their newfound awareness of context and subtext. In this case, student

Figure 2.7

Nat Turner's Rebellion: A Historical Marker

You have been commissioned by the state of Virginia Historical Trust to develop a historical marker that will be placed along the roadside adjacent to the area impacted by Nat Turner and his followers. Your task is to develop the inscription for the marker that describes your interpretation of Nat Turner and his actions. Your inscription should take into account:

- The specific factors involved in the event
- The various reactions to Nat Turner (artistic and other)

Why I came to this decision (What documents most impacted your decisions and why?):

_____
_____
_____
_____
_____
_____
_____

responses run toward the bland. Students depict the basic facts of the events and avoid the emotional, value-laden, and at times ahistorical interpretations of Nat Turner, as shown in Figure 2.8.

Figure 2.8

Nat Turner's Rebellion: A Historical Marker

You have been commissioned by the state of Virginia Historical Trust to develop a historical marker that will be placed along the roadside adjacent to the area to the area impacted by Nat Turner and his followers. Your task is to develop the inscription for the marker that describes your interpretation of Nat Turner and his actions. Your inscriptions should take into account:

- The specific factors involved in the event
- The various reactions to Nat Turner (artistic, and other)

> ## NAT TURNER
>
> Here, Nat Turner, an African American slave, lead one of the first rebellions and opened the doors to many more. Turner was considered a phrophecy of God and his visions gave him the idea and courage to take on such an impossible task. Although Turner and his followers were killed, they still made an impact on the society and will forever be remembered as heroes.

Why I came to this decision (What documents most impacted your decisions and why?): I decided to portray Turner as a hero because what he did was very courageous. He took on an impossible task and although he did fail it made a big impact. People will always remember Turner as for leading one of the first slave rebellions and thats how he deserves to be remembered, not as insane. People do see Turner as insane because his motives and ideas seem questionable but all along he just wanted freedom and to help his people. Cromwell and Gray's sources helped me come to this conclusion because Cromwell knows the whole story and Gray was there with Turner interviewing him. Therefore, Nat Turner deserves to be remembered as a hero.

Although this response might seem to defeat the purpose of the exercise, I interpret it as a solid first step toward thinking historically. When confronted with conflicting interpretations of Nat Turner, each driven by the implications of the combination of authorship and purpose, the student seeks to strip the documents of any overt point of view and simply depicts the basic facts surrounding the rebellion and its leader. I call these textbook interpretations. Most modern textbooks are absolutely devoid of any narrative tension, and students are generally not taught to question the interpretive structure of the text. They tend at times to reflect the types of writing with which they are most familiar, and in the case of history, that is the textbook.

Other students approach the telling of Turner's rebellion by seeking to find commonality among the interpretations they have encountered. As demonstrated below, these students are inclined to depict Turner's actions as heroic or Turner as a leader. In their minds, the common thread running through all six documents is that an enslaved man challenged an all-encompassing institution and that this action itself was brave. Students point to the fact that open, violent rebellion was not the norm and that Turner showed courage through his efforts to organize and execute a slave insurrection and his willingness to risk the consequences. For example, one student said the following in her analysis:

> I came to this decision [to depict Nat Turner as a heroic leader] because he gave people something to talk about and to fear. He made the slave owners scared because if he had done it other slaves could pull off a rebellion too. All of the documents impacted me. They all gave different views of the same man from different people. But they all show that he did something amazing because they are talking about it. The one that impacted me most was the *Richmond Whig*. It talked about how he was wrong for doing what he believed to be true.

In my evaluation, this and other, similar responses indicate the first phase of historical thinking. The students have questioned the sources, considered the implications of the context of the time period and the subtext of each source, and worked to rectify the problems raised by the contrasting viewpoints by seeking what they see as the common point of agreement among the authors. Although I have never conducted "think-aloud" protocols that might allow students to articulate their own thought processes, the writing indicates that something is going on upstairs that has led them to this conclusion.

As shown below, one student has narrowed her considerations to two sources. Her analysis, buoyed by the interpretations of Herbert Aptheker and William Drewry, demonstrates that she has formulated an interpretation. In depicting Turner as a leader, she says, "You need to have a strong following and accomplish your goals. Nat Turner had a following of over 40 slaves and they killed 55 whites. This, to me, shows great leadership." The one weakness—a common one I address later—is that she does not address the issues raised by Drewry and Aptheker's subtext. Another student argues that although the documents conflict, "they mostly agree that he led the slaves well." "History shows," continues the student, "that his rebellion was the most successful (if body count and impact are a measure of success), so he must have done something correctly as a leader."

On the other hand, Anna interprets Turner as insane and grounds her justification in one source. She argues that "His [Turner's] confession to Thomas Gray impacted me the most because I felt it was the most reliable source because he actually talked to Nat Turner." Her analysis indicates two elements of introductory historical thinking. First, she places the sources into context: Gray spoke to Turner. Then she assesses the sources' reliability (granted, lacking any real heuristic other than her own intuition) when she declared Gray's *Confessions* to be "reliable." Anna has come to learn that historians base their interpretations on sources and that understanding the subtext enables one to generate a more nuanced interpretation. By the same token, though, she—like many other students—fails to directly confront the problems that Gray's authorship of Nat Turner's confessions presents. Understanding the effect of authorship and incorporating it into the construction of a historical narrative is a skill that takes time to develop. Nevertheless, I argue that it is worth having students develop that acumen because it invigorates the teaching of the past and aids their reading skills.

Other students are frustrated by the whole concept that sources of information, be it their textbook, a historical documentary, or another source such as those used to examine Nat Turner, might need to be questioned. Previous years of history/social studies classes have trained them to simply identify the answer and be prepared to regurgitate that answer when asked. The notion that they possess some degree of agency in determining how to interpret the past, and that this process requires them to question the sources, is too foreign for some of my students to grasp. I remind them that learning something new is always an uncomfortable process. Because this is their first attempt at approaching history in this manner, I respond with encouragement.

My students' attempts to bail out of the process of investigating the past is consistent with any number of documented efforts to inculcate students with the idea of thinking historically (Barton 1997a, 1997b, 2004; VanSledright 2002). David Kobrin puts it succinctly in *Beyond the Textbook*: "When students think about it [contrasting interpretations], just the idea that history is constructed rather than retold can be disquieting" (1996, 24). Often, this category of students completely ignores the prompt to discuss how the documents influenced their conclusions. Student responses sometimes openly argue that "the documents were too confusing because they contradicted one another" or that "you cannot trust anyone's opinion because they are all biased," and they simply trust their own instincts when formulating an interpretation. As one student put it, "I tried to put everything together and sum up all of the true information, leaving out the bias." This statement is interesting, because to him, history is full of true facts that can be teased out if you eliminate the "bias." Bias as articulated in his response is a negative factor that dilutes or even destroys the utility of the information provided by a document. Per his description, this removal of bias is best accomplished by looking for commonalities between sources. But then he goes on to admit an interesting historical choice when he says, "However, he [Nat Turner] sounds a little like a hero because I didn't want him in a negative light." Emerging from a supposedly scientific process of thinking historically is the reality of the telling of history; perspective is inherent in all sources, and my students are as prone as professional historians to present their interpretations of the past with a bit of spin.

The positive news is that some students craft remarkably well-thought-out plaques and articulately explain their use of sources (see Figure 2.9). This student uses the sources in combination with his understanding of the role of rebellion to craft his interpretation. His analysis does not get caught up in the dismissal of sources because they are "biased." In addition, his justification for the language on the plaque indicates an effort to synthesize information and to connect it with his own preexisting beliefs. Clearly this response, and others like it, indicates that students have moved past the idea that history is about memory and have instead begun to use information to make source-backed historical arguments. They still have a long way to go, but something about every journey starting with one small step rings in my mind.

Some Conclusions

So, after teaching this lesson in a variety of iterations for the better part of a decade, what does it all mean? One of the interesting by-products of this

Figure 2.9

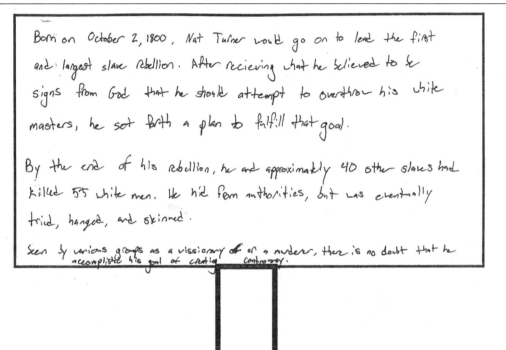

Born on October 2, 1800, Nat Turner would go on to lead the first and largest slave rebellion. After recieving what he believed to be signs from God that he should attempt to overthrow his white masters, he set forth a plan to fulfill that goal.

By the end of his rebellion, he and approximately 40 other slaves had killed 55 white men. He hid from authorities, but was eventually tried, hanged, and skinned.

Seen by various groups as a vissionary or a murder, there is no doubt that he accomplished his goal of creating controversy.

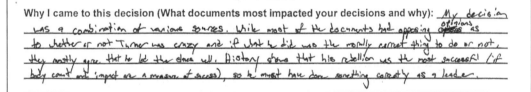

Why I came to this decision (What documents most impacted your decisions and why): My decision was a combination of various sources. While most of the documents had opposing opinions as to whether or not Turner was crazy and if what he did was the morally correct thing to do or not, they mostly agree that he led the slaves well. History shows that his rebellion was the most successful (if body count and impact are a measure of success), so he must have done something correctly as a leader.

lesson and the broader approach to history instruction that it represents is how my students often come to question me and their textbook. A teenager's natural inclination to question everything is facilitated by an approach that develops the skill set to do it effectively. "How do you know?" goes from snarky teenage query to legitimate investigation of the process by which textbooks, teachers, films, and museums reach their conclusions.

If my students have been challenged to reconsider all that they know about history, what about me? Lessons about Nat Turner and others designed to elicit the same type of student interaction with big historical questions and a variety of sources have energized me. As described earlier, my love of history stems partly from the dialogue it generates. Discussing and debating the motivations of historical figures, the meaning(s) of past events, and the effect of ideas, patterns, changes, and constants drew me into Clio's corner. Unfortunately, my initial foray into the classroom did not reward me with this dynamic. Now, as students slowly—and at times reluctantly or not at all—consider the tools of the discipline as they confront questions of the past, I am getting that dialogue I so desired. Let's face it: I am not teaching a graduate school seminar. My students are fifteen- and sixteen-year-old teenagers. But the history labs and disciplinary approach to teaching history have changed the atmosphere of my classroom, and that was one of my most important goals.

Another important goal was to ensure that content—the substantive stuff that we often pay too much attention to—is not lost. I am sure that it is not, because students always do well on the assessment items related to the causes and consequences of Turner's rebellion. In addition, Nat Turner is often referred to in other contexts. I address this concern at greater length in Chapter 10, and argue that in fact students explore and retain more content through this approach to history instruction than they do when using the more traditional lecture and textbook methods.

Nat Turner Outside My Classroom

I have taught this lesson for more than ten years and shared it with numerous teachers across the country via my involvement in Teaching American History (TAH) grants. Funded through the federal Department of Education, the TAH program has funneled hundreds of millions of dollars to school systems to promote effective teaching of American history (Ragland and Woestman 2009). "The program," as described by the U.S. Department of Education (2010) Web site, "is designed to raise student achievement by improving teachers' knowledge and understanding of and appreciation for traditional U.S. history." It goes further to state that "by helping teachers to develop a deeper understanding and appreciation of U.S. history as a separate subject matter within the core curriculum, these programs will improve instruction and raise student achievement." When presenting under the auspices of a TAH grant, I get interesting responses from audience members.

In some venues teachers challenge the notion of a student placing any spin on their interpretation of Nat Turner. Although I can agree with the need to avoid blatant emotional terms, I nevertheless question the concept of any historical interpretation that purports to be wholly objective. In *That Noble Dream*, Peter Novick (1998) argues convincingly that the historical profession aspires to an objectivity that it has never achieved. The stories of the past are always shaped by not only the questions asked of the sources but the social-political context that generates those questions and the racial-ethnic-political views of the historian. Any cursory examination of historiography will immediately indicate the tendency of historical inter-pretation to change.

The example I often refer to is Reconstruction. Students of William Dunning at Columbia University in the early twentieth century were taught to view Reconstruction as a failure because of the corrupt actions of African Americans and the rapacious and pernicious actions of Southern Scalawags and Northern Carpetbaggers. Dominating the telling of the story, and crystallized in D. W. Griffith's *Birth of a Nation*, Dunning's interpreta-tion of the past stood for more than fifty years. Historian Eric Foner has sys-tematically undermined the Dunning version of Reconstruction. His seminal *Reconstruction: America's Unfinished Revolution 1863–1877* argues that the period's failure was caused more by the decline in Northern commitment to racial equality and a growing support for industrialization than to any inability of African Americans to handle the demands freedom placed upon them (Foner 1988). If historians' interpretations change, often based on dif-fering conclusions drawn from the same sources, why can't students'?

The greatest lesson I have learned through sharing "Introducing Historical Thinking: Nat Turner's Rebellion of 1831" with audiences out-side my classroom is that, despite access to a greater range of materials with which to teach history and a growing body of research on cognitive rather than behavioral learning—specifically as it ties to teaching his-tory—teachers still cling to lectures, movies, and various other forms of "memory-centered" methodologies as the primary modes of classroom instruction. Part of this reluctance to change is driven by the degree to which teachers are required to cover material that is later assessed by some sort of external examination. In addition, the continual concerns about classroom management and the effect other forms of instruction rather than coordinated seat work and lecture may have on student behavior ham-string teachers' willingness to consider historical investigations and more discipline-centered forms of instruction.

Also, one constant question teachers raise when faced with instruction centered on source analysis, interpretation, and semiauthentic historical investigations is "How can I do this and cover it all?" Coverage is the fun-damental barrier to promoting historical thinking in the classroom. The pressures of coverage haunt the choices teachers make when they consider altering their instructional program, which I will address in greater depth in Chapter 10.

Finally, what becomes apparent in many instances is that teacher training in history instruction is truly a reflection of how individuals were taught by K–12 teachers and college professors, rather than a systematic application of what we know about how students learn. Concerns about time, student behavior, and assessment, in addition to habit, all converge to limit the willingness of many teacher participants to even consider altering their approach from a content-centered to a content-discipline marriage (McNeil 1988). Each of these reasons—classroom management, assessment pressures, coverage obsessions, and the "apprenticeship of observation" phenomenon—are pragmatic reactions to the incentives and expectations of their profession (Lortie 1975).

After sharing this lesson with teachers in a number of forums, I am often asked why I place such an emphasis on historical thinking. I respond by asking them to consider how Nat Turner would be taught in the classroom if historical thinking and historical sources did not form the basis of the lesson. I am hesitant to address this question because I have not been in many other classrooms. Nevertheless, instinct and some research indicate that a combination of one or two approaches would characterize how Nat Turner's rebellion would be taught. As illustrated by the research, an investigation of Nat Turner that was consistent with typical social studies/history instruction would center on the textbook and lecture (Baxter, Ferrell, and Wiltz 1965; Cuban 1982; Bracey 1991, 1997; Goodland 1984).

> *The most common pattern, employed by the vast majority of social studies teachers, is that of teacher-centered instruction. This pattern includes activities using the textbook and teacher as sources of information for assignments, recitation (now commonly called discussion), tests, and individual seatwork. Talking by the teacher (presenting information, explaining, and clarifying) exceeds talking by students, whose responses are generally confined to answering teacher's questions.* (Cuban 1991, 204)

Given the centuries-long persistence of this instructional pattern in history classrooms, it would follow that if there were not such an overemphasis on historical thinking skills in my iteration of Nat Turner, students would simply be asked to read the section in their textbook on slave resistance and rebellions and answer the corresponding questions. Without allowing students to examine a historical question about Turner and interrogate historical sources in an effort to develop an evidence-based response to the guiding question, they might confront Nat Turner through a lecture in which the teacher provides notes on slave rebellions and resistance on the plantation. In either manner—and this is painting with a wide brush—the focus is not on students' engagement with the past and the utilization of historical thinking skills but simply on acquiring the correct facts about the Southampton rebellion and its leader.

"Isn't this sufficient?" one might ask. Students are quiet, reading or listening, content is at the center of the lesson, and the entire activity can be measured with an objective and measured through a standardized test item. On one hand I would say yes. Pragmatically, either of these approaches would meet the needs of the curriculum, the students' perceived developmental abilities, and the time demands placed on most teachers. In reality, the main method of teaching that has predominated in K–12 education, whatever it is, has not generated great results. Sam Wineburg reminds us of this when considering the almost 100 years of dismal results on tests of student knowledge about history:

> *We learn that there has been little appreciable change in students' historical knowledge over time . . . the consistency of these results casts doubts on a presumed golden age of fact retention. Appeals to such an age are more the stuff of national lore and a wistful nostalgia for a time that never was than a reference to a national history whose reality can be found in the documentary record.* (2001, 33)

This observation, combined with the best research we have on how history/social studies is actually taught, pushes me to conclude that any way must be better. My hope with this lesson is to rattle students a bit and have them reconsider what "doing history is all about."

Looking Back and Looking Forward

What I have discovered from teaching this lesson at the beginning of my U.S. History course for the past ten years is that many students are caught off guard by the idea of having to use evidence to support their opinion. I often hear the refrain "Can't you just tell us the answer?" and to me that is a sign of success. Although it could be interpreted as students giving up and demanding that history return to an information-transfer model, I see it as a sign that they are at least considering the implications of having to engage the past from a disciplinary approach. Of course, the science teacher does not tell students how the lab experiment will turn out. The math teacher does not simply provide the answer to the quadratic equation. As these skills are carried over and applied to their investigation of other events, personalities, and ideas, students develop confidence in their abilities and look forward to the next time they will investigate the past rather than simply be told what happened and the teacher's interpretation of why it was important.

Moving to a more balanced content/discipline-based approach to history instruction is not easy. It challenges students' preconceptions about history and forces teachers, as it did me, to completely reconsider the structure of their course. As they say, the first step is the hardest, but once it has been taken, the dividends are high and rewards are frequent. Ultimately, Nat Turner sets the stage for where I hope to take my students during the course of the year. Exposed to the study of history as a series of questions to be formulated, debated, and answered, students are immersed in a discipline structured by a set of cognitive tools akin to those taught and used to learn English, math, and science. Students see history as an area of study that is debated rather than one that resembles a catechism.

With these goals established, my next task is to weave into the course the skills of source analysis and interpretation, along with other historical thinking skills. Easy enough to say, but I need to make sure that these skills are overt yet do not cause students to lose sight of the tested content. In many instances my students approach the concept of thinking historically, questioning sources, and developing interpretations as nothing more than the information needed to be successful in the first unit. In other words, they treat these skills as they would historical content—as information to be digested, regurgitated, and forgotten as it is replaced by newer content in the next unit. Sustainability is now the key to transferring these skills.

Despite all the questions generated and thoughts churned by their investigation of Nat Turner, my students still need more practice in developing and refining their abilities to think historically. Making these historical thinking skills explicit and overt in my instruction, along with continued practice, pushes students to reconsider their assumptions about the past and how its stories are developed and communicated. Often, my students think the approach I share and the skills of considering text, subtext, and context are just for the first unit and can be summarily forgotten when unit two begins. I remind them, and myself, that students in other disciplines do not simply forget the tools of their discipline. In biology they will always need to calculate measurement, in math they will always need to show their work, and in English they will always need to analyze a piece of literature for tone. If I am truly going to convert my students' understanding of the discipline of history, then persistence must be an ally.

CHAPTER 3

Text, Subtext, and Context

Evaluating Evidence and Exploring President Theodore Roosevelt and the Panama Canal

LA!

They were all different sources saying different things. Some were letters from Roosevelt which meant they were lies. Others were newspaper articles and political cartoons which were biased. It was hard to know which one to believe.

—Student comments during discussion of the lesson

Let's be honest for a moment. There are time periods, individuals, ideas, and events in American history that you simply do not find interesting to teach. For me it has always been military history in general and, more specifically, the Panama Canal. Military history mostly because when I was growing up, I was inundated with World War II films that my parents' and grandparents' generations used to remind themselves of the contributions they had made to promoting freedom around the globe. From *McHale's Navy* to *The Bridge at Remagen*, war films and military history often appeared to be the only venue for examining the past. The Panama Canal was anathema to me because for years I could not connect to all the fuss over digging a hole in the ground. Yellow fever, President Theodore Roosevelt, the locks, and the other associated stories fell flat for me. I am sure this stems from the fact that placing a hammer or saw in my hands is a recipe for disaster. The Panama Canal is historically significant, absolutely, and I did "address it"—code for "folded it into a broader examination of President Theodore Roosevelt's Big Stick Diplomacy." But it was not until I ran across a fabulous dog-eared, about-to-be-destroyed book titled *Selected Case Studies in American History* published in 1970 by Allyn and Bacon that I found the central question that could drive an investigation of the canal. The book reflected the Amherst History Project and was connected to the New Social Studies Movement of the 1960s and 1970s. Presciently enough, the four authors of the two-book series—two classroom teachers, their curriculum supervisor, and a university methods professor—made the following argument in the preface:

> *[A]fter more than a decade of discussion and debate something is still rather radically wrong with what is taught in social studies and how teaching proceeds in the field . . . [T]he social studies field is still dominated by notions of instruction that emphasize description, narration, and authority. Rarely are students encouraged to inquire, to investigate, to develop their own points-of-view using skills of critical thinking and analysis. (Gardner, Beery, Olson, and Rood 1970)*

Differences in vocabulary aside, the authors describe the central focus of my instructional program and what I am attempting to articulate in this book: historical thinking.

In the second volume of *Selected Case Studies in American History*, I came across the cartoon in Figure 3.1, which provides not only an interesting angle to incorporating a deep examination of the canal into my course,

Figure 3.1

THE MAN BEHIND THE EGG—From the *Times* (New York)

but also a platform for using the common language of text, context, and subtext more fully within my instructional dialogue. It is okay to come out of the closet and admit that not everything in the past is equally sexy to teach, but keep looking: even your least favorites can be opened up when students are given the opportunity to investigate the past rather than simply digest it.

The lesson forming the backbone of this chapter is one that deeply engages my students in applying their budding historical thinking skills, while simultaneously generating a deeper and more nuanced examination of American foreign policy during the Progressive period.

A Common Language for Investigating the Past

The vocabulary words that form the common language of my classroom are *text, context,* and *subtext.* As discussed in Chapter 1, these terms are derived from Sam Wineburg's work (2001). When I teach the Nat Turner lesson on the second and third day of school, I introduce students to the terms, define them, allow students to apply them, and then provide a laminated sheet with the definitions for their notebooks. In many ways this sheet serves as my periodic table of history or the formula sheet students now keep for geometry or physics. During day-to-day instruction I require students to consult this sheet, or the bulletin board with the same material, and to employ the vocabulary in class much as they would the theorems, atomic numbers, or formulas in science or math. The challenge for me initially was to ensure that I incorporated the vocabulary consistently so that it was not something "extra" but part and parcel of the names, dates, ideas, events, and personalities that also structured classroom dialogue. I have become much better with this over time, and it shows in the facility my students have developed with the terms.

One point of emphasis: Although I am highlighting this particular lesson to demonstrate the incorporation of text, subtext, and context into a classroom defined by discipline-based historical investigation, these are concepts that should be used almost daily. My students have used this common language since the first week of school. To be effective, it must be infused into a teacher's instructional dialogue on a daily basis. This lesson in a grander manner illustrates what must be the lingua franca of your course if students are to move away from history as memory and toward an investigative approach.

A Word on Selecting Sources

One of the most frequent mistakes I made early on when trying to promote student investigation was in my selection of sources. All sources are not created equal. They are not equal in readability, student accessibility, interest level, or their linkage to enough background information to enable students or teacher to determine subtext and context. The selection of historical sources will make or break any investigation of the past. Pick sources that do not correspond to the broader historical question being investigated and you will quickly hear the class discussion move off task. Select sources that are not accessible to students because of language and the hands will go up quickly as your students struggle and turn you into their own personal whack-a-mole game as you go from kid to kid, interpreting and explaining. Finally, use sources that do not provide information that aids in student analysis and identification of subtext or context, and watch meaningful investigation quickly fizzle. With these concerns in mind, I recommend several criteria to be considered when selecting sources for an investigation:

Key Sources

1. Do not use more than four to six sources, especially the first time you conduct a particular investigation. Keeping it simple will build your confidence as you shepherd students through the investigation and will keep you from spending too much time on the Internet Googling for historical sources.

2. Read the sources ahead of time. Make sure they facilitate student investigation of the focus question, are not plagued by vocabulary out of your students' reach, or are not so arcane that students cannot access the information in the text.

3. Balance your offerings so that there are visual sources as well as text, material objects, and ephemera from popular culture. In addition, do not have all the same types of visual, text, or material and popular culture sources. Include cartoons, artwork, pictures, formal photographs, data tables and graphs, oral histories, newspaper articles, interviews, and so on. Diversity is important for maintaining student engagement.

4. Aid students by defining difficult vocabulary, editing sources for length, contextualizing sources and their authors, and providing typed copies for students if written documents are in cursive.

5. Ensure that sources are comparable in length. Students will compare and, well, it can get ugly.

Initiating the Investigation

Essential to any successful historical investigation is drawing students into the central question. To initiate the Panama Canal lesson I ask students to distinguish among lies, half-truths, exaggerations, rationalizations, and obfuscations. Parsing the semantic differences is a useful discussion for understanding that human motivations might inform the use of one of these techniques to convey information. As one might imagine, high school students are full of examples of lies and its cousins. This discussion segues into introducing the questioning of a selected portion of President Theodore Roosevelt's autobiography as it relates to the acquisition of the territory for constructing the Panama Canal (Lesh 2005).

Source work for the lesson in the case of the canal investigation starts with a quote from President Theodore Roosevelt's autobiography. I use this quote because the canal is a central element of Roosevelt's list of presidential accomplishments and he serves as an important figure in the historical debate over the role the United States played in the Panamanian

Revolution. The source is placed in context for students with the following directions:

> Read the following excerpt from President Theodore Roosevelt's autobiography. On the left-hand side summarize the argument presented in each section of the writing. After summarizing, list all of the explanations Roosevelt provides to justify his actions in Panama. Pay particular attention to the adjectives he uses to describe his actions, the reaction of the Panamanians, and the benefits of his actions.
>
> **Context:** *The American desire for an Isthmian canal had its impetus as far back as the 1840s migration to Oregon Territory and the California gold rush of 1848. To protect the potential economic and strategic boon of a canal the United States signed the Clayton-Bulwer Treaty with Great Britain in 1850, in which both nations agreed to not to seek independent rights to a canal, but to maintain friendly relations as it pertained to a possible canal. After the American Civil War the craving for the monetary benefits of a quicker route from the East Coast to the West Coast of the United States drove President Ulysses S. Grant to appoint a commission to research the best potential location for a canal between the Atlantic and Pacific Oceans. Although the Grant and McKinley administrations both found that a canal route through Nicaragua would be the most advantageous, a French company began in 1878 to construct an inter-ocean canal in the Panamanian territory of Colombia.*
>
> *By 1898, the French effort to construct a canal, which cost more than $300 million and thousands of lives, was declared a failure and discontinued. At the same time, American needs for a quicker route between coasts was exacerbated by the growing Spanish-American and Philippine-American wars. Theodore Roosevelt, secretary of the navy and soon to be president, immediately saw the strategic importance of constructing and controlling a canal. Buoyed by the Hay-Poncefote Treaty of 1901, in which the British relinquished their claim to a canal, Roosevelt began an intensive search for territory to build one.*
>
> *As Roosevelt and the American government made the canal a priority, Philippe Bunau-Varilla, a former member of the French construction team in the Panamanian territory of Colombia, sought to contract with someone to continue the construction of a canal. Functioning as a private citizen, Bunau-Varilla hired American lawyer William Cromwell to lobby the U.S. Congress on his behalf. Working from New York City, Bunau-Varilla prepared maps and budgets to use while*

lobbying the U.S. Congress and President Roosevelt to sell the territory of Panama as the logical location for a transoceanic canal. As the U.S. Senate debated the possible locations for the canal, Bunau-Varilla and Cromwell leaked to the American press a Nicaraguan stamp depicting the eruption of volcano Mount Momotombo. Though dormant for years, the sight of an erupting volcano so close to the proposed Nicaraguan route, coupled with the mailing of the stamps to every member of Congress quickly killed the idea of a Nicaraguan Canal. Given the choice between active volcanoes in Nicaragua and the geologically safer Panama, the Senate agreed in 1902 to support a Panamanian route. By 1903, Bunau-Varilla's efforts had led to a change of administrative policy favoring a Panamanian canal and the negotiation of the American assumption of French debts and territory.

The result of the American change of policy was embodied in the 1903 Hay-Herran Treaty signed with the president of Colombia, José Marroquin. The treaty, approved by the U.S. Senate but not by its Colombian counterpart, promised the lease of a strip of land ten miles wide for a hundred years at the purchase price of $40 million and an annuity of $250,000 per year. Despite President Marroquin's signature on the treaty, the Colombian Parliament's refusal to ratify it set in motion a series of events that resulted in the revolt of the Panamanian people from Colombia.

Long frustrated with the government in Bogotá, citizens in the Panamanian province sought independence. The opportunity for freedom presented itself when the Colombian legislature rejected the Hay-Herran Treaty. Seeing the opportunity to win freedom and the benefits of American construction of an isthmian canal, Panamanian rebels overthrew the Colombian government. Supported by the presence of the U.S. navy off the coast of Panama, the revolution quickly resulted in an independent Panama. Having secured their independence, the Panamanian people watched as Philippe Bunau-Varilla's French canal company signed a treaty with the United States empowering the Americans to construct a canal through the new nation. The events surrounding the Panamanian Revolution have been interpreted differently by historians, and this debate serves as the heart of my lesson on the canal.

With the context for the autobiography established, students then probe Roosevelt's contentions within the document. In his autobiography, Roosevelt (Figure 3.2) declares that the United States did not directly influence the

Panamanian Revolution, yet the United States benefited greatly from the resulting situation. Specifically, Roosevelt makes the following argument:

> *No one connected with the American Government had any part in preparing, inciting, or encouraging the revolution, and except for the reports of our military and naval officers, which I forwarded to Congress, no one connected with the government had any previous knowledge concerning the proposed revolution, except what was accessible to any person who read the newspapers. . . From the beginning to the end our course was straightforward and in absolute accord with the highest of standards of international morality. Criticism of it can come only from misinformation, or else from a sentimentality which represents both mental weakness and a moral twist. To have acted otherwise than I did would have been on my part betrayal of the interests of the United States, indifference to the interests of Panama, and to the interests of the world at large . . . I did not lift my finger to incite the revolutionists . . . I simply ceased to stamp out the different revolutionary fuses that were already burning.* (1913, 564)

Figure 3.2

Class conversation about the excerpt from Roosevelt's autobiography focuses on the central argument made by the author and on the vocabulary that might indicate a subtext. Some students immediately gravitate to the effect an autobiography might have on the information presented. Other students immediately doubt the veracity of the source because they see all politicians as "corrupt liars." The upside is that kids are questioning the source and unconsciously applying subtext. As discussion winds down, I present the central question to guide this investigation: What is Roosevelt doing in his autobiography (lying, telling a half-truth, exaggerating, rationalizing, or obfuscating), and what role did the United States play in the acquisition of the territory used to construct the Panama Canal?

Digging Deeper

To facilitate investigation of the focal questions, students are provided one of several historical sources and asked to consider the information provided by the text, place the source in its historical context, and consider any information the subtext provides. The following list shows the sources used in my current iteration of this lesson:

(handwritten margin note: focused tasks)

- ⊕ "The Man Who Invented Panama," Philippe Bunau-Varilla's 1940 interview with Eric Sevareid
- ⊕ Private letter from President Roosevelt to his former secretary of state, John Hay, July 2, 1915
- ⊕ The Rights of Colombia: A Protest and Appeal, November 28, 1903
- ⊕ "The Man Behind the Egg," political cartoon, *New York Times*, 1903
- ⊕ "Panama or Bust," political cartoon, *New York Times*, 1903
- ⊕ *The Great Adventure of Panama: Wherein Are Exposed Its Relation to the Great War and also the Luminous Traces of the German Conspiracies Against France and the United States* by Philippe Bunau-Varilla, 1920

These sources are selected because they provide contrasting viewpoints, represent a cross section of the types of historical sources that students might encounter, and are generally readily available. To help facilitate student examination of the sources, I provide two short guide questions: According to this source, what role did the United States play in the Panamanian Revolution? And, is there any information contained in this source that challenges the assertions President Roosevelt makes in his autobiography? These questions help focus students on the key elements of the text.

Having examined their source, students are now asked to consider the sources examined by their peers. I organize groups so that each has one representative with each of the six sources utilized in this historical investigation. Students then share the information their sources convey. Key to this element of the lesson is that students are specific, using examples from the text, and, when appropriate, either reading segments or showing the visual to their group mates.

A word about implementation: Historical investigations do not require students to jigsaw into small cooperative groups to share their sources so they can develop conclusions. Jigsawing is a great instructional technique if student maturity, classroom organization, and time factors are all working in the classroom teacher's favor. Often, particularly when it comes to the level of management required by a group of students, the jigsaw can be problematic. If so, there are alternatives. The least attractive is to have individual students examine each source. This can dramatically slow down an investigation, particularly if there are many sources or the sources are textual rather than visual. Another option is to provide the same source to student groups of three or four. The students examine the source and derive the information that helps to inform the key question being investigated. Next, these groups present their source to the class using an overhead projector or some other device. This option can focus conversation because students are examining only one source. However a classroom teacher approaches the investigation, the key is to ensure that students gain exposure to the wide variety of historical sources being consulted.

Doing Source Work

A key component of a laboratory experience in history is what students do with the historical sources once they have analyzed the text, placed the sources into context, and addressed the questions of subtext. Much of this work is tied to critical literacy skills specific to the domain of history. The work of Sam Wineburg and his associates at Stanford University and George Mason University, as well as that by David Hicks and his colleagues at Virginia Tech, provide two potential frameworks to help scaffold students' source work. Sourcing, contextualizing, close reading, and corroborating dominate the approach outlined by Wineburg and the Historical Thinking Matters Web site, and summarizing, contextualizing, inferring, monitoring, and corroborating demarcate the steps in the SCIM-C Strategy outlined by Hicks and friends (Martin and Wineburg 2008; Historical Thinking Matters; Hicks, Doolittle, and Ewing 2004; Historical Inquiry). Both approaches emphasize the need for students to move beyond a single source and to critically examine the relationship between the information provided by each piece of evidence. It is in the corroboration stage that students can truly begin to develop and defend a legitimate interpretation of a historical question.

Complicating the Investigation

To assist my students with their analysis of the subtext of their source, I provide the following information:

President Roosevelt's Autobiography
- Published in 1913, one year after Roosevelt ran unsuccessfully for president on the Bull Moose/Progressive Party ticket
- Would have been the first three-term president if he had won

"The Man Who Invented Panama": Philippe Bunau-Varilla's 1940 Interview with Eric Sevareid
- Given to an investigative journalist
- Occurred thirty-seven years after the events
- Bunau-Varilla was almost ninety years old

Letter from President Jose Marroquin of Columbia
- Written to protest the presence of U.S. Navy and Marines in Panama at the outset of the Panamanian Revolution
- Marroquin supported the Hay-Herran Treaty but felt mistreated by the United States after the revolution
- Was worried that the loss of Panama might lead to his loss of power in Colombia

"The Man Behind the Egg" cartoon
- Published in the *New York Times* investigative story on the events in Panama
- Muckraking attempt to investigate the president

Letter from Theodore Roosevelt to Secretary of State John Hay
- Private letter
- Written after the 1912 election in which Roosevelt was denied a third term

"Panama or Bust" cartoon
- *New York Times* was developed to counter the yellow journalism of other New York newspapers
- Not supportive of American imperial efforts

***The Great Adventure of Panama* by Philippe Bunau-Varilla**
- Written after Roosevelt's death
- Written by former French engineer and first Panamanian Minister to America
- Written as a personal narrative of what happened in Panama
- Second book written by Bunau-Varilla about the Panamanian Revolution

Moving from individual analysis of sources to group corroboration enables students to compare, contrast, and corroborate information and move toward the development of a historical interpretation. Reflecting on this segment of the lesson, students have identified a series of problems created by various types of sources. The list below shows how they completed a sentence stem about the sources: "The various types of sources used to determine the purpose of Roosevelt's autobiography created problems because . . .

- "they weren't reliable sources; most of them had biased subtexts."
- "each source had different subtexts. Different authors created each source, which created biased information. Some authors agreed w/President Roosevelt, and some did not."
- "everyone had their own opinion about what they believe. Some were for and others against."
- "few of them challenged President Roosevelt's contentions while others supported the contention. Most of them were biased because news articles and cartoons usually only try to show their own viewpoint through untrue stories."
- "they were US sources. Some of them were created by Panamanians. They all had different views."
- "the truth was twisted in order to make Roosevelt look bad or good. The creators of the documents had a purpose in writing or making the source, so they gave what information they wanted."
- "we didn't know what the reasons were behind each source telling of the events. There was a whole lot of bias from the President [Roosevelt] and Philippe [Bunau-Varilla] who wanted to cast themselves in a good light."
- "letters and articles can't be changed because they are primary sources. Plus they are not written by the president."
- "they were all different sources saying different things. Some were letters from Roosevelt which meant they were lies. Others were newspaper articles and political cartoons which were biased. It was hard to know which one to believe."
- "they all varied in opinions of whether they agreed with what Roosevelt said in his autobiography."
- "they were from many different views and we could not determine the real story without the subtext."
- "they are biased and only present a certain viewpoint that can also be contradicting."
- "some were credible and some were not based on the subtext of the texts."

Student thinking indicates a degree of comfort with the idea of doing source work. They see the various historical sources as containing information that not only bears on the topic but needs to be analyzed and questioned. These positives are counterbalanced by the fact that over the years subtext has been the most difficult concept for students to grasp and apply. Student reflections on the Panama Canal lesson reinforce this conclusion. Often the difficulty with subtext arises because students must make the mental connection between background information on the author, audience, and purpose of the source and the information provided in the text. This cognitive leap is difficult for some students. Linking information from a historical source, then learning about the history/background of the source, and then extrapolating a connection from the two is complicated thinking.

Despite these difficulties, when students reflect on subtext at the conclusion of the Panama Canal investigation, they have indicated both a rote understanding of the definition and some footprint of having actually internalized the thought process. At the conclusion of this lesson, students are asked to reflect metacognitively on the historical investigation they have just completed by finishing the following sentence stem: "The subtext of the various documents was important to consider because . . ." The first group of student responses indicates recognition of the idea of subtext, but not necessarily a direct connection between the concept and the investigation of the sources. The students shared their thoughts about subtext:

- "[It] explains why they wrote the given document and whether there was bias intended."
- "[It] was important to know who created the source, when the source was created, and why it was made. Each author had different opinions on the Panama Canal."
- "Everyone had an agenda on what they wanted to try to fulfill, making them point out what they thought was important."
- "[It] showed who actually wrote the document and where the document came from."
- "It was important to consider subtext of the documents because the subtext determined whether the source was reliable enough to base our opinion on."
- "Reading between the lines gives you a much better insight on what people were really thinking and the true intentions of the character of the source."
- "[It] was important to see the background and views of the authors."

- "We took the sources a different way before we saw the subtext and they helped us find the real story."
- "If you only look at the document itself you will not be able to see if the truth is being covered in the subtext, so your document could be false."
- "Subtext tells us why and for whom the text was written so we can establish bias."
- "For who [*sic*] it was written and why it was written can vouch for the validity behind a source."

Although these responses do not reflect the depth and connections to specific sources I would like, they nonetheless show student progression in historical thinking. Students have moved away from the conception of history as a "story well told" or a list of discrete facts. Instead, students now see that understanding the past is part of an investigatory process. In addition, they realize that the interrogation of sources is central to understanding the past. Without prompting, students are questioning sources and linking them to the central question of the lesson. It is essential for students to break with preconceptions of "history class" if they are to progress to a deeper engagement with the past.

Two student responses indicate a more nuanced connection between text and subtext and may reflect some internalization of these questions. One student responded that "the whole ordeal was complicated by the various motives. The most helpful source was the letter between Roosevelt and Hay because there were no façades. In his autobiography, Roosevelt was obfuscating in order to make himself look better." Complementing this was the comment that "cartoons may show a skewed opinion only to sell newspapers. Letters are more reliable. Roosevelt's autobiography was hiding the truth. He did this to protect his legacy." Here students are making connections between subtext (author, audience, purpose) and the sources and then employing this in their interpretation of the past. In addition, they consider both the sources and their connection to the broader investigation. Instead of compartmentalizing their thinking on each separate source, students are linking them into a narrative interpretation of the lesson's focus question.

I teach the Panama Canal lesson about halfway through the second quarter of my school year. Students have been applying the concepts of text, subtext, and context for several months, and they have engaged in a number of historical investigations. A key question then is how they perceive the past and its interpretive nature. When asked to complete the sentence stem "Overall, when trying to interpret events from the past, you need to . . . ," students respond with some insightful explanations that indicate progress, confusion, and in many instances a deeper understanding of historical thinking:

- "know the context and subtext in order to prevent lies, half-truths, exaggerations, and obfuscations."
- "research the documents to find out who wrote them, why, and during what time period."
- "look at all of the sources, where they came from, and the bias. Most importantly, their intent on sharing the information should be looked at."
- "examine the source by looking at the sequence, the writer, time period, the intention of the document and putting it all together."
- "obtain data that has two sides of the argument."
- "find out who sources are, or are coming from, and consider why they may be telling an event in a certain manner."
- "identify key people in the event, determine the main idea and what is happening, and see how the time period affects it."
- "look at all the sources and know where they are coming from."
- "look at the context, subtext, and text and all the reasoning behind it and multiple sources."
- "think about the message of the source."
- "look at the date of the source, the author of the source, and the situation it was written about to understand why it was written."
- "leave my options open, and look up as many sources as possible and compare the information given."
- "look to see who wrote the source and where the source came from. When reading a source about a man, you should look to see if the man wrote the source himself."
- "evaluate the context and subtext, meaning why documents were written and for whom. People are unreliable so a variety of sources need to be considered."

The central area of confusion indicated by these comments centers on the differences between context and subtext. Even though students transpose the concepts, they are trying to apply the definitions, which is better than simply ignoring them. Their confusion indicates to me the need to consistently reinforce the definitions.

Persisting in student responses is the proclivity to take the mathematical approach to investigating the past. As discussed in the chapter on Nat Turner, and to be explored in later historical investigations, this attempt to quantify evidence is a perplexing route that many of my students take when conducting source work as part of a historical investigation. The approach is encapsulated in the following student reflections:

- "Review all sources and take out the biased."
- "Not be biased, and try to piece all of the puzzle together to try and find the truth."
- "Use a single strong evidence to eliminate sources that are contradicting each other."
- "Gather many sources, primary and secondary, and pick out the most common things."
- "Look at different sources and pick out information that you know is true. You must pull out only the facts and leave out information that you know could be biased or unreliable."
- "Analyze all different sources and have a background on the time period and events going on."

I am less concerned by the manifestations of this trend than I once was. Considering it over a number of years of experimentation with historical investigations I realize that the mathematical approach may actually indicate the deepest level of investigation. In articulating their responses in this vein, students are showing that they realize the need to look not just at one piece of evidence but at the relationship between a variety of historical sources. In addition, students are attempting to use historical evidence rather than simply unsubstantiated opinion to support their interpretations. It is vital, as Keith Barton has noted, for students to realize that evidence is central to historical investigation (Barton 1997a, 2004, 2005).

What still concerns me, and is an aspect of the historical lab process that still needs to be refined, is students' notion that bias eliminates a piece of evidence from creating a final interpretation of the historical question at hand. I have tried to ban the use of the term bias and spend an entire lesson on examining historical sources so that we search for the subtext rather than the bias, to no avail. Bias, and all the ugly connotations students attach to the term, still occupies portions of all discussions of historical sources. Thankfully, this has not been my experience alone (Sandwell 2003; Sipress 2008). Ultimately, I rest easy: despite the issues with the mathematical approach to history and the associated issues with bias, I feel strongly that my students are engaging historical questions, interrogating evidence, and using this community of inquiry to debate history rather than simply memorize a series of facts.

Student Interpretations

Although the Panama Canal lesson can be taught in forty-five minutes, I teach it in ninety. Having two forty-five-minute classes means there is a twenty-four-hour break in the investigation. To help bridge the gap, I have students do a quick-write at the end of the first portion of the investigation. This no-fault, ungraded writing allows students to unpack their thoughts about the sources and how they relate to the central focus question of the investigation. The example in Figure 3.3 clearly indicates that the student is connecting an examination of the sources to the lesson's focus questions.

These quick-writes indicate a high level of student confidence with the documents and a movement toward an interpretation that fully integrates the variety of documents encountered. Most pleasing to me is the number of student responses that refer to specific documents and the perspectives presented by the historical sources. This is a significant step. It reflects not only an application of the skills specific to historical investigations but also an improvement in their writing skills. Referencing specific sources and using evidence to support their interpretations increases the efficacy of their writing—a skill that will be of use to them far beyond the walls of my classroom—and is a significant benefit of the whole process. As demonstrated in the response shown in Figure 3.4, along with the quotations that follow, students use evidence to create a narrative about the events surrounding the acquisition of the land to construct the Panama Canal:

key skills

Figure 3.3

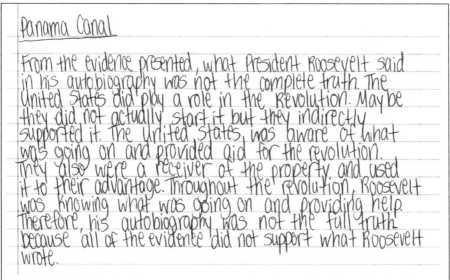

Panama Canal

From the evidence presented, what President Roosevelt said in his autobiography was not the complete truth. The United States did play a role in the Revolution. Maybe they did not actually start it but they indirectly supported it. The United States was aware of what was going on and provided aid for the revolution. They also were a receiver of the property and used it to their advantage. Throughout the revolution, Roosevelt was knowing what was going on and providing help. Therefore, his autobiography was not the full truth because all of the evidence did not support what Roosevelt wrote.

Figure 3.4

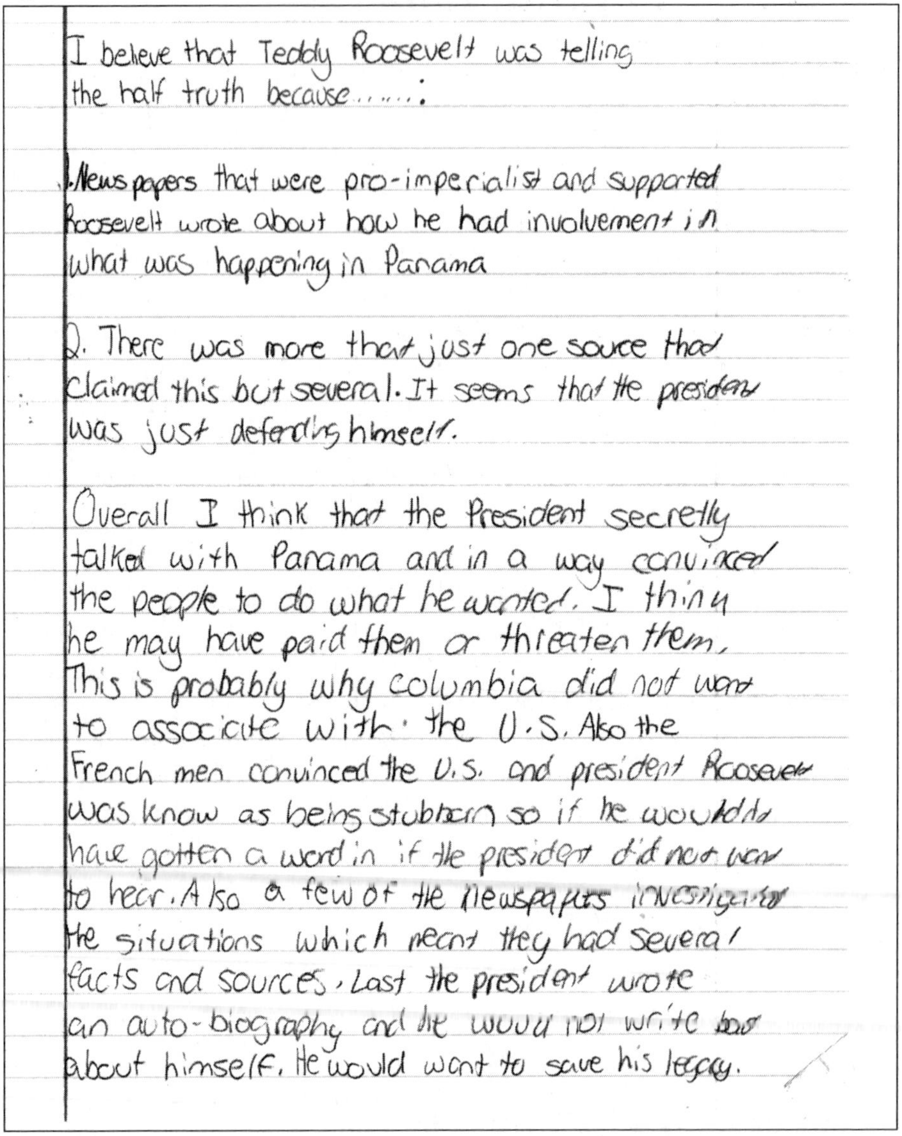

I believe that Teddy Roosevelt was telling the half truth because.......:

1. Newspapers that were pro-imperialist and supported Roosevelt wrote about how he had involvement in what was happening in Panama

2. There was more that just one source that claimed this but several. It seems that the president was just defending himself.

Overall I think that the President secretly talked with Panama and in a way convinced the people to do what he wanted. I think he may have paid them or threaten them. This is probably why columbia did not want to associate with the U.S. Also the French men convinced the U.S. and president Roosevelt was know as being stubborn so if he wouldda have gotten a word in if the president did not want to hear. Also a few of the newspapers investigated the situations which meant they had several facts and sources. Last the president wrote an auto-biography and he would not write bad about himself. He would want to save his legacy.

- "Also, the political cartoons are biased against him, so they are going to exaggerate the bad things Teddy did. The interview with Philippe B-V [sic] is also against him, and it was taken long after the issue of the Panama Canal."
- "I believe Roosevelt knew about the events in order to protect his own reputation. In a letter he wrote, he said he was tired of those Colombians; his intentions were there."

- "However, other sources such as political cartoons depict that Roosevelt took Panama over and broke laws, but also helped Panama to get free from Colombia . . . Even though the source may have biased opinions based on the point of view that is presenting evidence on whether or not he did nothing or he really did something, no source completely agrees with Roosevelt's point of view."
- "In one of Roosevelt's private letters [from Roosevelt to Secretary of State John Hay] . . . he writes that he is fed up with Colombia and is going to focus on Panama now."
- "The cartoons were biased but all of the events included in them, including Roosevelt breaking laws, could not have all been made up . . . The Muckrakers [creators of the cartoons or the newspapers and magazines in which they were published] might also be exaggerating Roosevelt's involvement b/c [*sic*] they didn't support Roosevelt."
- "However, others, like the Colombians and the Muckrakers, while not the most honorable sources, believe Roosevelt did play a role."

Despite the positives found in the above quotes, other responses indicate either the need to reemphasize the use of evidence-based examples or a lack of understanding of how to use evidence once it has been analyzed for text, subtext, and context and applied to the analysis of a historical question.

The non-evidence-based responses below are marked by two distinct trends. First, they address the central questions structuring their investigation. These students' responses do not indicate an inability to approach the past through a focus question. Instead, they show a reticence to use evidence to support their preliminary interpretation. This lack of evidence is frustrating, because I teach and encourage students to consider sentence starters such as "according to," "as shown by," "as indicated through," and other prompts that remind them to use specific examples and evidence.

The second trend is the persistence among many students who do not cite evidence in taking the mathematical approach to source work. As we saw during the Nat Turner investigation, and will continue to see throughout the book, this indicates an attempt to divine a mathematical answer that will produce a "true" interpretation of the sources.

- "Therefore, his autobiography was not the full truth because all of the evidence did not support what Roosevelt wrote."
- "According to all of the other documents that we have looked at in class, I feel that the Americans did have something to do with the war. I don't believe that they started or stopped the war, but I feel that they had some involvement in it."

Returning to the Investigation

On the second day of the investigation, students quickly return to examining the sources. It is during the final phase of small-group presentations that they encounter the source that most influences their analysis of President Roosevelt's autobiography: the interview with Frenchman Philippe Bunau-Varilla. This source intrigues students both because of the type of source—an oral history forty years after the event—and because of the frustrations generated by the information presented, or not presented, by the document. Given to CBS reporter Eric Sevareid in 1940, the interview investigated the events surrounding the Panamanian Revolution and the manner in which the United States gained access to the territory upon which the canal was constructed. Bunau-Varilla describes a meeting with President Roosevelt:

> *I called on Mr. Roosevelt and asked him point blank if, when the revolt broke out, an American warship would be sent to Panama to "protect American lives and interest." The President looked at me; he said nothing. Of course a President of the United States could not give such a commitment, especially to a foreigner and private citizen like me. But his look was enough for me. I took the gamble.* (Sevareid 1963)

"Mr. Lesh," my students often ask, "what is this look and how do we deal with it as evidence?" This query is evidence that students can engage the past by interrogating the evidence but that they still need to practice and refine the skills central to mastering this approach.

This source is challenging and intriguing. It often occupies much discussion as students present their narrative of the events leading up to American acquisition of the territory used to construct the canal and their positions on the veracity of President Roosevelt's autobiography.

Conclusions

The most significant conclusion I draw from this lesson is this: History instruction can be enlivened and made more meaningful for students when they are taught to conduct source work. Student facility with text, context, and subtext empowers them to investigate the past rather than simply digest and regurgitate. Although true internalization of the process and comfort with using the questions that underlie text, context, and particularly subtext are still in the developmental phase for many of my students, it is neither impossible nor impractical to incorporate these approaches into course work on history.

The strongest objection I hear from teachers when presented with historical investigations is that their kids cannot do it. The majority of the research on this approach has been conducted with elementary school students, including many in schools with high poverty rates. My students are not exceptional. They are not in an Advanced Placement course. They are generally college bound, but few if any have a deep love for studying the past. They want to be nurses and accountants, or, more commonly, just get out of high school as fast as possible. The goal is not to train a new generation of historians. Instead, the historical investigation model is designed to generate student interest in studying the past, engender competence with a set of thinking skills that will benefit them beyond the school walls, and promote an understanding of the major events, people, and ideas that populate the American past. It is also important to remember that it takes perseverance on the part of the teacher. Do not give up. Once students turn the corner toward thinking historically, you will never return to your previous approach to teaching the past.

As this chapter merges into the remainder of the book, I hope it becomes apparent that there is a different way to approach teaching history. It need not be the digestion of facts for the sake of "knowing" those facts. Instead, learning about the past can be mentally invigorating and promote student interest. The use of multiple historical sources, examined and applied to a historical question, invigorates instruction and increases students' abilities to think historically. No, this is not the panacea for all that ails education, nor is it the magic elixir that will erase student apathy. But the involvement of my students in debating the evidence and applying it to a central historical question is certainly food for thought. Be it about Nat Turner, the Panama Canal, or, as we will see with the Rail Strike of 1877, the Bonus Army, Little Bighorn, or the civil rights movement, my students are engaging the past. It is that engagement that I further illuminate as we examine chronology, multiple perspectives, and change and continuity over time.

CHAPTER 4

Using the Rail Strike of 1877 to Teach Chronological Thinking and Causality

You can't have a riot unless there is a reason, and there wouldn't be a need to ask for troops unless there was violence and you needed troops to enforce the laws.

—Student reflection on how she ordered the events relating to the Rail Strike of 1877

One day in the library, while my students were researching reformers from the Progressive Era, the proverbial Looney Tunes anvil was dropped on my head. Each student had been assigned a reformer from the Progressive Era and was conducting research on the accomplishments of that individual. The goal was to have them write a cover letter and résumé and engage in a series of interviews in which they would represent the assigned reformer. Ultimately, through the review of the résumés and the individual interviews, the class would select the five most significant reformers of the Progressive Era. Their library research included seeking out sources that provided an overview of their person and eventually identifying and using primary sources about their assigned individual. Basic stuff, right? I thought so, until one young woman approached me and said she had looked everywhere but could not find any sources about her person. I inquired whom she was researching and she said it was Upton Sinclair. No problem, I said, there are plenty of resources; go check in the *Dictionary of American Biography* for some general background information. The student responded that she had looked in all the *U* books and there was nothing on Upton Sinclair. All the *U* books, I thought? And thus the anvil descended: the order of things matters, but you cannot assume that students understand the importance of order. Chronological thinking and what causes certain factors to be related are essential building blocks for historical thought. One cannot assume, like I had done with proper names and research, that students understand how to think chronologically. As all teachers know, assumptive teaching can be painful for both student and teacher.

Chronological Thinking

Time lines: we have all made one. It might have been in elementary school when we were asked to place the events of our day in order or in middle school when we documented the major turning points in the American Civil War. Most textbooks use time lines to introduce a new unit so that students can have a quick visual overview of the major events of a period of the past. As teachers of history we have memorized the time lines of major political, diplomatic, and economic events, and the social history of our nation. Whenever we first encountered time lines, we were exposed to the idea that history unfolded in order. The American Revolution was before the Civil War but after the colonization of North America by English settlers. Time lines are possibly the most ubiquitous organizational tool used in history classrooms, and perhaps rightly so. They are effective in promoting the organization of events so that students can envision the temporal relationship between them, but time lines really disguise the true nature of the past: events unfolded, but it is not until historians order them that they take on a narrative structure.

What students rarely do—and the convulsive events surrounding the Rail Strike of 1877 provide a wonderful occasion for them to do so—is develop a chronology using the sources employed by historians. When they engage in this process, students move beyond the simple reflection of temporal order generated by the analysis of a time line to a more critical determination of how the events along the line were determined to have a relationship with one another. By challenging students to create chronology, they gain insight into how historians have determined what happened in the past and to practice the types of thinking skills relevant to the twenty-first century.

It May Be "One Damn Thing After Another," but It Is Still Important!

Many critics of historical study share the perspective of an oft-repeated aphorism that history is "one damn thing after another." The memorization of events in sequential order has been a constant in history instruction for generations. From the order of the presidents to dates of battles, memorizing things in order has been emphasized more than understanding relationships or making content-based historical arguments. Although this criticism of the traditional approach to history instruction is valid, the relationship between chronology and studying the past is nevertheless essential.

"In trying to understand or explain what happened and why," Stéphane Lévesque reminds us, "one has to look for the causes of the change as well as the consequences of the change . . . otherwise, history becomes a mere chronological list of disconnected events, having no historical meaning" (2008, 67). This is not to say that when it comes to chronological thinking, the baby should be thrown out with the bathwater. Indeed, time lines and the chronological awareness that they generate are an important part of any history classroom. Instead, if the emphasis in history instruction is on making evidence-based historical arguments, then chronological thinking takes on another, more important dimension.

When I started teaching, I assumed that students understood that events on a time line were related either causally or correlatively. Not true. What I have discovered is that students take for granted that the events on the time line have a particular relationship. They see the events as related only because one happened before the other—thus their proximity on the time line. In light of students' lack of facility with thinking chronologically, I emphasize it during many of the historical investigations in which they are engaged throughout the year.

After introducing the whole vocabulary and approach to thinking historically as demonstrated in the first chapter, I strip the process back down and emphasize particular skills: using text, context, and subtext (as we saw in the Panama Canal investigation, and as demonstrated in forthcoming chapters), as well as broader historical concepts such as chronology, multiple causality, and multiple perspectives. One of the earliest skills I teach is chronology. The National Standards for History identify chronological thinking as the first skill for all students to master. Key within those standards are the following skills:

- ⊕ Identify in historical narratives the temporal structure of a historical narrative or story.
- ⊕ Measure and calculate calendar time.
- ⊕ Interpret data presented in time lines.
- ⊕ Reconstruct patterns of historical succession and duration.
- ⊕ Establish temporal order in constructing historical narratives of their own.

When students come to understand that time-event relationships are important to deciphering the past, they are ready to delve more deeply.

As students see that the relationship between events is not simply sequential but that they are related by cause and effect, or historians have interpreted them to have a relationship that affects our understanding of the past, their facility with thinking historically increases and their understanding of the past deepens. This is not the death of content under the feet of process. Students cannot interrogate historical sources in an effort to develop a chronological narrative without understanding key vocabulary and the historical context in which these events occurred. Students placed in the position of a historian, whose job it is to examine historical sources and develop a historical narrative of their own, can do so. This process is best facilitated by teaching chronological thinking alongside causality.

Chronology's Close Friend: Causality

Causality is a fundamental building block of historical thinking. Although no surveys have been conducted, I would guess that after chronology, causality is the most frequently used historical thinking skill in the K–12 classroom. End-of-chapter questions in textbooks always stress the causes of major events, as do the associated resources. Essay questions, from the Advanced Placement exam to those designed by teachers, ask students to discuss the causes of a particular event, or to determine whether an event was caused more by political, social, or economic factors. Causality is also central to the documents, structuring much of the current approach to teaching history. Within the "Historical Analysis and Interpretation" standard found in the Voluntary National Standards, students are asked to "explain causes in analyzing historical actions." The National Council for History Education's *Habits of Mind* publication encourages students to "grasp the complexity of historical causation, respect particularity, and avoid excessively abstract generalizations."

Causality is central to many of my historical investigations because it gets to the heart of the discipline. Rather than memorizing a list of names, dates, and events, I want my students to examine the relationships between these factors to determine why a particular event occurred. What happened is important, but the various pieces of content are cognitively abstract unless they are attached to the exploration of a historical question that focuses on why. For example, when investigating the Cold War, students are exposed to a list of actions taken by the United States and the Soviet Union from 1917 until 1948, the leaders of the nations at the time, and the definitions of *capitalism* and *communism*. But if they are not challenged to integrate these *what*s of history into an interpretation of who or what caused the Cold War, causality is not achieved. If we hide from students the debates that roil historians who focus on the causes of the Cold War, we cheat them of both a more engaging approach to studying the past and a deeper appreciation of how to think historically.

Coverage, the driving force behind history instruction, demands that teachers obscure causality. The A–Z demands of a coverage-centered curriculum require teachers to teach events and their causes in a manner that assumes a relationship between content. The narrative nature of history coverage, be it via a textbook, lecture, or film, assumes causality but does not draw attention to it (Achugar and Schleppegrell 2005). To truly explore the multiple causes and the relationship between these factors, teachers must slow down, expose students to multiple historical sources, and open up the debate. Historical investigation, with its attendant demands for focus questions, historical source analysis, and student formation of historical interpretations, does not foster the occlusion of causality but brings the necessity of its study to the forefront of history instruction.

Although chronological thinking and causality are emphasized in a number of lessons I teach during the year, I have picked the Rail Strike of 1877 to serve as the portal for examining how to approach these tools for thinking about history in the classroom. Almost any topic in history lends itself to a chronological examination. Selecting sources that require students to construct a chronological narrative—rather than one that looks at multiple causality, multiple perspectives, or another historical thinking skill—allows students to practice this skill while simultaneously learning the important content prescribed in a local or state curriculum.

Why the Rail Strike of 1877?

My interest in the Rail Strike of 1877 really began with the question of how I could integrate local history into my course. Teaching in the suburbs of Baltimore, I was looking for ways to use what was familiar for my students. Starting with the familiar and then making connections to the broader national picture is an effective way to connect students to the past. Having affection for the Gilded Age and the strikes that roiled the nation during that time period, I remembered a photograph of the Rail Strike of 1877 that had the Camden Rail Station in the background. This was the same building that is incorporated into the Baltimore Orioles baseball stadium: Camden Yards. Students would be familiar with the location, and Baltimore's direct connection to the event would provide a nice segue from the local to the national (Figure 4.1).

A Little Background on the Rail Strike of 1877

While still mired in the calamitous politics of Reconstruction, the United States suffered from economic depression and an increasing tension between social classes. The economic malaise followed a panic on Wall Street in 1873 that sent waves of economic strife across the nation. In the wake of this panic, bankruptcies increased dramatically and many businesses closed as the economy collapsed into a depression. In 1874 alone, more than 6,000 businesses shut their doors (Painter 1987). Although this dramatic downturn swept over most sectors of the newly industrializing economy, it hit the railroads particularly hard.

In an effort to minimize the effects of the depression, many of the nation's railroads engaged in a rate war. The Baltimore and Ohio, Pennsylvania, New York Central, and Erie rail lines quickly set out to

Figure 4.1

Courtesy of HarpWeek.

reduce their shipping rates to attract business and damage their competitors. The continuous reduction in rates forced the railroads to look for other ways to reduce expenses. They found the answer in labor costs.

From the standpoint of the rail workers, the impact of the depression was exacerbated by the reduction in both wages and the number of workdays implemented by the railroad owners. By 1876 workers for the Baltimore and Ohio Railroad (B&O) averaged wages of $400 per year, $200 less than many of their competitors. In addition, many employees had been cut back to two or three days of work per week (Gillett 1991). To add insult to injury, the B&O forced many rail workers to pay their own way home from rail jobs that took them to other cities (Brugger 1988). By 1877 rail workers were discontented and concerned over the devastation the depression had wrought in their lives.

In April 1877 the railroad corporations consented to end the rate wars that had threatened to destroy them all and instead collectively agreed to reduce workers' wages (Brugger 1988). On July 13, 1877, John W. Garrett, president of the B&O Railroad, took the lead in this initiative when he announced a 10 percent reduction in wages and, simultaneously, a 10 percent increase in stockholders' dividends. The wage reduction affected all workers making more than a dollar per day and marked the second time since 1873 that the railroad had cut wages. This decision frightened and angered the workers, who launched a rail strike that quickly paralyzed the nation's transportation infrastructure.

The response to the wage reductions by the B&O brakemen and firemen was quick and decisive. On July 16, 1877, forty disgruntled workers walked off the job at Camden Station in Baltimore and were immediately fired. The effects of the wage cuts and fears of the workers quickly spread along the line to other cities. The same day saw frustrated workers burning and destroying railroad property in Martinsburg, West Virginia. By late July, discontent and anger had spread from coast to coast. Pittsburgh, Albany, Buffalo, Chicago, Cincinnati, Kansas City, St. Louis, and San Francisco all experienced violence and the destruction of property associated with the railroad strike (see Figure 4.2). At its height the strike included more than 100,000 workers nationwide (Foner 1977). The nation's railroads were shut down and businesses suffered even more than they had from the general economic depression.

By August 1, opposition by federal courts and the deployment of federal troops, coupled with a lack of central organization among the workers, brought the strikes to an end. The monthlong series of violent and destructive actions by the rail workers stirred many fears within the public. Some viewed the strike as analogous to the 1871 Paris Commune socialist uprising. Despite these anxieties and the destruction of life and property that occurred, the strike sparked a series of changes in the relationship between labor and management. Locally, the Baltimore and Ohio initiated reforms in 1880 with the creation of the Employees Relief Association. This entity provided death benefits and some medical services for the employees. In 1884 the company followed up with a pension plan for the workers (Gillett

Figure 4.2

1991). Nationally, the strike provided momentum for the Workingmen's political party and for the labor movement in general. The memory of a paralyzed rail system and the presence of federal troops in American cities highlighted some of the problems that industrialization was creating for American workers (Lesh 1999).

Ultimately, a version of this lesson appeared in the Organization of American Historians' *Magazine of History*. After the publication of the article, the lesson, as lessons always do when you spend more time teaching them to live teenagers, evolved. It is now the first lesson I teach that asks students to confront historical sources and to develop a chronology of events.

Implementing the Lesson

I initiate the lesson by projecting the image in Figure 4.3 and asking students to identify elements of the depiction that aid in understanding the artist's viewpoint. Students are immediately drawn to the woman with the baby in her arms and the smoking gun. Their answers will eventually include the dead body, the train wheel, the bricks, and the obscured landscape in the background. The image is intriguing, particularly when one considers the forlorn look of the man who serves as the focal point. At this

**Figure 4.3 "The Frenzy, and What Came of It"
(Drawn by E. A. Abbey)**

Courtesy of HarpWeek.

juncture I inform the students that the purpose of their investigation is to determine what event is being depicted and what the artist's message about the event is. With their mission set, the students begin their source work.

The Sources

A multitude of sources are available online relating to the 1877 strike. For my purposes I have selected four: a letter advertising the benefits of a Gatling gun to the owner of the Baltimore and Ohio Railroad; a broadside announcing the reduction of wages for all workers on the B&O line; a letter from the president of the B&O to President Rutherford B. Hayes requesting federal troops; and an insurance document listing the types and amounts of damages generated by the strikers. These four documents, when compared and contrasted to determine the causal relationships between the events they discuss and then placed in the correct chronological order, enable students to tell the tale of the strike and to place the initial image in its historical context.

"What's with All the Cursive?"

One of the challenges of this lesson is the fact that I use the true original sources, handwriting and all. Three of the four sources are handwritten in beautiful cursive, or what my seven-year-old son calls "scribble-scrabble" (see Figures 4.4 and 4.5). Cursive is not a central part of most elementary school curricula, so the presence of an entire document in this foreign script can be daunting. In most instances I solve this problem by retyping the documents so that the cursive does not become an impediment (real or manufactured) to student analysis of the sources. I do not make these adaptations unless my students' reading or motivation levels demand them. That confession aside, there is nothing wrong with adapting a historical source so that it is readable for students. We all love the old yellowing documents that scream, "I am old, look at me." But once we move beyond

Figure 4.4

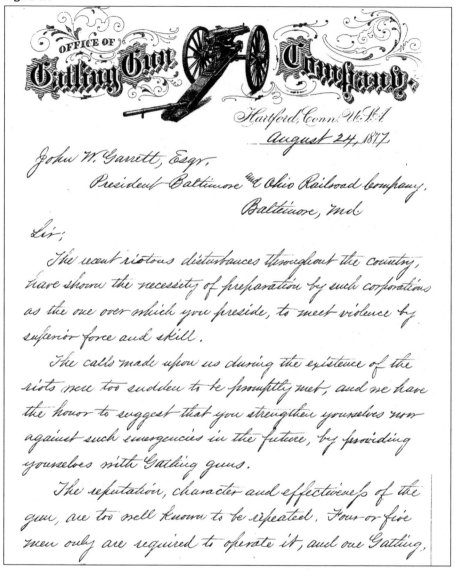

OFFICE OF

Gatling Gun Company.

Hartford, Conn. U.S.A.
August 24, 1877

John W. Garrett, Esqr,
President Baltimore and Ohio Railroad Company,
Baltimore, Md

Sir;

The recent riotous disturbances throughout the country, have shown the necessity of preparation by such corporations as the one over which you preside, to meet violence by superior force and skill.

The calls made upon us during the existence of the riots were too sudden to be promptly met, and we have the honor to suggest that you strengthen yourselves now against such emergencies in the future, by providing yourselves with Gatling guns.

The reputation, character and effectiveness of the gun, are too well known to be repeated. Four or five men only are required to operate it, and one Gatling,

the initial reaction, these same yellowing documents, with their archaic and sometimes misspelled words, can turn a good historical investigation into a battle with students who shut down because of the language or readability of a source. Making adaptations for vocabulary and style, and even placing them next to the original source, can empower students to conduct the source work rather than drive them away (Wineburg and Martin 2009). Allowing students to see and even interpret the original source can be useful, but if frustration wins out over motivation, then everyone loses.

Figure 4.5

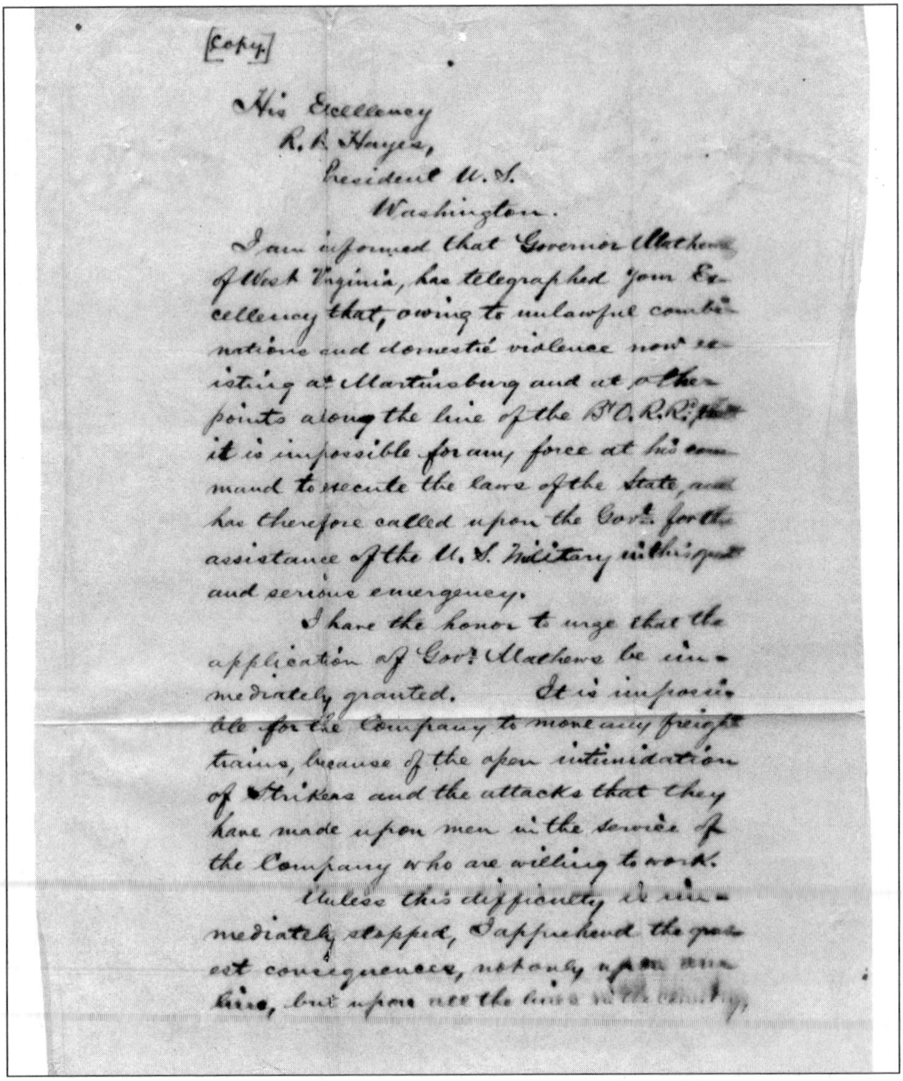

[Copy]

His Excellency
R. B. Hayes,
President U.S.
Washington.

I am informed that Governor Mathews of West Virginia, has telegraphed your Excellency that, owing to unlawful combinations and domestic violence now existing at Martinsburg and at other points along the line of the B&O. R.R., that it is impossible for any force at his command to execute the laws of the State, and has therefore called upon the Govt. for the assistance of the U.S. Military in this great and serious emergency.

I have the honor to urge that the application of Govr. Mathews be immediately granted. It is impossible for the Company to move any freight trains, because of the open intimidation of strikers and the attacks that they have made upon men in the service of the Company who are willing to work.

Unless this difficulty is immediately stopped, I apprehend the greatest consequences, not only upon our line, but upon all the lines in the country,

Developing the Chronology

Having identified the information their sources provided, students present their findings to the class. This phase of the lesson can accommodate a number of formats for delivery. Following a traditional jigsaw structure, students can be regrouped so that each new group has one person who reads each of the documents. Students then share their information and are asked to create a chronological narrative of the events that generated the artist's image they confronted at the outset of the lesson (Figure 4.6).

Figure 4.6

A Hot Summer's Day: An Incident in Baltimore

SOURCE A: A letter from the treasurer of the Gatling Gun Company to the president of the Baltimore and Ohio Railroad

> Examine the primary source—in this case, a letter—and answer the questions completely. Be sure to provide specific facts or direct quotations from the source to support your answers. You do not need to answer the question in the box; we will do that in class.

What opportunity is the letter writer discussing?

Why does the letter writer see a need for the president of the Baltimore and Ohio Railroad Company to make such a purchase?

What benefits does the letter writer envision stemming from the use of his product?

Summarize what you learned from the source.

> Develop a hypothesis based on the information contained in the source. What might motivate the president of the Baltimore and Ohio Railroad to accept such an offer?

The development of a chronology can also be accomplished by having each group present their document to the class. As each group presents, I have a sign with the document name taped to the wall, and we vote on the order of the documents based on the information they provide. As a new source is shared with the class, we collectively revisit the previous documents and decide where the new information fits and if any alterations to the existing chronology need to be made. I have come to prefer the second method of delivery because it enables me to have students unpack their thinking for a larger audience. The depth and quality of students' responses as we collectively develop a chronology of events through our analysis of the individual documents and the relationship among them is insightful and beneficial for a larger audience to hear, confront, challenge, and develop consensus on.

Of course you are probably thinking, "How hard can it be to build a chronological account of an event? Just use the dates on the sources." Gotcha! Yes, all of the documents have dates, but if the chronology were built with just the dates, students would not understand the strike. The insurance document that depicts in great detail the damages wrought by the rail workers is dated well after the conclusion of the event (Figure 4.7). If students simply made the decision based on the dates, their chronology would have the strike starting, the call for federal troops, the advertisement for a Gatling gun to stop future strikers, and then the riot that generated the damages. To effectively develop a narrative of the events surrounding the Rail Strike of 1877, students must consider not only chronology but also causality. In fact, as the student comments that follow indicate, it is causality that becomes the doorway to the development of an effective chronological telling of the story illuminated by the four documents they consulted on the Rail Strike of 1877.

Student Thinking on Determining Causality and Chronology

"How," one of my students argued, "can you have a letter asking for the president of the United States to send troops before there has been violence or destruction of property?" One student interviewed after the lesson said that the documents, when compared, created "a sequence of events" that indicated to her the natural flow of the events surrounding the Rail Strike of 1877. "You can't have a riot unless there is a reason [wages being cut], and there wouldn't be a need to ask for troops unless there was violence [illustrated by the list of destroyed products] and you needed troops to enforce the laws." Her logic, as drawn from her understanding of the infor-

Figure 4.7

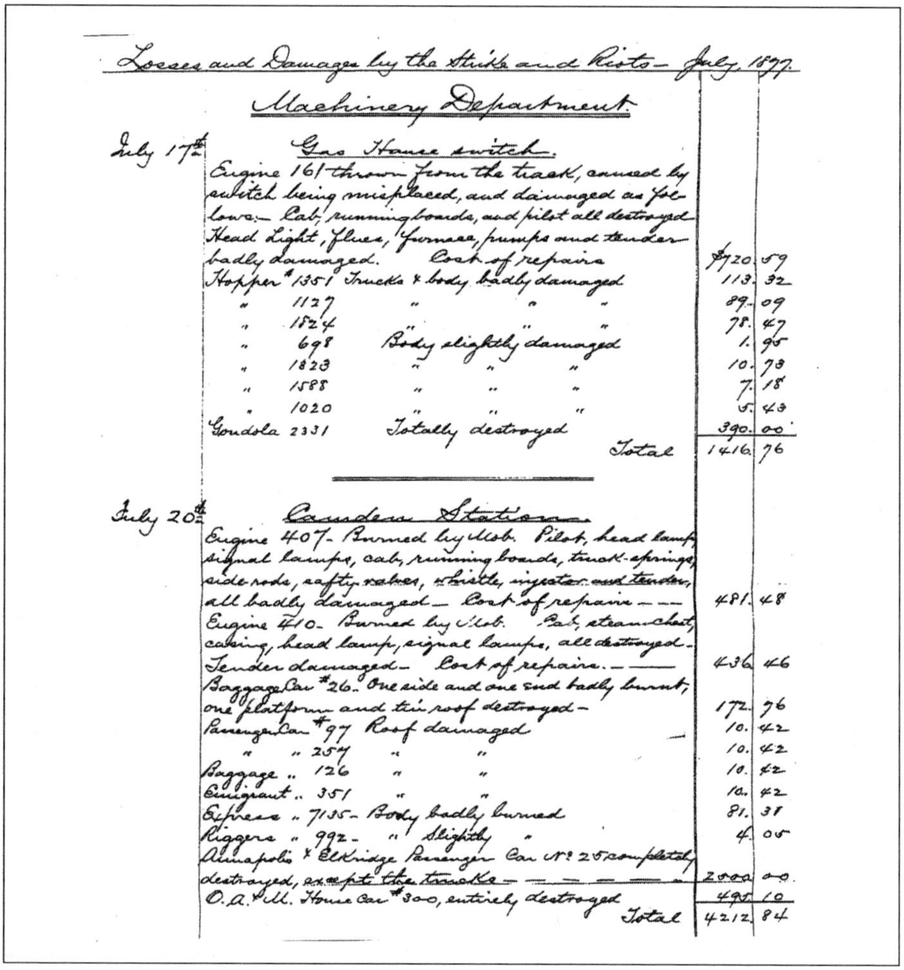

mation provided by the historical sources, is that "a sequence" of events should reflect a logical causal relationship among the components.

In short, she was describing what the Historical Thinking Skills section of the National History Standards calls establishing temporal order in constructing a historical narrative. Natalie said that because the "dates do not correspond with the logical sequence of events [as extrapolated from the class interpretation of the documents and their relationship to one another]" they actually interfere with an accurate telling of the 1877 strike narrative. Her comments hit the cognitive bull's-eye of the lesson: chronology, when developed by historians, is not simply placing documents in chronological order, but making determinations about the relationships among information contained within a historical source and then using that information to craft an accurate telling of the event. Just because a document is dated later than others does not mean that the information does not inform an earlier telling of the event.

Several things become clear as my students unpack their thinking on how they developed a chronological narrative of the events surrounding the Rail Strike of 1877. First, they are capable of thinking about history as more than an aggregation of information. As with any skill, there is variability among students to the degree to which they have arrived at this conclusion. Nonetheless, their discussion of how they approached the documents and the conclusions they developed hearten me to the fact that they are beginning to alter their thoughts about the discipline of history and what it means to study the past. Second, they are willing to make an effort to engage the past using the historical thinking skills within the investigations framework I have taught. This is important because it means they see, at least relative to their grade, the skills as an integral part of the rail strike investigation specifically, and the course in general.

Concluding the Lesson

With chronology established, and the context set, students return to the image examined at the lesson's outset. They immediately focus on the railroad ties, the train wheel, the smoke, and the gun and correctly place the picture at the conclusion of the 1877 rail strike. The connections among the information confronted in the historical sources are readily apparent. Next, the chronology they developed becomes useful as they attempt to discern the artist's message. Knowing the damages wrought by the rail workers and the use of federal troops to suppress the violence, students' responses quickly fall to whether the image is anti- or prolabor. After discussion of why the image may transmit one view over another, and after they refer to the chronology for the content to substantiate their opinion, I reveal the caption to the illustration.

Before this point in the investigation, students have not seen that the image is captioned "The Frenzy and What Came of It." Once this is revealed, they focus on the term *frenzy*. Given the context of the events, as understood through the chronology they developed, students speculate that the image is antilabor because *frenzy* is not a positive appellation for the workers' actions. Through class discussion and the revelation of how the workers were described by the newspapers of the time, students correctly interpret the image as a challenge to the use of violence as a tool for rectifying labor-management disputes.

Lessons for the Future

How much do chronology and causality aid in the development of an interpretation to the key focus questions of this lesson? Significantly! Students have confronted a series of documents that present evidence. If they examine the documents in chronological order, based on the date each one was produced, they encounter contradictory information. They tend to view a source produced during or close in time to an event as a "more accurate" depiction of it. They reflexively assume that a memoir, or any source distant from an event, is inherently less useful to the exploration of a historical question. Students think of the time gap as the occasion for senility, disingenuousness, or some other pernicious development to spoil the utility of the information provided by a source. They believe that when creating a chronological interpretation of an event, they must assume that there is an inverse relationship between time and utility. Ideally, students learn that this cheapens the usefulness of the evidence. Time, after all, can also allow participants to present a broader view of an issue, depoliticize it, or deepen its political value. At the end of the day, time does not destroy the utility of a source to a given problem. Even if other sources challenge the validity of the factual basis of the source, it opens up new questions (were the mistakes intentional?) and simply furthers the source's ability to inform the problem at hand or another historical issue.

Traditional time lines are still useful and important to the investigation and understanding of the past. In some instances, for students to conduct source work and draw conclusions about a central question, it is imperative that they have a clear picture of the chronology of events. A time line is a perfect tool for this. But instead of stopping with time lines as the only application of chronology in the classroom, I believe that for students to understand the past they must engage in creating chronological frameworks for historic events. As the rail strike example demonstrates, students can approach the study of the past by thinking chronologically when applying evidence to a historical question.

One of the big conclusions I draw from this lesson and others that emphasize chronological thinking is that students see the opportunity to generate a temporal story as akin to putting together a puzzle. The knowledge that a story is embedded within the historical sources promotes interest in the investigation. The downside is that sometimes students read too much into the sources as they create their chronology. Despite humorous results, I am open to their speculation. To me, this means that they are attempting to draw information from the sources and create a chronological narrative. As their version unfolds, it is not long before their peers point out the flaws in their logic or information from the sources that contradicts some of their central, albeit misguided, assumptions.

A second conclusion is that there is a broad change in students' impressions of history as a discipline. When asked after the lesson either in writing or in a one-on-one interview, students indicate that by building a chronological narrative of an event, they felt more engaged. Natalie, interviewed after the rail strike lesson, noted that she approached the sources looking for a "sequence" or relationship between the information provided by each. She was examining historical sources to develop a chronological telling of an event in order to place a historical image in its context. She was not examining a time line but creating one. Her analysis of the sources was not simply to glean information from them akin to the reading of a textbook, but instead to use the sources to approach a historical question. That students are engaged in doing history means that my efforts to simulate a more discipline-centered approach, rather than the more traditional memory-history paradigm, can work. In addition, and again this is anecdotal, I think my students retained the information better when it came to assessments on content in addition to their growing facility with thinking historically.

Just as students do with change over time, multiple perspectives, or causality, they can use chronological thinking in a manner similar to that used by historians. Of course chronology, like the other disciplinary concepts, does not simply disappear in one lesson and appear in another. Approaching any historical question will require students to think chrono logically to some degree or other. What is important, if a teacher is attempting a disciplinary approach to investigating the past, is to make each concept visible and apparent for them. Emphasizing one concept over the others in a lesson makes plain for students the mental apparatus necessary to employ that skill. Overtly and intentionally thinking chronologically in one lesson per unit, compounded over the course of a year, can truly promote historical thinking in the classroom.

By the way, when my student researching Upton Sinclair for the Progressive Era Hall of Fame project turned in her cover letter and résumé for a final grade, it was for the famous Progressive reformer Sinclair Upton, so perhaps I have more work to do with teaching the importance of order!

"Revolution in the Air"

Using the Bonus March of 1932 to Teach Multiple Perspectives

We got to make our own interpretation rather than you simply standing up there and telling us what happened. If you had just told us, we would not have understood how many perspectives there were.

—Student reflections on the Bonus Army lesson

Pluto is not a planet? When I heard in 2004 that the International Astronomical Union had downgraded Pluto from planet to trans-Neptunian object, I was happy (Inman 2006). My joy was not derived from some deep-seated anti-Pluto bias. It came instead because it spoke to the realities of the creation of knowledge and opened the door to discuss one of my personal bugaboos: people who declare an animus toward "revisionist" history. History, rather than memory, is a discipline that continually reexamines the past in light of the emergence of new evidence and the posing of new questions to existing evidence. By its very nature, then, the meaning of the past evolves and is not a static account of events. It is not the who, what, when, and where that is open to reinterpretation, but the meaning of those events, personalities, and ideas. When Pluto was demoted, it became an opportunity to discuss how our understanding of even the supposedly peer-reviewed immutable laws of science are open to revision when new information is discovered and new questions are posed. Science, just like history, is open to revision in light of new evidence. The key ingredient is evidence.

Carol Berkin, Presidential Professor of History at Baruch College, often tells the story to Teaching American History audiences of the selection of her dissertation topic. Having completed her course work at Columbia, she told her adviser she would like to take her research in the direction of women in the age of the American Revolution. "But there is nothing important to write about—and there are no sources from which to write it," responded her adviser. If we were to believe that history occurs without revision, Carol Berkin and the other historians who blazed the path that led to a deeper understanding of the role of women in American history would never have been able to so radically alter and deepen the American story. Berkin, Mary Beth Norton, Kathryn Kish Sklar, Linda Kerber, Nancy Cott, Carol DuBois, and numerous other historians reexamined sources, asked new questions, and discovered previously ignored sources to revise our understanding of the role of women in American history.

It is not, as is so often implied, that they revised history by inventing details, but that their revisions came from the evidence and their interpretation of the evidence. "Only recently," argues Linda Levstik, "have historic sites such as Monticello or Mount Vernon attributed much importance to life in the slave quarters. Yet many of these facts were there all along, largely unnoticed until historians revised both the questions they asked about the past and their assumptions about what data might help answer those questions" (Levstik 1997, 49). Just as Pluto suffered demotion from planetary status as the result of new evidence, enslaved people and women have been elevated in their significance to the telling of the American story. So to think historically, students must be able to deal with new evidence brought to bear on historical questions. Revision is central to interpreting the past and becomes a key focal point as I use multiple perspectives to examine the Bonus Army of 1932.

Multiple Perspectives

For my purposes, I define multiple perspectives as an approach that examines a historical event, person, or idea through the lens of its contemporaries, participants, or proximate chroniclers. I am often asked why I limit the definition. It is arbitrary because of the contrast I draw between multiple perspectives and historical interpretations. When comparing historical interpretations, I take an approach that is more historiographical. Examining the evolution of historical research about an event is a more longitudinal investigation, whereas I limit multiple perspectives to an investigation that emphasizes historical sources of greater proximity to the event or individual being studied. The types of historical sources—diaries, pictures, and material culture versus historical monographs, films, or textbooks—bring the distinction to greater clarity. Although students ask the same questions of text, context, and subtext about all sources, those I tend to use in examining multiple perspectives often offer more narrow insights into the individual or event than those employed in the service of contrasting historical interpretations. When working with students as they develop greater facility with historical thinking, I find it very beneficial to distinguish between multiple perspectives and historical interpretations.

When teaching a lesson that makes the historical concept of multiple perspectives visible, a few guidelines are in order. Key, in my estimation, is that students not confront too many perspectives at once. Balancing one-dimensional sources when students are considering only the information presented in the text is easy. It is a much more daunting task to have them balance multiple sources from a multiple-dimensional perspective. Having to consider not only text but also subtext and context for an individual source, students must now examine, compare, contrast, and synthesize multiple sources. Too many perspectives, and kids will shut down. Yes, this is artificial to the process that historians undertake when confronting an issue from the past. But these are teenagers, and authenticity of approach must at times be sacrificed to student and teacher sanity. Confidence is communicable, but so is frustration. Just as Jerome Bruner reminds us that "the trick is to find the medium questions that can be answered," the trick with multiple perspectives is to inject just enough so that students can see the differences but still generate an interpretation for the question at hand (Bruner 1961).

A second warning is this: when students are dealing with multiple perspectives, it is essential that they be provided with a significant understanding of the context and subtext of the documents used (Westhoff 2009; Reisman and Wineburg 2008). As we witnessed in the Panama Canal lesson, studying context and subtext is paramount to students' development of a historical interpretation. Without understanding when, why, and for whom a source was created, it becomes impossible to seriously interrogate the evidence and apply it to the development of an interpretive argument. In the Bonus Army lesson, identity of the authors, their connection to the events, and the ideological tendencies of their publications are essential pieces of information for students if they are to deal with the questions at hand. Making the perspectives explicit greatly facilitates students' ability to engage their historical thinking.

"Why the Bonus Army? Did They Really Have an Impact?"

"Why the Bonus Army?" queried a teacher in a professional development workshop I was running. For me, one of the things lost in the examination of the Great Depression is the choices that Americans made to deal with the economic decline of the late 1920s and 1930s. The travails of the Oakies and Arkies have found a place, and pictures of hobos riding the rails and the ubiquitous Hoovervilles (Figure 5.1) populate the texts, but are the individuals represented by these images lost? The courage that it took for former veteran Walter Waters to leave Oregon, travel the length of the nation, and exercise his constitutional rights to petition the government speaks volumes about the impact of the Depression. The story of the Bonus Army is a way of humanizing the Depression and serves as a good segue from President Herbert Hoover's attempts to rectify the steep economic downturn to those of President Franklin Roosevelt.

The Bonus Army

On a warm July day in the nation's capital, 20,000 Americans, engaging in their constitutional right to peaceably assemble, found themselves staring

Figure 5.1

at American soldiers ordered to remove them from the swampy edges of Washington, D.C. By the dawn of the next day, issues of governmental power, the widening impact of economic depression, the potential growth of Communist influence, and the electability of the incumbent president were all brought to a head. The actions taken by the United States military, in violation of direct orders from President Herbert Hoover, drew to a close the desperate plight of numerous World War I soldiers. Yet it cast great doubt on the ability of the president to effectively govern the United States and bring it out of the Depression. And it cast additional doubt on the decision-making abilities of American General Douglas A. MacArthur.

The impetus for these events in the summer of 1932 can be traced to the return of American veterans from the Great War in Europe. In the midst of the prosperous 1920s, American soldiers, led by the newly formed American Legion, petitioned Congress for monetary recognition of the sacrifices they had made as participants in World War I. Angered by the dramatic difference in pay earned by civilians working in domestic military jobs and soldiers serving in the military, the Legion and millions of veterans secured the payment of a bonus that recognized service to their country. The Adjusted Compensation Act of 1924, referred to as the Bonus Bill by its proponents, promised that in 1945 all veterans would be paid $1.00 for every day of service within American borders and $1.25 per day for service overseas. All veterans who were eligible for more than $50.00 of bonus were issued Bonus Certificates redeemable beginning in 1945, whereas those eligible for less than $50.00 were immediately paid in cash. A major victory for those who had served their country, the delayed payment was a concern for some (Daniels 1971; Dickson and Allen 2004; Kennedy 1999). These concerns were exacerbated by the deepening of the economic depression that struck the nation in the early 1930s.

One of those reacting directly to the declining economic environment was World War I veteran Walter W. Waters. Recently unemployed and concerned about the shared plight of many American veterans, Walters thought veterans could become an imposing lobbying force as the United States Congress debated a bill calling for the immediate payment of their World War I bonuses. The bill could provide hundreds of dollars to veterans immediately rather than a decade later, in 1945. Waters decided to emulate a strategy used by American Communists and other homeless workers. In December 1931 the Communist Party of America had organized and executed a hunger march on Washington, D.C. On the heels of the hunger marchers in early 1932 came a contingent of 12,000 jobless men who marched from Pittsburgh to Washington demanding government assistance for their condition. Although neither effort was successful, the stage was set for a major and visible campaign to aid a specific category of unemployed: American veterans of World War I. Beginning in early 1932, Waters organized unemployed veterans in and around his Portland, Oregon, home for a cross-country march on the nation's capital. Playing off the American Expeditionary Force, which had served in the Great War, Waters and his followers nicknamed themselves the Bonus Expeditionary Force (B.E.F.) and began their eighteen-day trek across the nation to demand an immediate payment of their bonuses. Newspapers quickly picked up on the emerging story of the Bonus Army, and Waters gained followers from Texas, Louisiana, New York, Pennsylvania, Ohio, and numerous other locations (Daniels 1971; Dickson and Allen 2004; Kennedy 1999; Klehr and Haynes 1992; Howe and Coser 1974; Lisio 1974).

The target of the marching army was the United States Congress, where an oft-introduced bill by Congressman Wright Patman of Texas called for the immediate payment of the bonus promised in 1924. To facilitate the veterans' demands the federal government would need to provide $4 billion beyond the existing contents of the bonus trust fund. This would exceed the entire federal budget for the year 1932 and was considered by many to be fiscally irresponsible. They argued it would impede congressional desires to eliminate deficit spending and rein in the expanding federal debt. Despite opposition from both Republicans and Democrats, as well as a reluctant chief executive, Waters and his followers set out to lobby the legislative branch, hoping to pressure a disinclined Congress (Hoover 1952; Lisio 1974; Daniels 1971; Dickson and Allen 2004; Kennedy 1999).

By Memorial Day 1932, the first of the Bonus Army had arrived in Washington and set up camps in areas designated by the district's police chief, Pelham Glassford (see Figure 5.2). Glassford, a former World War I veteran himself, secured condemned government buildings several blocks from the White House as well as space on the Anacostia Flats, across the river from the Capitol. In addition, he worked to provide food and water for the marchers. Having successfully navigated the Communist and homeless

Figure 5.2

marches, Glassford knew that providing provision and shelter would ensure that the veterans would be more malleable and willing to adhere to the strictures of local law. The former brigadier general's efforts paid off when President Hoover himself allowed the Bonus Army to use several old federal buildings a few blocks from the White House and the Capitol, set for demolition, as temporary shelter. By early June, food, supplies, and order had been brought to the veterans who complied with the demands of the D.C. police because of the commitment of their leader (Daniels 1971; Dickson and Allen 2004; Lisio 1974).

Walter Waters responded to the accommodations provided by Chief Glassford by imposing military-style discipline on the Bonus Marchers encamped in the nation's capital. Drinking, freeloading, and radical talk were strictly forbidden, and military police patrolled the compound. The marchers were openly opposed to any Communist or radical elements within the B.E.F. and at one point had to be corralled by the D.C. police force to stop the public beatings of Communists who were caught attempting to stir up trouble among the marchers. The families accompanying many of the Bonus Marchers were provided with many of the trappings of a regular town. A newspaper was published, a library was established, and nightly entertainment was provided to help ease the frustrations of the camps' inhabitants as well as distract them from the boredom. By early June 1932 the encampment on Anacostia Flats was the largest Hooverville in the United States and the source of constant worry for Hoover and other government officials. The growing number of protesters demonstrated their collective will and their ability to gain attention when 8,000 of them marched down Pennsylvania Avenue on June 7 (Daniels 1971; Dickson and Allen 2004; Lisio 1974).

Much of the concern over the presence of so many unemployed and disgruntled veterans stemmed from their potential effect on the reelection bid of President Hoover. Warning signs showed that the November election against the governor of New York, Franklin Delano Roosevelt, was going to be close and that it promised to be a potential referendum on Hoover's ability to address the issues stemming from the Depression. In addition, there was concern among many in Washington that the Bonus Marchers' agenda was more radical than simply securing passage of the Patman Bill. President Hoover, General Douglas MacArthur, and J. Edgar Hoover, director of the Bureau of Investigation in the Department of Justice, shared varying degrees of concern over the connections between Communist ideology and the Bonus Army encamped in the front yard of the world's most prominent, democratic Capitol. The fears of the United States Army and the Justice Department were fanned by representatives of the Communist movement in the United States who used the B.E.F. to generate publicity for their goals. Soon after Walter Waters's army left Oregon, Emmanuel Levin, organizer of the California Communist Party, announced that the march was organized by the party and that he would place pressure on the other marchers to agitate for change. Despite the vocal denials by Waters and other veterans, the perception of Communist involvement raised the stakes for Police Chief Glassford and President Hoover as they faced a crowd of disappointed veterans, frustrated by the failure of their bill to become law (Klehr and Haynes 1992; Klehr, Haynes, and Firsov 1995; Daniels 1971; Dickson and Allen 2004; Kennedy 1999).

On June 17 the U.S. Senate voted to reject the Patman Bill, which had been approved by the House of Representatives two days earlier. At this time many of the marchers left the capital and headed home or in search of work. Many were assisted by the $100,000 appropriated by Congress at the request of President Hoover. This money paid for train trips home. Despite the thinning of numbers and the failure in the halls of Congress, between 10,000 and 15,000 marchers remained encamped in Washington, willing to continue their efforts. Frustration and boredom soon set in and were exacerbated by oppressive summer heat, declining food quality, waterborne diseases, and a small but vocal element of radicals pushing for more drastic efforts to draw attention to the veterans' plight (Daniels 1971; Dickson and Allen 2004; Kennedy 1999; Lisio 1974).

After much internal discussion, the federal government, in cooperation with the Washington, D.C., municipal government, agreed that the Bonus Army would be removed from the condemned buildings they had been allowed to occupy in the Federal Triangle. July 28 was established as the date for their eviction, and leaders of the army were informed. On the morning of the 28th, Police Chief Glassford and his force moved in to remove the troops and escort them across the Eleventh Street Bridge to the encampment on the Anacostia Flats. Agitated by some of the more radical elements among the remaining marchers, Bonus Army members threw bricks at the police. A brief but intense struggle ensued (see Figure 5.3). Despite the short duration and limited number of casualties generated by the veterans' outburst, President Hoover issued orders to the U.S. Army. Commanded by General Douglas MacArthur, the army was to proceed to Washington and remove the B.E.F. from the condemned buildings, over the Eleventh Street Bridge, and to the safety of Camp Marks. Upon issuing his orders, President Hoover expressly refused to declare a state of insurrection and instructed MacArthur not to cross the Eleventh Street Bridge and

Figure 5.3

enter the Bonus Marchers' compound. The initial removal of the Bonus Army went quickly. Armed troops under the command of MacArthur, Dwight D. Eisenhower, and George S. Patton used tear gas, bayonets, and physical force to remove the occupants of the buildings and to march them down Pennsylvania Avenue and across the bridge to Anacostia Flats. At this juncture, General MacArthur stopped his troops and waited. On two separate occasions, he was informed of the president's orders not to cross into the Bonus Army's camp. But these orders proved to be of no avail. MacArthur ordered his troops into the makeshift Hooverville and routed the veterans. Flames quickly engulfed both the hovels and the marchers' possessions (Eisenhower 1967; MacArthur 1964; Hoover 1952; Daniels 1971; Dickson and Allen 2004; Kennedy 1999; Lisio 1974).

Even before the flames had died out, the debate over why the Bonus Army was forcibly removed began. For most contemporary observers the treatment of the veterans was the final evidence of President Hoover's callous attitude toward the poor in general and veterans in particular. Hoover was openly castigated for what many saw as the wanton attack on American citizens by the armed forces. For others, however, the government's actions were justified. The Bonus Army, according to this line of argument, was made up of Communists bent on destroying the government of the United States, and Hoover's actions saved the nation from a "red plot." On June 29, despite General MacArthur's direct contravention of his orders, President Hoover issued a press release declaring the end to this threat to American unity. The necessity for his actions was couched in the evidence of the Communist conspiracy to overthrow the United States government. Despite these public pronouncements, Hoover remained angered by MacArthur's actions. Finally, investigations by the Justice Department, the Secret Service, the Metropolitan Police Department, the Immigration Bureau, and the Military Intelligence Division of the War Department failed to find any evidence linking a Communist conspiracy to the rioters' actions (Eisenhower 1967; MacArthur 1964; Hoover 1952; Daniels 1971; Dickson and Allen 2004; Kennedy 1999; Lisio 1974).

Historians' interpretations of the Bonus March have been divided into three distinct periods. Immediately after the dispersal of the marchers and until the 1950s, much of the blame was placed squarely on the shoulders of President Herbert Hoover. Many of the contemporary accounts, including books published by Walter Waters and Police Chief Glassford, argued that Hoover did not care about the plight of the veterans or others unemployed as a result of the Depression. For many, the Bonus March and its violent outcome were the final symbol of the Republican president's uncaring nature. In the 1950s another view of the march gained prominence, focusing on the role and influence of the Communist Party and other radicals within the Bonus Army. Although they did not exonerate Hoover, historians writing during the Cold War and the height of the McCarthy era argued that the president and General MacArthur acted to protect the nation's capital from the pernicious influence of Communists on the veterans in Washington. It was not until 1966, when President Hoover's personal papers were opened, that his role in the incident was revisited and a new historical interpretation developed. This interpretation shifted some of the responsibility onto MacArthur. It is this debate over why the marchers were removed from the nation's capital and who should bear the responsibility for the decision that drives my investigation of the Bonus Army. It is the thinking skill of multiple perspectives that students must employ to develop and defend an answer to this question (Dickson and Allen 2004; Kennedy 1999; Lisio 1974; Daniels 1971).

From Idea to Historical Investigation

When first researching the Bonus Army in preparation for developing a historical investigation, I was surprised to find that there was much more to the story than presented by the sentence and picture that appear in most textbooks. Within this event lay the inevitable debate among historians about causality. In this case it was not a debate over the causes of the marchers' discontent. Instead, it was the question of why the marchers were forcibly removed from Washington, D.C., and the degree to which those actions were the result of a disobedient military general or a legitimate fear about the influence of Communism on the protesting veterans.

The Web being my friend, and unfortunately sometimes my enemy, I quickly found a treasure trove of sources that provided insight into the historical debate about the removal of the marchers. Jana Flores, onetime director of the California History Project, once mentioned to me that the materials used by University of California at Davis professor Roland Marchand were available on the Web (The History Project 2006). Wow! What I soon discovered was a college professor whose approach to teaching the past was in some ways consistent with the one I was attempting to foster in my own classroom. Marchand's resources are clustered around a historical question. One of the questions he posed was about the ill-fated efforts of Walter Waters's veterans. Marchand's resources were complemented by those on the Herbert Hoover Presidential Library Web site as well as a variety of other online repositories.

Roads I Should Not Have Taken

Because this was one of the first lessons I designed to meld content and historical thinking, it has undergone numerous revisions. My first mistake was to focus on the wrong question. My first two years teaching the lesson I asked the students to determine what had happened to the Bonus Marchers and why. The answer to the first part was so easy that it blunted the depth of student investigation of the second part. In addition, what happened really was not in dispute—they were forcibly removed by a combination of the Metropolitan Police and the United States military. After rethinking the results of the investigation, I focused the question on why the Bonus Army was removed. This provided a narrower focus for students to investigate—always key to a high-quality experience for students—and required them to ask critical questions of the sources.

The second major adjustment I made to this investigation is the number and type of sources I use. The Internet is both friend and enemy. As the volume of digitized sources increases, the Web has become a gold mine of materials for teachers. A simple search for "Bonus Army Primary Sources" can reveal several hours' worth of letters, telegrams, newspaper and magazine articles, political cartoons, and numerous other historical sources. Unfortunately, when designing a historical investigation, not every source is created equal. Some sources, though interesting and informative, distract rather than assist students' investigation of a historical question. In addition, too many sources can overwhelm students as they sift through the evidence, consider each source and how it may affect the information provided, and begin to develop and apply the evidence to the historical problem at hand. Over the years I have found that limiting investigations to about eight sources helps students focus and reduces my tendency to include all the sources I find interesting. Limiting the number, although artificial to the manner in which historians approach the investigation of a historical problem, nonetheless presents students and teachers with a more manageable task. So, with these mistakes behind me, let's investigate the Bonus Marchers.

Teaching the Lesson

The current version of the lesson starts with students listening to the song "Brother, Can You Spare a Dime?" Music is an amazing tool to use in the classroom, with the caveat that it is not all like the rock-and-roll, pop, and rap music that students are accustomed to hearing. The earliest phases of a history course using music as a source will be dominated by drinking songs, martial songs, and folk music. Danceable they are not, but they are an interesting diversion and an important window into American popular and political culture. Music can form the basis of an investigation. For example, I examine the Ludlow Massacre through Woody Guthrie's "Ludlow Massacre" or the Detroit race riots of 1967 via "Black Day in July" by Gordon Lightfoot. Aside from forming the central focus of an investigation, songs can also be used as evidence brought to bear on a historical question. In the instance of the Bonus Army, "Brother, Can You Spare a Dime?" provides a perspective both on the deepening economic depression of the 1930s and the plight of these World War I veterans. It also allows me to segue into a homework reading that sets up the finer points about them.

Projecting a series of images helps debrief students' homework reading on the Bonus Army. While reviewing students reading, I place particular emphasis on the treatment of the army as it arrived in Washington, the relationship between D.C. Police Chief Pelham Glassford and the marchers, and President Hoover's position on the Bonus Readjustment Act and the marchers. The images draw students into the event, especially pictures of the U.S. military, armed with guns, tanks, and other accoutrements of war, burning the makeshift homes occupied by the remaining marchers. After establishing the basics of the march, I pose the questions that will frame their investigation: Why were the marchers forcibly removed, and who should take responsibility for that decision?

To facilitate student examination of the questions, I provide one of eight sources (see below). The variety of historical sources encourages students to confront the challenges presented by memoirs, the effect of time on memory, political bias as expressed through journalism, and ultimately what happens when new information is introduced about an old question.

Low skills

Bonus Army Sources

SOURCE 1: Telegram from Secretary of War Patrick Hurley

SOURCE 2: Presidential press release one day after the removal of the marchers

SOURCE 3: General Dwight Eisenhower's memoirs, written thirty-six years after the event

SOURCE 4: Excerpt from General George Van Horn Moseley's unpublished autobiography, written between 1936 and 1938

SOURCE 5: General Douglas MacArthur's memoirs, published thirty-two years later

SOURCE 6: Article from the liberal magazine *The Nation*

SOURCE 7: Article from the liberal magazine *Harper's*

SOURCE 8: Speech by Senator Hiram Johnson, a liberal Democrat and supporter of the Bonus Bill

---

When students read and analyze any of these sources, it is important to provide them with a "who's who" list of the people involved in the Bonus Army situation. Just as one identifies and defines important vocabulary words so that students can comprehend a written passage, students need to be reminded to identify people mentioned in a historical source. Without placing a name into a position and context, writers assume readers already know the individuals and the role they played, an assumption that can be toxic. I always provide a list like the one below when students are reading about a broad issue.

Bonus Army Who's Who

Pelham Glassford	Police chief in Washington, D.C.
General Douglas MacArthur	Commander of U.S. military
Major Dwight Eisenhower	Assistant to General MacArthur
Patrick Hurley	Secretary of War
Walter Waters	Leader of the Bonus Marchers
General George Van Horn Moseley	MacArthur's chief of staff
John Pace	Leader of the Communist protesters

After completing their reading, students are grouped so that each collection of eight includes one student who has read each source. Students are then instructed to share the information provided by their source. Once the sharing has been completed, each group is asked to complete the following sentence stems:

why + who responsible

- ⊕ "We believe that the Bonus Army was forcibly removed from Washington because . . ."
- ⊕ "We believe that _____ was/were responsible for the decision to remove the Bonus Marchers because . . ."

In a traditional jigsaw activity, students present their sources and the evidence they provide, and discuss how the subtext and context of each source might affect the evidence. It is crucial during this phase that students apply the information about text and context to their evidence. Frequent reminders, spot-checking groups, and pausing to review the information presented as a full class can help ensure a greater level of compliance among students.

Student sharing during this phase of the lesson tends to emphasize definitive statements from their sources. "Not abiding by the Constitution," "challenging the government," "violating civil law," "removed to maintain peace," and "disturbing the peace" are the phrases students gravitate toward when sharing reasons their sources provided for why the Bonus Marchers were removed. Sources of blame are also easily identified from the evidence. Students are quick to demonstrate their sources' identification of D.C. Police Chief Pelham Glassford, General Douglas MacArthur, or President Herbert Hoover as the key instigator of the violence against the Bonus Army.

When engaged in sharing, Maria—one of my students—points out that it became important to realize that there were different perspectives, and that it was essential to "figure out where the source was coming from." Even with a historical sense more advanced than that of some of her peers, Maria approaches the final decision about causality and responsibility as a mathematical formula. She says her group identified how many sources were stacked "against one and then threw it out [eliminated that cause of the removal or that individual as being responsible]."

Once the various pieces of evidence are presented, students discuss the two question stems. The challenge becomes their ability to link the text of a source with context and subtext and then bridge that connection to a reasoned interpretation based on weighing the historical evidence.

Debating the Evidence

After small-group work concludes with the completion of the two sentence stems, the debate about the Bonus Army and its removal really comes to life. Student outrage and frustration with the image of American soldiers attacking veterans is now given greater depth as they consider the evidence and bring it to bear on the historical question at hand. On the issue of why the marchers were removed, discussion quickly comes to the threat of a Communist revolution that is purported by several of the sources. My more nuanced historical thinkers will challenge the first-blush assumptions of their classmates. These challenges are reflected in the following student exchange:

Student 1: "There is no evidence of an actual threat, just that the government said there was a threat."
Student 2: "But all the sources say that there were Communists, and the government was obviously reacting to something."
Student 1: "But the only evidence of the threat comes from government sources, and the others [magazines] do not indicate that there was going to be a Communist riot."

Eavesdropping on this conversation, I took this exchange and others at this point in the school year as evidence that some students have internalized the process of thinking historically. Their arguments are based on the evidence, and they are applying the concepts of subtext and context as they debate. Though their vocabulary does not include the actual terms, the core of the first student's comments that the "only evidence of the threat comes from government sources" implies that they appreciate the need to consider authorship as a part of their evaluation of the evidence.

More interesting, and over the past few years occupying more of class discussion, is the question of responsibility. Contextually, President Hoover bore the mantle of responsibility for the fate of the marchers because 1932 was an election year. Political opponents painted Hoover as the perpetrator of the violence against the veterans. Students, of course, see an apparent acquiescence to this responsibility in the presidential press release issued one day after the removal of the marchers:

> A challenge to the authority of the United States Government has been met, swiftly and firmly. After months of patient indulgence, the Government met overt lawlessness as it always must be met if the cherished processes of self-government are to be preserved. We cannot tolerate the abuse of Constitutional rights by those who would destroy all government, no matter who they may be. Government cannot be coerced by mob rule. The Department of Justice is pressing its investigation into the violence which forced the call for Army detachments, and it is my sincere hope that those agitators who inspired yesterday's attack upon the Federal authority may be brought speedily to trial in the civil courts. There can be no safe harbor in the United States of America for violence. (Hoover 1932)

As the class discussion develops, my student Eli argues that responsibility is obvious because the telegram from Secretary of War Hurley to General MacArthur sent at the behest of the president clearly shows that the "president orders" the military to deal with the marchers. Daniel interjects that "MacArthur's account of the president's order thirty-two years later might be off because of his memory." (MacArthur says that "the orders not to cross the Anacostia Bridge were followed as we were in the midst of crossing the river, to suspend the operation at my discretion. I halted the command as soon as we had cleared the bridge, but at that moment the rioters set fire to their own camp. This concluded the proceedings for the night.")

But, Maria says, the "president actually says do not use violence and do not cross the bridge," according to Dwight Eisenhower's memoirs: Instructions were received from the secretary of war, who said he was speaking for the president, that forbade any troops to cross the bridge into the largest encampment of veterans, on the open ground beyond the bridge.

Maria continues that Hoover is the obvious choice to blame because he is president, but that her source, General Dwight Eisenhower's memoir, seems "concrete" because it clearly says that "MacArthur was ordered not to cross the bridge." At this point the debate rages and students move toward implicating either MacArthur or Hoover as the key perpetrator of the decision to rout the marchers encamped on the Anacostia Flats.

Within this exchange I see strong evidence that students' historical thinking has evolved from the beginning of the year. Occurring just after the midpoint of the school year, the debate about the Bonus Army's forcible removal is one that has them directly associating their conclusions with the evidence presented. Students, either without prompting or with a gentle reminder from me, started their arguments with "according to source number." Some students of course continue to make arguments based on hunches rather than through a critical application of evidence. They are teenagers, as I often remind myself, and I am asking them to approach history in a completely new manner, so I cannot expect every one of them to make an immediate transition to thinking historically. Nevertheless, I am fairly sanguine that by the time many of my students reach this lesson, they are consulting text, considering the subtext, placing evidence in context, and arguing like historians.

"More Evidence? Seriously, Mr. Lesh!"

Once students have developed their initial interpretation, I present them with a final piece of evidence. I ask them to reconsider the chronology of events and how this new source might challenge their interpretation. Because historians do not always find all the sources they need as soon as they approach a historical problem, this activity is not any less genuine than those experienced by any historian researching a historical issue. The new evidence comes from President Herbert Hoover's memoirs. For the first time, the president speaks at a distance from the event. As shown in Figure 5.4, he supports the contention that a Communist conspiracy was at hand, challenges the idea that MacArthur had the authority to cross the Anacostia Bridge, and challenges assertions made by Police Chief Glassford.

Besides their perturbation that the lesson is not over, students are frustrated by the fact that the new evidence challenges the interpretations they previously developed. The new source runs counter to their original thought that it was President Hoover who bore responsibility for the forced removal of the Bonus Marchers. Some of the evidence previously discounted by stu-

Figure 5.4

> ### Excerpt from *The Memoirs of Herbert Hoover: Volume 3: 1929–1941, The Great Depression* (1952)
>
> *In the midst of this riot the District Commissioners, upon Glassford's urging, appealed to me. They declared that they could not preserve order in the Capital, that the police were greatly outnumbered, and were being overwhelmed . . . they asked for military assistance to restore order. At my direction to Secretary of War Hurley, General Douglas MacArthur was directed to take charge. General Eisenhower (then Colonel [actually major]) was second in command.*
>
> *Certain of my directions to the Secretary of War, however, were not carried out. Those directions limited action to seeing to it that the disturbing factions returned to their camps outside the business district. I did not wish them driven from their camps, as I proposed that the next day we would surround the camps and determine more accurately the number of Communists and ex-convicts among the marchers. Our military officers, however, having them on the move, pushed them outside the District of Columbia.*
>
> *General Glassford, shortly afterwards, published a series of articles stating flatly that he had opposed calling out the troops, and that he could have handled the situation without them. The Attorney General, however, took sworn statements from the District Commissioners proving that Glassford had implored them to call for troops. Among the statements to the Attorney General was one from General MacArthur stating flatly that General Glassford had appealed to him directly for help and accompanied him throughout.*
>
> *I was portrayed as a murderer and an enemy of the veterans. A large part of the veterans believe to this day that men who served their country in war were shot down in the streets of Washington by the Regular Army at my orders—yet not a shot was fired or a person injured after the Federal government took charge.*

dents, particularly General Dwight Eisenhower's memoirs and the excerpt from General George Van Horn Moseley's unpublished autobiography, written between 1936 and 1938, now becomes more applicable to the question at hand. Although both sources attribute the decision to rout the Bonus Army on the Anacostia Flats as a direct violation of orders by General MacArthur, students discount it in the face of the presidential press release and

MacArthur's memoirs. Curiously, some students often base this discounting of evidence on the time lapse between the Bonus March and the publication of Eisenhower and Van Mosley's writings. One student remarks that "both generals published both of the memoirs over thirty years later," and another says, "Thirty-six years after the event, he [MacArthur] was older; he could have forgotten or thought differently, making us unsure whether or not it was true or not." The time lapse for some students is enough to discount the perspectives of Eisenhower and Van Mosley. Interestingly enough, the time lapse is not much of a consideration when students add President Hoover's memoirs to the mix and contrast his contentions with those of MacArthur, Eisenhower, Van Mosley, and the 1932 press release. In fact, for some students the compounding of evidence from three separate memoirs is enough to seal the deal in their minds about who bears responsibility for the events on the Anacostia Flats.

One-third of my students from the 2009–2010 school year identified Hoover's 1952 memoirs as the most important piece of evidence for determining responsibility for the expulsion of the Bonus Army from the Anacostia Flats. Their interpretation of the evidence led them to the following conclusion:

- "The memoirs are [published] past the point when people were angered about the event, so the truth of the disobeyed orders can be revealed."
- "Memoirs . . . show more than one person's opinion on what happened."
- "Memoirs   give a perspective from people who were involved in the event and they [the memoirs] were more abundant [than the press release]. The press release one day after shows one broad point of view while the memoirs show many points of view."

Student analysis goes deeper as some question the context and subtext of the press release.

- "If you read into it [the press release] the president wanted to make sure everyone knew he gave the order because otherwise it would make him look bad, especially if his orders were ignored."
- "The press release would not tell what was happening behind the scenes like what the president was say[ing] at the time."
- "Thirty years later, the president could tell the truth without worrying about hurting his image and damaging anyone's career including his own."

- "Later, when he isn't president, he tells the true story because it doesn't affect him anymore. The memoirs will allow the ex-president to reveal the true story without any repercussions, because he is out of office."
- "After a while things could be more clear as to what happened and why."
- "The press release is merely an outside summary of a witness in the case. They are given the big picture and document the information they are given. Meanwhile, the memoirs are a primary source in which president can tell all without the worry of having his tenure in office cut short or reputation tainted."
- "He [President Hoover] has less at stake and can tell the truth in his memoirs."

Unfortunately, despite the analysis discussed above, some students accept the memoir as an unvarnished account of the events of that fateful day in 1932. Gone from their analysis of Hoover's perspective is any of the analysis of the subtext and context evident in their examination of the other sources. Oddly, gone also is the reticence of some students to give Eisenhower and Mosley's memoirs any credence to the argument. Hoover, despite meeting the criteria for time lapse, seems immune to any critical analysis. In my own defense, the results of every historical investigation differ depending on the motivation, reading levels, maturity, and chemistry within a group of students. In years past, students have not taken Hoover's memoirs as a commandment from the history gods about what happened and why. Conversely, the other two-thirds of my students from 2009–2010 considered the presidential press release, Eisenhower's memoirs, Moseley's autobiography, and General MacArthur's memoirs as most useful to the investigation.

Student Interpretations

When the lesson concludes, most students lean toward a disobedient General MacArthur as the actor bearing the most responsibility for the forced removal of the Bonus Army from the Anacostia Flats. Students ask why President Hoover would have issued his press release twenty-four hours after the devastation of the Bonus Army's shantytown and then twenty years later so overtly expose General MacArthur. "Why," they ask, "doesn't the president say in 1932 that his general disobeyed orders and that he as president was not responsible?" This, and the question of the legitimacy of the concerns about a Communist uprising as justification for removing the marchers, is at the heart of the historical debate over the Bonus Army, and my students (not me, but my students) have raised that question. As Maria said at the outset of the chapter, "If you had just told us, we would not have understood how many perspectives there were." Maria further argues that she prefers the investigative approach because she "would not have realized how much debate there is. . . . We got to make our own interpretation rather than you . . . telling us." That is exactly what I was hoping she would say!

Conclusions

Multiple perspectives can be a challenging concept to implement. Students confront these perspectives and must decide how and why to use evidence from a particular perspective to develop an interpretive response to a historical question. The pedagogical challenge is to ensure that they do not simply reject evidence because it promulgates a particular perspective. Instead, if they are taught to recognize the perspectives as reflections of particular contexts and subtexts, and then to corroborate the various pieces of evidence, considering multiple perspectives becomes a tool by which they can develop a nuanced understanding of historical questions.

Each time my students wrestle with the Bonus Army, they have questioned historical sources and applied this information to the discussion of a historical question. This is the essence of a disciplinary approach to studying the past. Content is present throughout the lesson. Discussions of President Hoover's presidency; the growth of the Communist Party; the treatment of veterans; the constitutional right to assemble, petition, and protest one's government; the election of 1932; causes of the Depression; and the relationship between civilian and military authorities all become part of the discussion of this historical question. In addition, students are interrogating a variety of historical sources through the use of critical literacy skills; formulating, defending, and refining a historical argument; and thinking deeply about how history is created.

CHAPTER 6

Continuity and Change over Time

Custer's Last Stand or the Battle of the Greasy Grass?

I believe people created the memory of "Custer's Last Stand" because they did not want to believe in an Indian victory. They wanted Custer to be depicted as a hero and not a loser.

The memory of "Custer's Last Stand" was created to promote patriotism. The media was controlled by whites. They wouldn't want to show the Indians as heroes or victorious so they depicted it as the whites being heroes.

—Student reflections on the memory of the Battle of the Little Bighorn xiting Yellowstone National Park, my wife, Christine, and I decided to head to the Black Hills via the Little Bighorn Battlefield National Monument (Figure 6.1). After an arduous pass through the Bighorn Mountains—which did not look as big on the map—we arrived in Gillette, Wyoming. The next morning we traveled north to visit the site of Custer's infamous last stand, and into what, unbeknownst to me, would be a transformational occasion in my approach to teaching history.

What I discovered in the beautiful scenery of Montana was history alive, not in an artificial manner, but intellectually alive. In 1998, my wife and I arrived on the coattails of a prolonged debate over what to name the site where Custer's Seventh Cavalry fought Crazy Horse, Sitting Bull, and the various Indian tribes encamped along the banks of the Little Bighorn River. What immediately struck me that day, beyond Montana's endless sky, was the interpretive exhibit at the National Park office. At the time Christine and I were there, we were confronted with a multitude of popular culture manifestations of Custer and his "Last Stand." Children's lunch boxes, board games, movies, television shows, toys, and numerous other artifacts depicted Custer as a hero, fighting to the last man against the "savage" Indians. Because I am a huge fan of popular culture, this immediately resonated with me. Why, I wondered, would American culture so venerate the guy who had not only died, but, I knew, made several poor tactical decisions?

Figure 6.1

My curiosity was soon stoked by our discussion with the park ranger about the site and its history. He explained that as a result of a brushfire that had burned back much of the tall grass that covers the battlefield, archeologists were able to reexamine much of the historical data about the battle, bringing into question many of the traditional assumptions about General Custer's decisions on that fateful June day. In addition, political lobbying by members of the Native American community had generated sympathy for reconsidering the name of the park as well as its interpretive exhibits. Much to Christine's chagrin and with great detriment to our credit card bill, I swept through the park service bookstore and purchased a number of resources on the battle and its participants. Although military history had long been anathema to me, I saw within this battle a chance to discuss much broader issues with my students.

Throughout the remainder of our vacation I read books on Custer, Sitting Bull, and the Little Bighorn and considered how I could translate my own historical epiphany into a useful classroom experience. As outlined below, I use the Little Bighorn events as a forum for reinforcing the idea of continuity and change over time, introducing the relationship between history and memory, and continuing my emphasis on historical thinking, source work, and my overall approach to teaching the past.

Continuity Versus Change over Time

For many students there is little difference between themselves and those who populated the past other than the fact that people in the past were "stupid" and those living now are much brighter. For developmental reasons, and as a way of simplifying discussion, students tend to conflate the actors of the past with themselves. The subtleties of change over time are sometimes lost on them. Thus it is essential for students to gain a historical sense, and to ask questions and draw conclusions about change and continuity over time. If they leave our classes with the notion that people in the past were less intelligent than we are or that the past is just a stage play in which current people debate ideas in period clothing, then we have not assisted them in understanding the past as both a foreign country and one that has direct connections to their present-day lives (Lowenthal 1985). In addition, the ability to understand that some concepts, ideas, beliefs, and other historical factors have remained constant, whereas others have changed, makes the historic landscape continuous rather than simply segmented into units to be momentarily learned and quickly forgotten.

I Pledge Allegiance

The technique I use to establish the concept of continuity and change derives from an opportunity I had to work on a Teaching American History grant with Robert Rydell, who is the Michael P. Malone Professor of History at Montana State University. During one of his presentations Bob discussed the evolution of the Pledge of Allegiance. As he moved through the metamorphosis of the words and the procedures for pledging to the flag, the famed lightbulb went off in my head: continuity and change over time! Since that day the development of the pledge has been the vehicle by which I introduce students to the ideas of continuity and change over time. There are of course limitless choices a classroom teacher could use to introduce this topic, but saying the pledge has been such a customary routine in the lives of my students that they simply assume it has been the same for time immemorial. The realization that this is not true creates a great deal of dissonance. The gap between what they thought they knew and the historical record enables me to cement in their minds the need to understand that the past and the present are vastly different landscapes.

Emerging in the 1870s, the Pledge of Allegiance, as written by Edward Bellamy, started as a poem to recognize the 400th anniversary of the expeditions of Christopher Columbus. When making the pledge, students were to stand and face the flag, place their hand on their heart, and then extend that hand outward—palm facing the flag—and recite the words: "I pledge allegiance to my Flag and to the Republic for which it stands, one nation indivisible, with liberty and Justice for all" (see Figure 6.2).

Figure 6.2

The 1920s saw the first major revisions to the pledge. Emerging from the Great War, the United States was plagued by domestic concerns about the influence of anarchists and Communists. This fear fed a generalized xenophobia about immigrants. Paralleling the legislative efforts to restrict immigration was an alteration to the pledge. Still performed with the Bellamy salute, the words were altered to reflect the changes in the purpose of pledging allegiance: "I pledge allegiance to the Flag of the United States of America and to the Republic for which it stands, one Nation indivisible, with liberty and justice for all," as in Figure 6.3.

A year after the Japanese attack on Pearl Harbor, President Franklin Roosevelt pressured Congress to change the Bellamy Salute. During the 1930s, both Italian Fascists and the Nazi Party in Germany had adopted national salutes similar to the Bellamy flag salute. In an effort to differentiate American democracy from European fascism, the U.S. Congress altered the Flag Code. On December 22, 1942, the Bellamy salute was replaced with the right hand over the heart.

The 1950s provided us with the pledge that students have recited their entire school lives. In the depths of the Cold War, the phrase *under God* was added to the pledge to distinguish the United States, and its support for religious freedom, from the Soviet Union, where religion was officially banned by the state (Ellis 2007). Thus a simple function of my students' daily routine becomes the platform for teaching about an important element of historical thinking—the concept of change and continuity over time.

Figure 6.3

PLEDGE allegiance to the Flag of the United States of America and to the Republic for which it stands:
One Nation, indivisible, with liberty and justice for all.

The Pledge as a Teaching Tool

On the first day of school, as part of an introduction to the course, I ask students to stand and recite the pledge. They of course place their hands on their hearts and recite the words of the modern iteration. As soon as they divert from the original wording, I ask them why they have their hands on their hearts and why they said "the flag." After several starts and stops in an attempt to complete this simple task, some frustrated but insightful student will blurt out something akin to "Has the pledge changed?" This query allows me to segue into my introduction to the concept of change and continuity over time.

To facilitate the introduction of change and continuity I display the three iterations of the pledge and ask students to identify the major differences. Identifying the changes to the wording as well as the shift away from the Bellamy salute leads to a brief discussion of why these changes might have occurred. Lacking any substantive knowledge of the 1920s or 1950s, students still generate thoughtful speculation about the reasons why the words changed. They immediately grasp the concept of change over time. Regardless of the time of year, a quick reminder about the pledge always reinvigorates student understanding of change and continuity. As we examine the reasons for the creation of the Pledge of Allegiance, the initial manner in which we saluted the flag, and finally the political climates that generated changes to the wording, students are drawn to the fact that although most things change, what is important in history is determining why these changes occur and what factors lead to some aspects of political, economic, and social life remaining constant. Later in the year the ideas of continuity and change in history are related to events on the Montana prairie.

Beyond applying an understanding of text, context, and subtext, the central disciplinary concept emphasized in this lesson is change and continuity over time. Student examination of the events and remembrance of the Battle of the Little Bighorn provides insight into why this event has remained a constant query among historians. In addition, the investigation allows students' insight into how and why the telling of an event changes over time. What changes over time is not the event being examined. Instead, what changes is the interpretation of the event and what that event tells us about the relationship between the present and the past.

Teaching the Lesson

This lesson falls within an examination of the post–Civil War population movement westward. At this point students have examined the Transcontinental Railroad, the Homestead Act, the Exoduster migration out of the South, and the Indian Wars through representative examples such as the Sand Creek incident, the pursuit and capture of Geronimo, and the rounding up of the Nez Perce. The Little Bighorn lesson allows students to examine the event as a historic symbol of the broader movement westward. The intention is to allow them insight not only into the concept of memory but also why this event, unlike others in the long and bloody Indian Wars, captured the attention of contemporaries and has sustained potency across time. The lesson is taught over one ninety-minute period, but is easily adaptable to one forty-five-minute period or a variety of other teaching situations.

The lesson begins, as you may have deduced by this point many of mine do, with visual images. In this case I project copies of the 1896 bar poster published and distributed by Anheuser Busch (Figure 6.4). There are numerous other images that depict the white version of events but that this was used as an advertisement is an intriguing element for students. When projecting the image I initially cover up the bottom portion identifying the event and the source. As students examine the first image, they are instructed to list their initial reactions to it and to describe what they believe to be its focal point. *Stupid, brave, suicidal, strong, courageous*, and other terms are bandied about in the description of General Custer. Students see him as either extremely foolish, preternaturally brave, or the creation of a fanciful artist. I ask them what motivations may have prompted the artist to depict this person and these events in such a manner. Class discussion ensues, and then I reveal the purpose, creator, and time period in which the image was created. Students are always fascinated to see up close that the painting includes Indians holding Zulu shields—not the traditional war accoutrements for Plains Indians.

Figure 6.4

CUSTER'S LAST FIGHT.

The Original Painting has been Presented to the Seventh Regiment U S Cavalry

BY ANHEUSER BUSCH BREWING ASSOCIATION.

Figure 6.5

Next, I project the 1898 images painted by Kicking Bear (Figure 6.5). In this image students are first caught off guard by the variation in artistic styles, but are generally quick to reorient and examine the artists' viewpoint. *Victorious, brave, angry, strong*, and other similar adjectives populate students' conversation about the piece. Discussion inevitably leads to someone asking if the event depicted was the same as the one in the previous picture. This query allows me to unveil the origins of the images and to move toward the central question driving the lesson.

The Native images were generated at the close of the nineteenth century when Kicking Bear returned to the reservation after completing extended employment with Buffalo Bill's Wild West Show. He was asked by artist Frederick Remington to produce a series of images depicting his remembrances of the battle on the Little Bighorn River (Kicking Bear). Twenty years after the fateful battle, his images reflected his memory of the events and the meaning he ascribed to the defeat of Custer and the Seventh Cavalry. In contrast, the similarly inaccurate Anheuser Busch depiction titled *Custer's Last Battle* was a vehicle for selling beer. The advertisement, distributed throughout the United States, drew on the bravery of General Custer as an American hero to link patriotism to the consumption of Budweiser.

When asked their thoughts about the images, students convey refined degrees of historical thought.

- "I wasn't surprised about the two different images of the Battle of the Little Bighorn because every side has their own story. The whites depicted Custer as a war hero and the Indians as villains. Indians thought the white army was evil and so was Custer . . . Time also changes stories because the memory is altered by the media, who has a biased opinion."

- "The images just showed how biased images can be and that you can't just take one historic image for a fact. They both showed two different sides of the story and two different perceptions of the Battle."
- "Both versions contradicted each other. The Indian version depicted them as the heroes for killing the whites. The white version saw Custer as heroic that died victorious. I think that they both have some truth to them, but aren't completely the true story."
- "They were both completely bias[ed]. The Indian version, however, showed more truth than what actually happened."
- "The white version was very biased because even when everyone knows that Custer was a bad leader, Americans still want to make him look like a good guy . . . I believed the Indian version because even though it shows themselves winning, some Indians are dead, so it seems more honest."

I interpret these comments to mean students are internalizing the questions that should be asked when confronting a historical source: about authorship, purpose, audience, intent, and so on. Frustrating, however, is the prevalence of the term *bias* in so many of the responses. I intentionally do not use this word when discussing sources and pooh-pooh it when students use it in class discussion. My displeasure with the term is that students equate bias with either lying or ignorance. Instead of accepting that historical sources inherently have a point of view, students see bias as a pernicious disease that erodes a source's utility. In addition, their use of the term always has a negative connotation. In a historical context, *bias* is a neutral word, because all sources have one. Despite my dislike for it when referring to historical source authorship, students still default to it. My efforts to eliminate *bias* border on censorship, but students continue to use it as part of their historical investigation. Frustration aside, I have decided to take advantage of its persistent usage, and more important the fact that many students approach bias as a negative appellation, and turn it into a teachable moment. Instead of chastising (well, instead of chastising too much) I ask students why they use the word *bias*, what it means to them, and how it might affect their interpretation. By drawing attention to the term I force them to confront their own thinking. It also furthers my emphasis on historical thinking.

Another troublesome term populating students' responses is *truth*. Postmodernism and literary deconstruction have led to innumerable debates about the existence of truth and whether it is a legitimate concept in an examination of the past. These debates have roiled the historical professions for much of the last forty years (Novick 1988). In microcosm, this debate about truth infects my students' discussion about historical evidence.

My consternation has to do with how students understand the idea of truth as it applies to their analysis of historical evidence. My students' perspective is not grounded in postmodern theory but instead grows out of the fact that they are teenagers. For them, truth is an absolute. Students interpret the sources as completely true or as a lie: black and white, no gray. The majority of my students miss the idea that sources simply represent the perspective of a person at a particular point in time. *Truth*, then—at least as my students express it during their analysis of evidence—is a black-and-white term that is synonymous with bias.

In searching for the truth, students are going back to the mathematical approach to historical investigations. They are looking for a "right answer." My students' responses when queried indicate that sorting "truthful" sources from "untruthful" sources simplifies their investigation. By simply dismissing a document as untruthful, they can plow forward and try to find the "smoking gun" document that holds all the truth necessary to aid their development of an evidence-based historical interpretation.

Levstik reminds us that students are "trained to seek correct answers to their questions more often than they are asked to consider multiple perspectives. As a result"—and the words of my students attest to this—"many children will find this kind of historical approach unfamiliar and even threatening" (Levstik 1997, 51). Just like the word *bias*, the use of the word *truth* produces a teachable moment with kids. Ultimately, despite the appearance of these terms in students' descriptions of historical sources—and my frustrations over them—the bigger picture indicates that students are transforming how they approach source work and thinking more like historians than they were when the school year started.

The student responses above also indicate an evolution in their facility for thinking historically. Students are approaching historical sources not as one-dimensional repositories of information but as three-dimensional reflections of an author and a time period. This is a significant step in their evolution away from memory-history and toward a deeper and more nuanced understanding of history as a discipline.

Delivering Context

Before the lesson, students read about the causes, course, and consequences of the Battle of the Little Bighorn. Segueing from their analysis of the images, I lead a brief overview of the events that led to and defined Custer's final act as a military general. Establishing the context for the events students will be discussing is an important component of any historical investigation, but unfortunately my arrival at this seemingly obvious fact was convoluted at best.

Trained in or at least exposed to the ideas of discovery learning, I first approached historical investigations and their like as an opportunity for students to use a variety of historical sources to figure out what happened in a particular event (Bruner 1961). This is a useful strategy for some historical events, but it does not lend itself well to asking the deeper historical questions that occupy much of the time of professional historians. Using a series of historical sources to identify who, what, when, where, and why can be a useful strategy particularly when students are first becoming comfortable with the idea of approaching the past through questions. As their comfort levels increase, and the routine of who, what, when, where, and why recedes, it is necessary to generate more thoughtful questions to frame their investigations.

As students encounter questions focused on the historical thinking skills outlined in Step 1 of the historical investigations model (see Figure 1.2 in Chapter 1), they need to understand the context for the events, ideas, or personalities being investigated. An examination of the work that Sam Wineburg has done with high school students in San Francisco, and Bruce VanSledright with elementary school students in the suburbs of Washington, D.C., solidified my belief that context is essential for any historical investigation (Mandell 2008; Mandell and Malone 2007; The Stanford History Education Group; VanSledright 2002). The manner in which context is provided should be based on students' needs and teachers' strengths. My preference is to have students complete some reading before the class in which they will conduct their investigation. The readings are usually teacher generated, compiled from summaries of historical monographs or reputable Web sites. How context is provided is of course a much debated question within the social studies/history community: to lecture or not to lecture?

"Anyone? Anyone?"

As Ben Stein so painfully reminded us all in the 1986 hit movie *Ferris Bueller's Day Off*, a lecture can be deadly business:

> *In 1930, the Republican-controlled House of Representatives . . . in an effort to alleviate the effects of the . . . anyone? Anyone? . . . The Great Depression, passed the . . . anyone? Anyone? The tariff bill? The Hawley-Smoot Tariff Act? Which—anyone? Raised or lowered? . . . Raised tariffs, in an effort to collect more revenue for the federal government. Did it work? Anyone? Anyone know the effects? It did not work, and the United States sank deeper into the Great Depression. Today we have a similar debate over this. Anyone know what this is? Class? Anyone? Anyone? Anyone seen this before? The Laffer Curve. Anyone know what this says? It says that at this point on the revenue curve, you will get exactly the same amount of revenue as at this point. This is very controversial. Does anyone know what Vice President Bush called this in 1980? Anyone? Something-d-o-o economics. "Voodoo" economics.* (Hughes 1986)

As the camera moves across the room, students are depicted chewing on their pens, sleeping with their eyes open, blowing bubbles, and drooling. This is an extreme example of a painfully dull approach to the study of history. And yet, many of us can remember having professors who could lecture in an engaging manner and ensure that everyone learned the material. These two types of lectures—dull and engaging—exist at the opposite ends of this particular continuum in the classroom.

Lecturing to establish the context for an investigation is something I almost never do. It is neither a personal strength of mine nor something that generates much interest from my students. In fact most observations of history/social studies teachers demonstrate that, for most high school teachers, lecturing means actually having students copy information from an overhead projector or PowerPoint slide show (Gough 2004). Lecture, when effective, is the presentation of an oral argument, in which the teacher lays out for students the factual information that supports the argument. This rarely happens in high schools. If students are simply asked to copy information, or feel pressured to copy the information delivered by the instructor as close to verbatim as possible, they are not engaged with the information. Problem-centered lectures, comparative lectures, and thesis-driven lectures all provide a mechanism for packaging information for students where the intellectual work is, for all intents and purposes, done for them (Stacy 2009).

Defenders of lecture often refer to how it quickly, efficiently, and concisely presents information to students (Hertzberg 1985; Trifan 1999; Oberly 1997; Stacy 2009). This I believe to be accurate. Lecture puts information in front of students and can be used to provide context for a historical investigation. Saying "never lecture" is an overreaction to the fact that too many teachers simply make this their primary instructional methodology. When asked why I do not lecture, I remind teachers that we now have more than a hundred years of results demonstrating that students do not like to study history and do not retain what they do study (Wineburg 2001). Because lecture has been the dominant approach for studying the past, and it is clear that there has never been a period when students understood, appreciated, retained, or loved studying the past, there has to be at least a coincidental relationship between method and result. Why continue down a path that is so clearly not working? Thus, my default position is that students benefit more from engaging with text than passively listening. But again, this decision is ultimately driven by teacher strength.

Back to the Lesson

Releasing myself from the reticence to provide deep backgrounds enabled me to broaden the types of questions that structure my historical investigations. In the case of Custer, students must fully understand the relationship between the various Plains Indian tribes and between the settlers, the Plains Indians, and the United States military. In addition, on an at least a superficial level, students must be exposed to the actions taken on the battlefield. This enables them to understand the context in which the battle took place and the realities of that day in 1876.

With interest prompted by the visuals and the short- and long-term contexts established through the homework, it is time to pose the question that will structure students' examination of the events at the Little Bighorn. It is here that my visit to the battlefield and my transformational experience there is translated to the classroom. I was fascinated by the debate over what to name the area on which the battle was fought. I now place my students in the position of a member of the National Park Service who must determine the name for the site. On the overhead I display the following names, and students discuss the relative merits of each.

- ⊕ The Battle of the Little Bighorn National Monument
- ⊕ Custer's Last Stand National Battlefield
- ⊕ Sioux Victory National Battlefield
- ⊕ Custer's Battlefield National Monument
- ⊕ Native Victory National Battlefield

- ⊕ Greasy Grass National Battlefield
- ⊕ Little Bighorn National Memorial
- ⊕ Fill in the blank with your own choice

Clarifying the difference between a memorial and a monument and providing a definition and discussion of the Greasy Grass are important. The Native name for the Little Bighorn River, Greasy Grass, refers to the cottonwood trees adorning its banks. With student interest whetted and the purpose in place, it is time to get into the history lab and do a little history.

"Killing Custer"

To introduce the idea of change over time and memory versus history, I show a six-minute segment from the end of the PBS *American Experience* series titled "Killing Custer." This video clip discusses in a way that no other source can the thought process generated when I witnessed the popular culture representations of Custer while at the Montana site. The memorialization and then perpetuation of the notion that Custer made a valiant last stand against the uncivilized Indians is explored in the film through brief examinations of how the mass media—plays, movies, and especially performances by Buffalo Bill's Wild West Show—provide the vehicles to glorify and often distort Custer's defeat. The film challenges students with the idea that an event with significant documentation could be appropriated in such a manner. At the conclusion of the clip, I pose a series of questions. I ask students to unpack the video as a historical source, and then to connect the battle for the memory of the event to the two former names of the battlefield. From its dedication in 1880 it was called the National Cemetery of Custer's Battlefield; in 1946, the site of Sitting Bull's victory was renamed Custer Battlefield National Monument. By the late 1980s pressure was again brought to bear on the National Park Service to alter the name of the site to better reflect both the events of the day and the role played by Natives in the subsequent history of the United States. Driven by identity politics and a deeper exploration of Native history, the Park Service set out to rename the battlefield and again alter our memory of that day.

Conducting the Investigation

Context established, purpose for the investigation set, and ideally student's curiosity roused, I begin the investigation. Students are provided one of several sources that consider the events of June 25–26, 1876, and its main players from a variety of perspectives. Working in pairs or triads, students are instructed to read the source and identify how it depicts the events of the day, its participants, and the outcome. In addition, students, as always, are reminded to consider the subtext of the source and how that might influence the source's perspective. The sources, outlined below, represent a cross section of impressions both historical and contemporary. As student groups present their findings, the audience records the perspective of each source.

Sources Used for Little Bighorn Lesson

Source A: "Uncle Sam's Crook: Will He Straighten the Sinuous Sioux of the Yellowstone?" *Chicago Times*, July 1, 1876

Source B: Robert M. Utley, *Cavalier in Buckskin: George Armstrong Custer and the Western Military Frontier*, 1988

Source C: Bruce A. Rosenberg, *Custer and the Epic Defeat*, 1974

Source D: *New York Times* articles and editorials

Source E: Tatiana Yotanka, Sitting Bull interview with a *New York Herald* correspondent

Source F: Sitting Bull quote

Source G: Lieutenant Jessie Lee, U.S. Military Court of Inquiry (March 1879)

Source H: Tashunkewitko (Crazy Horse), through Horned Horse as his spokesman, told to a correspondent for the *Chicago Times*, May 28, 1877

Source I: Nelson Miles, *Personal Recollections and Observations* (1896)

Source J: *Chicago Tribune*

Source K: The Reverend D. J. Burrell, sermon in Chicago about the Battle of the Little Bighorn (August 1876)

It is interesting to see, at this point of the investigation, how students react to the varying opinions. Some have begun to habitually ask questions about the author(s) of the sources. In addition, they often ask why sources' interpretations and perspectives have changed over time. This is a key indicator that they are starting to think historically. As they ask about change over time as well as authorship, I sense that they have begun to consider that interpretations require a more active set of skills than simply memorizing facts. It is essential that teachers ask questions that require students to link their analysis of the sources to words within the text. More penetrating questions require students to consult information about the context surrounding the sources' creation or the effect of authorship, purpose, or audience on the creation of the source. In either case, central to students' responses must be information gleaned from, or about, the various historical sources they are consulting for the investigation. By having students verbally show their work as they would in written form in math class, teachers can reinforce the content to be retained also in addition to the historical thinking skills that structure the course.

Halfway through the presentations, I ask students to consider potential choices for naming the battle site. The break is intended to alter the flow of the lesson. Continuous presentations have the same effect as lecture—that is, attention and comprehension decrease with time. The break also requires students to incorporate new information into their preexisting opinions. To facilitate full participation, I hang signs around the room representing the potential choices for the historic site and ask students to stand by the sign that best represents their preliminary thoughts about its naming. You can also have students write their names on a sticky note and then attach the note to the sign of their choice. The sticky notes make it easy to call on a variety of students to explain their opinions.

The discussion that ensues finds students sorting out the entirety of the unit (up to this point) on the movement westward. As much as their comments reflect an understanding of the actions taken by General Custer on the days leading up to the battle, they also speak to a desire for examining the battle in the larger context of the time period. This is very satisfying to me because kids are engaging in the same debate as historians. Historians, when considering an event's significance and making decisions about coverage and commemoration, rarely consider it in isolation. Instead they place events, ideas, or personalities into the context of the times—and this is what my students are doing. Terms such as *Manifest Destiny, assimilation, acculturation, genocide, Peace Policy,* and *extermination* populate the discussion. In addition to the desire to discuss Custer in historical context, students make connections between how he was remembered by popular culture—as illuminated in the PBS video clip—and how this affects both their reading of the sources and their opinions on naming the historic site. Finally, I am often struck by the emotions that students invest in the defense of their selection of names for the site. The decision, and in fact the past, has become important to them, and they are willing to argue persuasively—using examples from the sources—to support their opinions. This is, in the immortal words of Jerry Seinfeld, "doing history."

Student Decisions

When it comes to naming the battlefield, students consider the information from the various accounts presented and attempt to synthesize their responses, as seen in Figure 6.6.

Figure 6.6

Name of the Site

> Little Big Horn National Memorial

> I believe this area should be commemorated as Little Big Horn National Memorial because it doesn't give favor to either side. The title tells an unbias story of the battle. Although the Sioux were victorious, Custer and his men were brave fighters through it all so they should also be honored in this fight. Custer, although many saw him as a hero to people, should not have his name be a part of the memorial. Custer was doing the government's job of try to exterminate the Indians for refusing to move on a reservation — something many during this time period would feel upset and outraged about. This battlefield should be called Little Big Horn National Memorial because the new title helps explain both sides of the fight. Therefore no one visiting the area would be upset with the way the battle between both parties was being portrayed. Although the Indians won the battle, the whites won the fight after being able to remove the Indians from the Black Hills and onto a reservation.
> *Well argued — just needs details.*

Student Use of Evidence

The lesson on Custer comes during my fourth unit of the year. At this point students have used a variety of historical sources, approached historical questions about intent, significance, causality, and chronology, and been thoroughly exposed to the idea of historical thinking and to some of the tools necessary to approach the study of the past. In addition, they have been assessed on many of these ideas. The Little Bighorn experience is a measuring stick for how much they have begun to internalize and feel comfortable with the idea of thinking historically and using the attendant skill set. One indication of their comfort level is found in how they use the various sources. I have asked students after the activity to consider their thoughts as they shared and discussed the various viewpoints about the battle and its participants. Some of their responses are included here:

- "The information from my classmates . . . [gave] several different angles and perspectives of this event. You see whose fault it was and how Indians/Custer should be remembered. From it I realized in a way the Indian won from mistakes made by the U.S."
- "It gave me more details and was in the Indians' point of view."
- "[It] showed me how each side, the Indians and whites, tried to make their side look better. Also, most sources favored that Custer was a bad leader, so I didn't want to give him too much credit. The Indians (from my source) said they had an easy win so I decided to commemorate the battle in general because no one group had a very good win."
- "The information from the sources further informed me of the perspectives of the battle. However, I just used the history portion from the sources. For example, from the sources, I learned that Custer did not follow his orders, and that he lost all of his men. I also learned that Custer was seen as both arrogant and a hero. Finally, the sources also depicted the Native Americans as rude and as victors."
- "I feel like some of the information swayed my opinion and the others supported . . . but I also had to look where those sources came from and be careful what information to trust."

Within this body of responses I see signs of progress. Students have come to recognize the need for multiple sources when addressing a question about the past. Simple reliance on the textbook, the teacher, or one source has been replaced with the recognition of "different angles," "perspectives," and "points of view." In addition, they openly express the need not only to consult a multiplicity of sources but also to "look where those sources came from and be careful what information to trust." Critically important on one level, this idea is frustrating on another. The student who wrote this has clearly become aware of an important process related to historical thinking. Recognizing authorship and its importance to understanding the past is significant. By the same token, however, the student still demonstrates the frustrating default of thinking of historical sources as either trustworthy or untrustworthy. I am not sure whether this persistent thought is related to how I teach the idea of historical sources, the developmental proclivity for teenagers to see life as mostly black or white rather than its more complicated gray, or the true difficulty involved in thinking historically. As we progress I explore this and other persistent elements of student thought. Nevertheless, I emphasize the positive here: students are more comfortable with thinking historically—woo hoo!

Some student responses are more problematic. They continue to reveal either confusion resulting from the sheer volume of conflicting information, reliance on a mathematical summation of the sources, the need to strike what they consider a neutral interpretation, or the creation of interpretation colored by their own personal beliefs. Some students mathematically aggregate the sources in an attempt to discern a result that indicates the "right" answers. Others challenge the opinion of one of the authors of the sources presented. Finally, others make an argument based on how they have interpreted the events through the lens of the sources. Strangely enough, this process is similar to the one students engage in on the second and third days of class when they are introduced to historical thinking during their investigation of Nat Turner. Some students still approach the investigation of the past as something that requires them to find "the right answer" rather than something that is based on the debate among evidence-based arguments. Some convey the desire to seek out a correct answer:

- "All of the information seemed to balance out."
- "[I'm] confused, because there are so many sources, and everyone has their own opinion about what they believe."
- "It didn't affect me completely because I live in America and I'm not going to name it some Indian name, even if the Indians won. It did affect me in a way that I'm not going to name it anything with Custer because he should be neutral because Custer didn't win."
- "Some sources said that the Indians were the heroes where others said that Custer was the hero. This showed me both sides of the story so I named the battlefield a neutral name."
- "There were many sources leaning towards the white side and leaning towards the Indian. Therefore, I wanted to name the battlefield something that represents both sides."

In some ways their response to the evidence is on par with their initial experience in the Nat Turner lesson. In others, students subtly demonstrate progress in their thoughts. The key is that they are considering the information, sifting through the perspectives, and taking ownership of the past. To me this is a huge sign of progress. Instead of simply digesting history as "other people's facts," they are using facts to make their own arguments about the past (Holt 1990).

Conclusions

This lesson has become a personal favorite because of the quality of student responses generated by class discussion. Students do a great job of applying evidence to support their opinions, questioning the sources of the information, and engaging in thoughtful analysis of a historical event.

What I have come to enjoy most about this investigation is how it takes a battle that occurred on the western plains and transforms it into a living piece of history. To steal a phrase, this lesson makes history come alive. Its breath comes not from an artificial simulation but from students contemplating the actions of Sitting Bull, Crazy Horse, General Custer, and Major Reno and using these facts to confront the past. The Indian Wars—particularly for my students, who are so ensconced on the East Coast—can feel like a distant and oftentimes esoteric topic. But the leadership, hubris, bravery, and sacrifice of General George Armstrong Custer, Sitting Bull, and Crazy Horse humanize the broader issues of the settlement of the West. The intertwining of the events of June 25–26, 1876, with the broader telling of the American past empowers students to engage with the past as historians. Approaching the past through the lens of a question, and interrogating, comparing, and drawing conclusions from a variety of historical sources to develop an evidence-based interpretation, makes my eleventh graders much more engaged in thinking historically.

Students get engaged in the idea of having to name a historical site and undo the memory that was created and perpetuated for almost a hundred years. They are empowered by the idea that history could still be alive enough for them to control the story that is told and, at least in the context of the classroom, to formulate and justify a new interpretation of a seminal event in American history. I am always intrigued by how this lesson brings students to use facts that they would often find too mundane to commit to memory to make sophisticated arguments about what to rename the Little Bighorn battle site. Minutiae about battle tactics and thoughtful evaluations of subtext and context are brought to bear as students present the reasoning behind their names. Analysis of the written assessments of the lesson and some postlesson interviews crystallize my reflections.

Other Applications

Debates over the public interpretations of history extend well beyond the rolling hills of eastern Montana. Issues ranging from the use of slave auctions in Colonial Williamsburg, to the manner in which the *Enola Gay* would be exhibited at the Smithsonian Museum of Air and Space, to the naming of elementary schools after slave-owning Presidents Washington and Jefferson all present teachers with the opportunity to examine the concept of change and continuity over time as expressed through the debate over history and memory. Framing these issues so that students use the historical record, rather than emotions, deepens their appreciation for the power of history and strengthens their abilities to formulate, articulate, and defend an opinion.

Currently, the decision to place a historical marker in Mississippi to memorialize the murders of Andrew Goodman, James Chaney, and Michael Schwerner is a fantastic example to be used in a manner similar to the Little Bighorn example. History is alive and being retold, co-opted for political purposes, lost, and refound all the time. Finding the right topic can open students up to how and why the telling of a historical story has changed or stayed the same over time (Curry 2002; Nash, Crabtree, and Dunn 1997; Linenthal and Engelhardt 1996).

So, where are we? At this juncture I have introduced my understanding of historical thinking; outlined the tools, vocabulary, and structure used to foster this approach in my classroom; and provided representative examples using change over time, chronology, causality, and significance. We have seen that students can engage the past using the intellectual approaches of historians. This process allows students not only to develop an understanding of the content of the past but also to develop, refine, and implement a set of skills that parallel those in higher education and are valued in the workplace. Though far from perfect, these results give credence to the argument that history education does not need to follow lockstep in the footprints of the past hundred years. Lecture, recitation, textbook reading, and multiple-choice measurements do not need to remain the norm. There is another option, and in the remaining chapters I cement the applicability of that approach.

CHAPTER 7

Long or Short?

Using the Civil Rights Movement to Teach Historical Significance

Martin Luther King, Jr., is a good icon for the movement, but it wouldn't be fair for him to get credit for what thousands of others helped to do.

Everybody always thinks it was Martin Luther King, Jr., but there was [sic] a million other people before him, but he gets noticed.

Martin Luther King, Jr., and Rosa Parks are the only people we ever hear about, so when they lived must be the start of the civil rights movement.

—Student comments during my lesson on the beginning
of the civil rights movement

How do you feel you will do teaching in a school that is overwhelmingly minority?" the principal asked during the interview for my first teaching position. "I have no idea," I replied. "I have been raised to treat everyone fairly and to not judge people based on race or gender." Leaving the interview, I figured that my answer to a difficult but important question was just above the cliché response "Some of my best friends are black." Thankfully, I got the job, and my first teaching assignment challenged me in more ways than I thought possible in an entire teaching career.

Educated in an overwhelmingly white suburb of Washington and Baltimore, I never experienced much in the way of diversity. My first teaching position was in a suburban district surrounding Baltimore City. The school population was 98 percent African American and representative of a broader range of socioeconomic divisions than I had been exposed to growing up. It was in this environment that I learned more about the confluence of race, socioeconomics, and history than I had at any point in my formal education.

The tenure at my first school corresponded with the trial of O. J. Simpson. On October 3, 1995, the decision in the Simpson case was announced. Staff members at our school were asked not to have televisions on or to disturb instruction by announcing the decision to our students. Because I was not teaching during the period the decision was announced, I was in the hallways when the verdict was conveyed. Despite the request not to draw attention to the decision, the building erupted in cheers, boos, and shouts of joy, indicating a clear lack of compliance with the request.

As the day progressed, my students presented a variety of opinions on the outcome of the trial. Some saw it as a miscarriage of justice, others an indictment of the legal system, and for some the decision exposed the vestiges of racism lingering in America. Spirited debates about the not-just-semantic differences between someone being declared innocent versus not guilty emerged within my classroom. The variety of reactions from an overwhelmingly minority student body was an education for me. They demonstrated that race, just like gender, is divided by region, age, class, ideology, and numerous other factors. Race does not presume a monolithic thought process. To accept race as such precludes a rich understanding of how it has functioned as a catalyst in American history. My students have taught me that to truly understand race as a historical force it must be approached through nuance, not with a broad brush. The four years that constituted my first as a classroom teacher enabled me to learn that issues of race are difficult, but when approached in a history classroom structured with the idea that the past is to be investigated, not promulgated, race can be explored and discussed as an important historical force.

To illustrate the intersection of race and historical investigations I share the second lesson in my unit on the post–World War II rights revolutions. These revolutions changed many of the political, economic, and social relationships in the United States. Equality for woman, protection of the environment, awareness of homosexuality, the expansion of rights for those accused of a crime, and the expansion of civil rights for African Americans populate this unit. After establishing the origins of the rebellions that came to dominate the 1960s, I focus on the civil rights movement. Specifically, this investigation emphasizes the historical thinking skill of significance. Students are asked to decide when the modern movement for African American civil rights began.

A Long or Short Civil Rights Movement?

Jacquelyn Dowd Hall's 2005 presidential address to the Organization of American Historians and Eric Arnesen's 2009 response provide confidence that the question posed to structure this investigation is aligned with the course of current debates over the origins of the civil rights movement (Arnesen 2009). From Dowd's perspective, the "dominant narrative [of the civil rights movement] chronicles a short civil rights movement that begins with the 1954 Brown v. Board of Education decision, proceeds through public protests, and culminates with the passage of the Civil Rights Act of 1964 and the voting rights Act of 1965" (Hall 2005, 1233–1234). To rectify this myopic view of the movement, Dowd reminds us that the story of the civil rights movement should be examined from its origins in the 1930s and not brought to a conclusion with the legislative victories of the mid-1960s. It is this historiographical question I want my students to consider: When does the modern struggle for African American civil rights begin?

Tackling the question of the origins of the civil rights movement requires students to access their understanding of continuity and change over time and, more important, to explore their understanding of what makes an event, individual, or accomplishment historically significant. To achieve this, students will be asked to develop and apply a class definition of what makes something historically significant. The use of student-developed criteria then provide the launching pad for a spirited historical debate about what people, events, ideas, and actions indicate the origins of the civil rights movement.

Heresy! There Aren't Any Primary Sources in This Lesson

The lesson, as designed and implemented, does not contain any primary sources to structure the heart of the student investigation. Instead, the reading that constitutes the stepping-off point for investigating the lesson's key question is more along the lines of a selective summation of important events in the battle for civil rights that occurred during the twentieth century than one might find in a textbook. Sometimes, when presenting this lesson to teachers, I am asked how this can be an activity that promotes historical thinking when it does not contain any primary sources. My response is that I do not think primary sources are a magical panacea for the lack of interest that students attribute to the study of the past. Keith Barton reminds us that "what historians work with is evidence," but that evidence takes on a variety of forms not limited by being original sources (2005, 749). Primary sources are a type of evidence that historians use to formulate and answer questions about the past but are not the alpha and omega of historians' work. Some historians make their hay by creating a synthesis of the work of others. The evidence they use is not exclusively primary; oftentimes this evidence includes the monographs, articles, and other residue of previous historians' investigations of a historical question.

For this historical investigation, the focal question asks students to consider when the modern movement for African American civil rights began. To develop a response to this question, the analysis of primary sources would take too long and encompass so much time that it would prohibit a useful student investigation. In addition, investigations that are too lengthy actually cause students to disengage. I have found that any investigation that goes beyond 120 minutes in total time generates minimal returns. So, instead of structuring students' source work for this investigation with primary sources, I rely on historiography to empower my students to make the judgments necessary to participate in a reasoned investigation of a key historical question.

On My High Horse for a Moment

The overemphasis on primary sources as the savior of history education is one of my big issues with the movement by school systems, textbook companies, and supplementary resources to reinvigorate history instruction. Over the past twenty years textbook companies have placed sidebars with excerpts of primary sources on their pages, or co-published readers with primary sources to accompany the main text. In addition to commercially prepared resources, the advent of the Internet has fostered an explosion in the number and type of primary sources available. The base assumption of the majority of these resources is that the presence of a primary source makes the study of history interesting. This is simply not true. If historical sources are not examined for context and subtext, then they are treated as repositories of information—just like the textbooks that are supposedly anathema to students learning history (Green 1994; Stahl, Hynd, Glynn, and Carr, 1995; Sandwell 2003; Danzer and Newman 1991). If a student uses a diary entry to gain information about the beliefs defining a particular time period, but never asks questions about the author and source, then the diary is simply another textual source of information rather than a piece of evidence that can be explored in an effort to develop an interpretation of a historical question. Students must be taught to ask these questions of all historical sources. This is essential to the discipline of history and central to conducting historical investigations in the classroom (McKeown, Beck, and Worthy 1993; Wineburg 1991a, 1991b; Nokes, Dole, and Hacker 2007). It is not just primary sources that make for a reinvigoration of history teaching, but what is done with them in the classroom.

But what about the Document-Based Question (DBQ) that has become the staple of many history classrooms? In short, the DBQ does not ask students to consider a historical question with more than one answer, but instead teaches them to treat historical sources as repositories of information that, when organized in a particular manner, indicate an understanding of the given question. As a signpost of the evolution in assessing historical thinking, the DBQ deserves recognition as a good first attempt, but it ultimately falls short of truly asking students to apply their facility with evidence analysis. As the College Board revamps the AP United States History exam, it will be interesting to watch how they adapt such an influential assessment to reflect the scholarship on teaching and learning in history. To the doubters in the audience who firmly believe that historical investigations must have primary sources, let me try to persuade you to reconsider.

Starting the Investigation

At this point you should be able to guess that the lesson starts with a series of visual images I show my students. From that collection, I ask the students to select the two that they most closely associate with the fight for

Figure 7.1a

Figure 7.1b

African American civil rights. The top two vote getters are invariably images of Martin Luther King, Jr., and Rosa Parks (Figures 7.1a and b). Less frequently, students identify other images I've shown them, including pictures of protesting (Figure 7.1c) or the sit-in at the Woolworth store in Greensboro, North Carolina. Rarely, if ever, do they identify images I've shown of the Shelley House or the Black Power Salute of Tommie Smith or John Carlos from the 1968 Olympic Games as those they most associate with the struggle for civil rights.

After tallying student responses, I posit a series of questions to explore why the images of King and Parks are so overwhelmingly associated with the civil rights movement. Student discussion invariably comes around to what they were taught in elementary school. In addition, they point to the Martin Luther King, Jr., holiday, in which they get a day off from school.

Despite King's and Parks's positions as the class's top vote getters, the discussion quickly moves to an examination of why they are not necessarily the most representative of the movement. Martin Luther King, according to student Ashana, "is the face of the civil rights movement," and "Rosa Parks just sat on the wrong seat on a bus" and therefore did not rise to the level of

Figure 7.1c

representing the totality of the movement—an interesting statement that, upon subsequent interview, reveals the influence of popular culture on her thinking. Ashana's statement is derivative of a bit from the movie *Barbershop*. Despite the source of her interpretation of Parks as not a full representative of the civil rights movement, Ashana thought the image of the protesters with posters better represented the movement. The presence of both "white and black protesters" and "signs representing all sorts of issues [segregated schools, jobs, and voting]" was a fuller telling of the issues and participants related to the movement. Drew described comparing the pictures to discussions he had with his grandfather. "They verified what he said," but Drew ultimately thought the image of the protesters was the best selection because it served as "a broad umbrella for what people were fighting for." Sorting through their own preconceived ideas about civil rights, students are beginning to determine their own criteria for determining historical significance.

To raise the problem of historical significance, I ask students to focus on the image of the Shelley House (Figure 7.2) and tell the story of J. D. Shelley and his family's battle to defeat the practice of racial covenants. The Shelleys, who moved from the rural South to St. Louis, wanted to purchase a home. Their efforts were thwarted on a number of occasions by a racial covenant. Covenants were portions of mortgage agreements

Figure 7.2

that in this case stipulated to whom a home could or could not be sold. Home owners were legally forbidden from selling or transferring their property to African Americans, Jewish people, Catholics, Chinese people, and other immigrant groups. Shelley was able to purchase a home in an exclusively white neighborhood when he found an owner willing to look past the covenant. Another resident of the block, Louis D. Kraemer, filed suit, and the case found its way to the United States Supreme Court. In 1948, the court unanimously ruled that racial covenants could not be enforced by state courts because they violated the Fourteenth Amendment, which guarantees equal protection. This decision paved the way for minority pioneers to gain access to home ownership in traditionally white neighborhoods. The Shelleys bravely stood up to discrimination and won. And yet their efforts, in 1948, are invisible to my students. This invisibility enables me to challenge their assumptions about how historians decide what in the past is significant enough to be remembered.

An important caveat: I remind my students that our efforts during this investigation are not to diminish the bravery of Rosa Parks or the leadership of Martin Luther King, Jr. For some students they come across as an attempt to do exactly that. Instead, I remind the class that our goal is to place King and Parks into a larger context so that we can understand why their roles become so prominent and why their actions are traditionally more associated with the civil rights movement. The Shelley case is only one entry point into this discussion. Suits filed under President Roosevelt's Fair Employment Practices Commission during World War II, the Supreme Court's decision in *Mills v. Lowndes*, the struggles of Jackie Robinson, and soldiers serving in the integrated armed forces during the Korean War all illustrate the same point: some of history is invisible and deserves new consideration. How then do we develop a sense of what is significant in the past and then apply that information to the focal question of our investigation?

Historical Significance

Modeling the concepts laid out by Bob Bain and Peter Sexias, my students and I establish some criteria for determining what makes an event, idea, organization, or individual significant (Bain 2000; Sexias 1997; Hunt 2000). Developing them can be laborious, so I try to move quickly through the process and help students identify at least three key criteria that help determine whether an event, person, idea, or organization is significant.

Lévesque discusses five criteria that historians have applied to the discussion of significance: importance, profundity, quantity, durability, and relevance (2008). In some ways these terms are confusing for my students, but the ones they generally arrive at are, if not synonymous, then at least derivative of the core idea embodied in each. Peter Sexias reminds us that when discussing historical significance, teachers must keep in mind that their students come into the classroom with ideas about the past based on "family stories, historical films, television" and numerous other sources of historical information (Sexias 1997, 22). This can be seen in both Ashana's referencing of *Barbershop* and Drew's consideration of his grandfather's stories about the past.

In many ways the narrowing process that occurs in this phase of the lesson consists of students sifting through their own historical baggage to determine what makes someone or something historically significant. The group of students I taught in 2009–2010 selected the following criteria as they debated the starting point of the African American civil rights struggle: how long it lasts; government involvement; visibility; things I have heard of before; and how many people were affected by the action, idea, or person.

Lévesque/Partington/ Martin Criteria	Students' Criteria
Importance ⟶	Visibility
Profundity ⟶	How many people were affected
Quantity ⟶	Not stated, but refers to number of laws or Supreme Court decisions rendered that were beneficial to the movement
Durability ⟶	How long it lasts
Relevance ⟶	Government involvement/ Something we have heard of

So, When Did the Civil Rights Movement Begin?

After identifying the terms we will use as a class to determine what events, people, or ideas are significant historically, we now set out to apply these ideas to historical content. Students are provided an annotated time line showing seminal moments in the civil rights movement from 1900 until 1955 (Figure 7.3). The annotated time line is not exhaustive. Often when I share this lesson with other teachers and scholars, someone suggests another event, court ruling, or organization to add to the list, but I want to avoid creating a tool that becomes too cumbersome for students to get their minds around. Keeping the resource to both sides of one page provides more than enough content for students to develop an understanding of the length of time that encompasses the civil rights struggle. My intention is not to test them on every item that occurs on the time line. Instead, I want them to consider this information and apply it to the focus question of the investigation: when did the civil rights movement begin? To do so they must now match the criteria for significance they develop with the institutions, individuals, success, and ideas that defined the movement for African American civil rights during the first fifty-five years of the twentieth century.

Upon completing their reading, students discuss their decisions with several peers. Next, they attach a sticky note bearing their name to one of several large signs that correspond to the periods of time on the reading. Having established criteria to determine historical significance and examined a thorough list of the events, organizations, and accomplishments related to the fight for civil rights, students must now defend their thesis about the beginning of the movement. Let the evidence-based, civilly argued debate (or as close as you can get to it in a high school classroom) begin!

Debating Student Interpretations

What is so enlightening about this discussion is the overpowering manner in which Martin Luther King, Jr., is almost the sum total of students' knowledge of the civil rights struggle. The National Association for the Advancement of Colored People (NAACP), Marcus Garvey, and the threatened march on Washington and Double V campaign during World War II have all been examined in previous units. Despite having used this knowledge in other investigations, students still return to Martin Luther King, Jr., as their icon of the movement. This does not surprise me, though.

Figure 7.3

When Did the Civil Rights Movement Begin?

The American civil rights movement generated some of the most defining changes of the twentieth century. Despite these results, historians debate when the movement actually began. Examine the major time periods and the changes that took place and decide when you believe the civil rights movement began. Circle the time period and complete the chart on the bottom of the page.

Early 1900s

- The National Association for the Advancement of Colored People (NAACP) forms in 1909. The NAACP relies mainly on a legal strategy that challenges segregation and discrimination in courts to obtain equal treatment for blacks.
- NAACP lawyers win court victories over voter disfranchisement in 1915 when "grandfather clauses" are declared unconstitutional in *Guinn v. the United States*, but fail to have lynching outlawed by Congress.
- The National Urban League is created (1910) to help blacks make the transition to urban, industrial life.
- The Association for the Study of Negro Life and History creates research and publication outlets for black scholars with the establishment of the *Journal of Negro History* (1916) and the *Negro History Bulletin* (1937). In 1926, Dr. Woodson initiates the celebration of Negro History Week, which corresponds with the birthdays of Frederick Douglass and Abraham Lincoln
- Marcus Garvey incorporates the Universal Negro Improvement Association (UNIA) and begins publishing *Negro World*. Garvey is an admirer of Booker T. Washington's philosophy of self-improvement for people of African descent; he arrives in America from Jamaica and becomes a black nationalist. His political goal is to take Africa back from European domination and build a free and united black Africa. Garvey studies all of the literature he can find on African history and culture and decides to launch the UNIA with the goal of unifying "all the Negro peoples of the world into one great body and to establish a country and government absolutely on their own." *Negro World* is the UNIA's weekly newspaper founded in 1918; in each issue, African history and heroes are glorified. By 1919 there are more than 30 branches of the UNIA throughout the United States, the Caribbean, Latin America, and Africa. In nine years, Garvey starts the largest mass movement of people of African descent in this country's history.

1920s

- Congressman Leonidas Dyer introduces the Dyer Anti-Lynching Bill to the U.S. Congress. Supported by the NAACP, the bill is ultimately blocked in the Senate.
- A. Phillip Randolph organizes the Brotherhood of Sleeping Car Porters (1925), the first union of predominantly black workers to be granted a charter by the American Federation of Labor. Randolph's union wins recognition as a bargaining agent with the Pullman Company.
- *Nixon v. Herndon* (1929) strikes down a whites-only primary. The Supreme Court finds that the whites-only primary is a denial of equal protection under the law as guaranteed by the 14th Amendment.

1930s

- The NAACP creates a separate organization called the NAACP Legal Defense Fund. The fund, led by Charles H. Huston and Thurgood Marshall, selects cases that will challenge the constitutionality of "separate but equal."
- President Franklin Roosevelt hires twenty-three African Americans to serve in his cabinet as advisers, including the heads of the National Youth Administration (NYA), the Works Progress Administration (WPA), the Civil Conservation Corps (CCC), and the Departments of Labor, the Interior, Commerce, and Justice.
- In *Gibbs v. Board of Education of Montgomery County, Maryland*, the Supreme Court declares that setting unequal salaries based on race is unconstitutional. This is a major win for the NAACP's Legal Defense Fund.

World War II

- Black newspapers campaign for a "Double V"—victories over both fascism in Europe and racism at home.
- In 1941, A. Philip Randolph, head of the Brotherhood of Sleeping Car Porters, plans a March on Washington to demand that the federal government require defense contractors to hire blacks on an equal basis with whites. To forestall the march, President Roosevelt issues an executive order to that effect and creates the federal Fair Employment Practices Committee (FEPC) to enforce it.

(continued)

Figure 7.3 *(continued)*

- A new organization, the Congress of Racial Equality (CORE), is founded in 1942 by James Farmer. Dedicated to the use of nonviolent direct action, CORE initially seeks to promote better race relations and end racial discrimination in the United States. It first focuses on the desegregation of public accommodations in Chicago and later expands its program to include nonviolent sit-ins in the South. CORE becomes involved in most of the major civil rights activities of the 1950s and 1960s, including organized sit-ins to end segregation in restaurants and public transportation facilities, sponsored voter registration and voter education drives, and political pressure placed on lawmakers by means of large public demonstrations.
- The U. S. Supreme Court, in the case of *Primus King v. State of Georgia*, declares the whites-only primary to be unconstitutional, thus removing a significant legal barrier to black voting in Georgia.
- In *Irene Morgan v. Commonwealth of Virginia*, the Supreme Court bans segregation in interstate (within one state) bus travel.
- From 1940 to 1946, the NAACP's membership grows from 50,000 to 450,000.

1945–1954
- President Truman makes racial equality part of his postwar Fair Deal domestic program. He calls for the establishment of a Civil Rights Commission, the strengthening of laws related to civil rights, federal protection against lynching, protection of blacks' right to vote, and the prohibition of discrimination in interstate transportation facilities. These proposals are defeated by Southern Democrats who control Congress.
- In 1947, Jackie Robinson becomes the first African American to cross the color line and play major league baseball when he takes second base for the Brooklyn Dodgers.
- In 1948, President Truman issues Executive Order 9981, which integrates the U.S. military. This requires all branches of the military to have integrated units, companies, and platoons.
- In *Shelley v. Kramer*, the Supreme Court strikes down racial covenants—parts of mortgages that block racial minorities from owning homes—as unconstitutional violations of the equal protection clause of the 14th Amendment.
- In *Sweat v. Painter* (1950), the Supreme Court declares that the University of Texas has to integrate its law school.
- In *McLaurin v. Oklahoma*, the Supreme Court declares that racial segregation in higher education is unconstitutional.
- The Supreme Court hears arguments in five cases that challenge elementary and secondary school segregation. In May 1954 it issues the landmark ruling in *Brown v. Board of Education I and II* that states that racially segregated education is unconstitutional and must end with "all deliberate speed."

1955–1956
- On December 1, 1955, Rosa Parks, a member of the Montgomery, Alabama, branch of the NAACP, is told to give up her seat to a white person on a city bus. When Parks refuses to move, she is arrested. The Montgomery bus boycott, organized in response, gains virtually unanimous support from the 50,000 blacks in Montgomery. It lasts for more than a year and dramatizes to the American public the determination of blacks in the South to end segregation. In November 1956, the Supreme Court, in the case of *Browder v. Gayle*, upholds a federal court decision that rules bus segregation unconstitutional. A young Baptist minister named Martin Luther King, Jr., serves as president of the Montgomery Improvement Association, the organization that directs the boycott. The protest makes King a national figure. His eloquent appeals to Christian brotherhood and American idealism create a positive impression on people both inside and outside of the South.

Important Leaders	Major Organizations	Methods Used	Successes	Ideas Behind the Movement

Considering King's recognition via a federal holiday and soon a monument on the National Mall, and his central presence in the elementary school curriculum on Black History Month, it is no wonder that his visage is so popular with students. But I am still amazed that they do not appreciate the depth and breadth of the movement. Of course this is also the point of the focus question. Students are generally drawn to King and the post-Brown element of the struggle because they are most familiar with those images and events. Based on their criteria for significance, students emphasize "something I have heard of before" over effect or duration. As they examine the annotated time line, many of them apply different criteria to determine when the civil rights movement commenced. Initial student responses valued the criterion of "something I have heard of before." But as the lesson progressed, this generality was soon replaced with the criteria of how long it lasts, government involvement, visibility, and how many people were affected. As the discussion evolves, more students are willing to make determinations about significance and challenge the post–*Brown v. Board* period of the movement as its birthplace. The offspring of this conversation and how students applied the ideas of significance to develop their interpretation can be seen in their written assessment.

A Birth Certificate for the Civil Rights Movement

The lesson concludes with students having to complete a birth certificate for the African American civil rights movement (Figure 7.4), Although the exercise is somewhat unconventional, students must humanize the movement and consider when it was born, learn who or what its parents were, and, most important, explain what made that time period and the events, ideas, organizations, and individuals who birthed the civil rights struggle significant. The birth certificate has become an assessment that both my students and I enjoy. For me, I like the fact that by requiring students to select a date (in this case, a decade) of birth forces them to consider how events, people, and ideas from various periods of time impacted the push for civil rights. In addition, by having to select people, organizations, or ideas that brought forth the movement, students must access specific content. My students like the latitude to make a reasoned historical argument. They are not confined by the need to parrot back what they are told. Instead, they consider the content, assess the information against what they feel makes something historically significant, and then develop an

Figure 7.4

The Modern Civil Rights Movement: When Did It Begin?

Based on your knowledge of the events, ideas, organizations, and personalities that defined the civil rights movement, you must decide when the movement actually was born and the events, ideas, organizations, and personalities that should be considered the "parents" of the movement. Decide the birth date (can be a decade or specific year) and explain why you selected it, and who/what gave birth to the movement and why you give them credit. Be specific in your justifications, and be sure to point to specifics from your homework and class discussion.

Birth date of the Civil Rights Movement and why.

Certificate of Birth

_____
was born

On _____

At _____

_____   _____
Weighing   Measuring

_____   _____
Mother   Father

Who or what gets credit for giving birth to the Civil Rights Movement and why?

evidence-based response. As students interpret the past in a manner parallel to historians, they are empowered by the occasion to do history rather than having it done for them.

As seen below, the students suggest the criteria for significance rather than make explicit use of the phrases we used to describe the criteria that set the parameters for our discussion.

> "The President [Franklin Roosevelt] became involved with African Americans during this decade and the NAACP made a major legal victory when they got the Supreme Court to declare unequal salaries based on race to be unconstitutional."

> "The NAACP lawyers won court victories that declared grandfather clauses unconstitutional."

> "The [formation of] the NAACP gets credit for the birth [of the civil rights movement] because it was the first organization that did something for civil rights."

> "The basis of civil rights is making everyone equal. This movement started to end segregation through the government. This time period [1945–1954] focused on . . . President Truman . . . [who] issued the Executive Order 9981, which integrated the U.S. military."

Although they do not use the specific vocabulary, the criteria of how long something lasts, government involvement, visibility, things I have heard of before, and how many people were affected by the action, idea, or person are implicit in many of the students' justifications on the birth certificate. They are applying criteria for significance to historical information in order to draw some conclusions about our focus question. Instead of sticking with the comfortable—in this case Rosa Parks and Martin Luther King, Jr.—they begin to incorporate new people, events, and ideas into the discussion. The presence of Truman's executive order, Jackie Robinson's pathbreaking efforts, and court cases related to issues such as racial covenants and equal pay show that new historical content is given purpose when grappling with the inauguration of the civil rights movement.

Conclusions

I really enjoy this lesson. As the quotations at the outset of the chapter indicate, my students are surprised by the notion that King and Parks sat on the shoulders of thousands of individuals and groups who were fighting similar battles before either was even born. They also have a greater context for the efforts of both King and Parks. Students gain an understanding that the most noticeable civil rights figures did not magically appear in Montgomery but inherited the goals of those who preceded them in the fight for equality. What strikes me the most is how vested in the learning process they feel developing their own interpretation of the past. Instead of memorizing the personalities, events, and ideas that define the freedom movement of the twentieth century and then matching up those items on an exam, students are employing the information to make an evidence-based argument. Using the criteria they establish, they can determine what constitutes the origin of the civil rights movement. They do not need to rely on their textbook but instead can think historically.

Though the discussion and student assessment do not reach the sophistication of Jacquelyn Dowd's argument or Arnesen's counterargument, they do mirror the essence of the debate. How far back, and how far forward from 1964, do we trace the development of the civil rights movement? That is at the heart of the debate over whether the civil rights movement has been going on for a long time or a short time. When the same question can become part of students engaging with the past, then everyone wins.

CHAPTER 8

Trying on the Shoes of Historical Actors

Using the Truman-MacArthur Debate to Teach Historical Empathy

His [MacArthur] disregard for higher authority and poor decision making has led to this decision. He has spoken out a number of times while leaking information to the media. This led to the Order 157 prohibiting any public statements without clearance.

—Student explanation of the dismissal of General MacArthur (told from the point of view of President Truman)

T he year 2006 found a Florida middle school teacher providing "eighth-grade students whose last names started with the letters L–Z yellow five-pointed stars." These students were designated the "persecuted," whereas their peers received "privileged" treatment. "Throughout the activity the star-wearing students were subjected to enforced rules which ranged from forcing them to stand at the back of the class or the end of long lunch lines, to barring them from using some bathrooms and preventing them from using school drinking fountains" (Anti-Defamation League 2006). In 2008 a New York City teacher bound the hands and feet of two African female students and placed them under a desk in a simulation of the transatlantic portion of the slave trade (nbcnewyork.com 2008). These unfortunate practices, along with mock transatlantic slave-ship journeys with students packed head to toe, or reenacting battles in the gymnasium, crop up too often in history classrooms. Intended to help students understand what it was like in the past by placing them in a position to empathize with a moment, idea, or person in history, these activities generate emotions unconnected to the historical experience. Such instructional efforts do not generate historical empathy, are ahistorical, and are antithetical to the idea of thinking historically in the classroom.

The easiest way to define empathy is by what it is not. Historical empathy is not putting students in positions where they will have the same beliefs or feel the same emotions experienced by people living in the past: these are impossible goals for students and historians. Students cannot adopt an identity as if they possess the body and soul of someone or sometime in the past (Lévesque 2008; Shemilt 1984; Lee 2005). Empathy is not an "exercise in imagination (e.g., 'Imagine you are an Apache warrior'), over identification (e.g., asking students to identify with Adolf Hitler), or sympathy (e.g., encouraging students to sympathize with victims of slavery)" (Yeager and Foster 2001, 13). In a nutshell, empathy is not being the person. That is impossible. Historical figures are dead, and the confluence of conditions that gave rise to the event or person has dissipated. What then is historical empathy? Following are some thoughts from the leading researchers in the field of historical thinking:

> *[Historical empathy is] the understanding of past institutions, social practices, or actions as making sense in light of the way people saw things . . . [It] is just not having the inert knowledge that people saw things in the way they did, but also being able to use that knowledge to make sense of what was done.* (Lee 2005, 46)

[Historical empathy asks,] "Why did an individual or group of peo-ple, given a set of circumstances, act in a certain way?" (Yeager and Foster 2001, 14)

[It] involves having students appreciate that the past was a very dif-ferent place from the present and that careful attention to historical evidence and historical context offers students the possibility of understanding and appreciating why people in the past acted as they did. (Foster 2001, 170)

[It encourages students] to judge past actors in their own historically situated context and on its terms. (Lévesque 2008, 167)

[Historical empathy can] deepen historical understanding only if we remember that we are observers of the past, not actors in the past . . . Students must listen to the voices of the past without preconceptions. They must let people of the past begin and end their own sentences. (Mandell and Malone 2007, 22)

Unifying these definitions is the idea of understanding the past on its own terms and developing interpretations of the past with full consideration of the universe of issues affecting the event, individual, or idea being investigated.

Much of what historical thinking entails is stripping away the present and immersing students in the past on its own terms. To do so requires them to understand the political, social, and economic universe of the actors populating the past's stage. Empathy is the ultimate historical thinking skill. Empathizing with a historical actor, idea, or action requires students to use not only historical thinking skills, but historical imagina-tion. This is not the imagination that spurs a toddler to envision his Legos battling on some distant planet. Instead, it is the imagination rooted in stu-dents' understanding of historical context and their analysis of historical evidence. Historical imagination is not making up information but is the intellectual leap between information in historical sources and the gaps within that evidence trail.

Unfortunately, historical imagination is often taken too far. When teachers attempt to fill in the gaps of evidence by conducting a slave auc-tion, a sophisticated cognitive process is cheated for an inauthentic histori-cal investigation. Having students attempt to understand the past on its own terms is the most rewarding manifestation of historical thinking in the classroom. Examining the movement westward from the point of view of an

Exoduster, or seeing the Cuban Missile Crisis unfold as did President Kennedy is a powerful cognitive accomplishment but one fraught with pitfalls and false steps.

With Whom Should We Empathize?

Because historical empathy takes longer to generate with students, picking the right topic is key. Providing students with a "structured dilemma" that requires them to examine evidence can facilitate the most successful platform for generating empathy (Stockley 1983, 63). Although any event, historical personality, or time period is ripe with options for investigations that promote historical empathy, my preference is to structure students' investigations on key presidential decisions. The availability of historical sources, the presence of large numbers of these types of decisions within my curriculum, the tendency for students to immediately condemn presidential decisions, and the fact that the empathy being generated is focused on one individual has motivated my arrival at these types of topics to support the teaching of historical empathy. Lincoln's Emancipation Proclamation, Jackson's removal of the Eastern tribes, Franklin Roosevelt and the question of whether to bomb Auschwitz-Birkenau, Kennedy and the Cuban Missile Crisis: for fostering historical empathy these and other presidential decisions are the lowest-hanging fruit on the curricular tree.

How Do You Promote Empathy?

Promoting empathy has nothing to do with classroom slave auctions or the like. Efforts to promote this disciplinary concept are often attempted through role-playing activities, simulations, historical debates, trials, and so on. But it is not the activity that brings out the potential for empathy. All of these formats are excellent mechanisms for facilitating student engagement with the past. Instead, promoting empathy has to do with employing historical evidence to generate an understanding of the social, political, economic, intellectual, religious and geographic context of a historical time period. Role plays, simulations, trials—all miss the mark if they do not allow students to invest themselves in historical evidence so they can attempt to understand the past on its own terms.

Take slavery, for example. The transatlantic slave trade, and its associated atrocities, is an important part of global and American history for students to examine. Slave auctions were a component of the transfer of human beings from Africa to plantations in the Western Hemisphere. Students will never be able to feel the same emotions experienced by those who were treated as chattel and transported to distant lands. Nor will students ever be able to share the beliefs of those who captured, transported, sold, and owned other human beings. This is not empathy. What students can do in the classroom is examine multiple sources of historical evidence in order to understand the past on its own terms. As Lee (2005, 47) argues, it "is not just having the inert knowledge [about slavery in this case] that people saw things in the way they did, but also being able to use that knowledge to make sense of what was done." It is beyond the scope of this chapter to lay out a full lesson on the transatlantic slave trade, but the plethora of historical sources, both visual and text, would enable students to determine the motivations and effects of the transatlantic trade on both the enslaved and enslaver. Take the image in Figure 8.1. Historically, it promoted more opposition to the practice. It was a catalyst in Britain for the movement to ban the trade in slaves and dedicate the British Navy to interfering with other nations still engaging in the trafficking in humans. The ability to see an issue such as slavery through the eyes of its participants generates empathy, not a false attempt to be a slave.

A Few Caveats

A word of caution on exercises that attempt to have students practice historical empathy. It is very easy for the focus questions and the attendant investigation to become more ahistorical than historical. Mandell and Malone (2007) contrast historical imagination with what they call "imagined history" to help teachers determine if empathy or sympathy is being employed. For example, they discuss the debate that occurs in many classrooms over how to bring the war in the Pacific to a conclusion. Imagined history would be asking students to debate whether the atomic bomb should have been dropped. This question asks students to render historical judgment from the decontextualized perspective of modern times. It does not require them to consider the historical realities that complicated the decision in the summer of 1945. Historical imagination—empathy—would instead ask students to debate whether President Truman's decision to drop the atomic bomb was "consistent with or a departure from American wartime ideals, goals, and tactics." This question demands that students investigate the historical evidence that explains the political, diplomatic, technological, and emotional context and place their debate within the

Figure 8.1

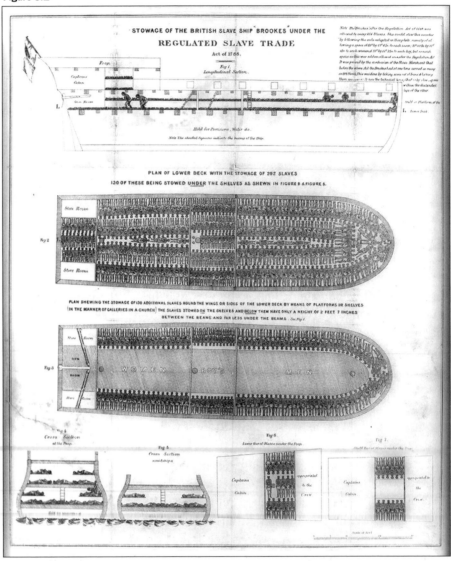

actual parameters that the decision occurred. Focal questions that promote student inquiry must put students into the past to generate empathy.

This chapter focuses on President Harry Truman's decision about General Douglas MacArthur and the course of the Korean War. Students are asked to consider this action from the president's perspective and to empathize with the political realities he faced in the late winter and spring of 1951. They are to consider the options facing the president at the time and to render a decision. Although they cannot know exactly what the president was thinking at all times, historical evidence can shorten the gap between the present and the past and ignite an empathetic understanding of Truman's decision to fire General MacArthur (Lesh 2008).

The Korean War

The Korean War evolved from a practical application of the policy of containment to a test of the boundaries of fighting a "limited war." After the invasion of South Korea by North Korea in 1950, the United States, under the auspices of the United Nations, entered the region to contain the expansion of Communism on the Korean peninsula. The conflict, never declared a war by the United States Congress, was a dynamic military situation, altered in November 1951 by the presence of 200,000 Chinese Communist troops and the haunting specter of a potential third world war. The clash became the impetus for questions about the ability to fight limited wars under the confines of containing versus rolling back and defeating Communist forces. It also led to the removal of an American icon, General Douglas MacArthur.

Intervention to defend South Korea was a measured decision made by President Truman and his advisers. Although many in the administration saw Korea as "the Greece of the Far East," stopping Communist aggression and avoiding an all-out Asian war was the more immediate concern for American policy makers. Truman confirmed these fears when he wrote in his diary on June 30, 1950, that the United States "must be careful not to cause a general Asiatic war" (McCullough 1992, 781). Nonetheless, Korea was an important market for the rebuilt and growing Japanese economy as well as for protecting the anti-Communist Chinese on the island of Taiwan. Despite these important considerations, global war over the invasion of South Korea was not a possibility the United States wanted to risk. Public opinion supported intervention, as did the United States Congress—Republicans and Democrats alike—but American policy makers were more restrained in their enthusiasm than the general public (Patterson 1996; McCullough 1992). Intervention, under the auspices of a United Nations resolution, was authorized in 1950. President Truman's initial goal was to contain Communism within North Korea, not to defeat North Korea and unite Korea under one democratic government (Schaller 1989). With these goals in mind, the vagaries of military strategy and challenges of preparedness interfered with initial progress.

By August 1950, two months after the initial invasion of the south by 90,000 North Korean troops, momentum favored North Korea (Patterson

1996). South Korean military forces and their United Nations allies were trapped in the southeastern corner of the Korean peninsula. The Pusan Perimeter, as this refuge was named, was the site of massive casualties for the U.N. and U.S. forces as they desperately attempted to defend the remaining portions of their territory. Hampered by poorly trained troops, ignorance of the landscape, outdated weapons, rampant dysentery, and the numerical superiority of the North Korean troops, U.S. and U.N. forces were cornered in a situation reminiscent of Dunkirk. Casualty rates were in the 30 percent range, and the fighting became bloodier and bloodier as the perimeter shrank in size (Patterson 1996). Emblematic of the difficulties facing American troops was the "stand and die" order issued on July 29, 1950. Despite desperate military leaders and the 6,886 American casualties suffered since intervention by the United States and the United Nations (McCullough 1992), Korea would not be abandoned because of the contributions of one of the nation's most famous military leaders, General Douglas MacArthur.

MacArthur's daring and ambitious plan for an amphibious landing behind North Korean lines at Inchon harbor changed the course of the war. On September 15, 1950, American military forces executed this daring and dangerous landing at the South Korean port of Inchon and broke the frustrating stalemate at Pusan. The invasion plan was questioned by many of MacArthur's military advisers, in part because of the tidal patterns in the port. The fear was that the water, which peaked at thirty feet at high tide, and at low tide was so low it would leave the landing vessels beached, created too much difficulty for the troops. The natural barriers were enhanced by a man-made barrier, a thirty-foot-high seawall that surrounded the city (Weintraub 2000). MacArthur argued vehemently that these negative elements would secure the surprise necessary to ensure the success of the landing. He was right. With the loss of only twenty-one American lives, U.S. and U.N. troops flanked the North Koreans, loosening the pressure on troops sequestered in the Pusan Perimeter and forcing the North Korean Army onto its heels. The dramatic invasion was accompanied by a drive by American troops out of the Pusan Perimeter. By September 27, Seoul—capital of democratic South Korea—was recaptured, North Korean troops were spilling back over the 38th parallel, and the president and his Joint Chiefs of Staff were revisiting their goals in Korea (McCullough 1992). The dramatic invasion at Inchon had changed the course of the war and enabled American policy makers to consider a more aggressive approach to the situation in Korea.

In the aftermath of the daring Inchon invasion, American policy makers considered and then approved the move from containing Communism at the 38th parallel to rolling it back to the Chinese border and defeating the North Koreans. The Joint Chiefs of Staff unanimously agreed to roll back Communism to the Chinese border, a plan that was supported by the president (Schaller 1989). American opinion was openly in support of pushing beyond the 38th parallel, and most military advisers (particularly General MacArthur) were convinced that Soviet and Chinese troops would not be willing to engage American forces (Kaufman 1999). On September 27, 1950, President Truman authorized General MacArthur's forces to cross the parallel and aggressively pursue the defeat of Communist forces. By late October, two months since the seemingly intractable situation in the Pusan Perimeter, troops from the United States, United Nations, and South Korea were overlooking the Yalu River, the border between North Korea and Communist China. Communism had been rolled back, but ominous signals from China foreshadowed a completely different war.

Potential became reality on November 26, 1950, when 260,000 Chinese troops spilled across the border and engaged American, United Nations, and South Korean troops. Although Chinese troops had been massing along the Chinese–North Korean border since July and pushing over the border in small numbers since Inchon, it was not until November that their full force was brought to bear against American-led troops (Schaller 1989). Early in the Korean War Chairman Mao Tse-tung of China decided he wanted to make Korea a place to confront what he saw as "American aggression." When pushed in August to intervene, Mao at first responded with what historian John Lewis Gaddis called "cold feet" (Gaddis 1997, 80). It was not until October, when Mao received assurances of Soviet air support for Chinese efforts in Korea, that the Chinese leader sent nine divisions to the border. Upon deciding to confront the Americans head-on in November, Mao believed that his superior forces would be enough to push the United States out of Korea. "After we have consumed hundreds of thousands of American lives," said Mao in a March 1951 letter to Soviet Premier Joseph Stalin, "the Americans will be forced to retreat and the Korean problem will be settled" (Gaddis 1997, 81–82). With this newfound confidence, the Chinese entered the conflict and dramatically altered its momentum and potential consequences.

The advent of a quarter million Chinese troops reversed the course of the war again. Bloody battles ensued, and geographically divided American and U.N. forces suffered massive casualties at the hands of the Chinese and the brutal winter weather. By January 1951, Chinese and North Korean soldiers crossed the 38th parallel, reoccupied Seoul, and caused a massive retreat. Before the Chinese invasion in November, General MacArthur publicly pledged to have American troops "home by Christmas." Military realities forced American policy makers to reconsider their goals and techniques implemented in Korea. On November 28, 1950, the National Security Council and President Truman agreed that Korea could not be allowed to escalate into a global conflagration. As Truman said in his diary, "We should not allow the action in Korea to extend to a general war. All-out military action must be avoided" (McCullough 1992). President Truman, the Pentagon, and the Joint Chiefs of Staff agreed that the war in Korea could not be escalated. "What we are doing in Korea is this," said President Truman. "We are trying to prevent a third world war" (Nishi 2003, 91). Truman, despite the fact that "the aggression against Korea is the boldest and most dangerous move the Communists have yet made," wanted to avoid fighting the wrong war in the wrong place. Although he believed the attack on Korea was "part of a greater plan for conquering all of Asia," what America needed to fight was a limited war in order to avoid a third global conflict in the twentieth century (Nishi 2003, 92–94). For the majority of the Truman administration the real war to contain or destroy Communism would happen in Europe, which would require the United States and its Western European allies to fight the Soviets. Truman did not want to fight in Asia, which he saw as a secondary concern (Schaller 1989). This decision ran counter to the views of General MacArthur, who saw the war in Korea as just as important an effort to contain Communism as any war that might happen in Europe.

Injected into the decision to reduce the American commitment to rolling back Communism in Korea was the tenuous relationship between the president and his lead general, Douglas MacArthur. MacArthur, nicknamed "Mr. Prima Donna" by President Truman, was the victorious commander in the Pacific during World War II and the supreme commander of Japan who oversaw that nation's rebuilding after the war. MacArthur, in reaction to the troubling inclusion of more than a million Chinese troops into the North Korean theater, called for the ability to widen the war. As reflected in his speech to Congress on April 19, 1951, MacArthur argued that limited war was impeding America's ability to be victorious. The "American Caesar," as author William Manchester labeled MacArthur, said the "communist threat was global" and must be fought in Asia as well as Europe. MacArthur wanted to unite Korea and make use of Chinese Nationalist troops even before executing the dramatic invasion of Inchon. To facilitate his agenda, MacArthur met with Chiang Kai-shek and made public comments about America's need to support Taiwan (Schaller 1989, 193–197). MacArthur continually pushed his civilian superiors to increase the latitude he had to make decisions about military policy. Blockading China, deploying Chinese Nationalist troops to invade the mainland, initiating bombing raids on Chinese industrial sites, and correcting the course for U.S. policy in Asia were all visible elements of MacArthur's agenda and served as the grist for his disagreements with the Democratic administration in Washington.

Early in March 1951 the MacArthur-Truman dispute escalated when the general went so far as to give interviews in Tokyo about the need to avoid limited war and how the "Europhiles" in Truman's cabinet were blocking his ability to effectively defeat the Chinese (McCullough 1992; Patterson 1996). On March 24, 1951, General MacArthur again trumped his president's authority by offering the Chinese the opportunity to negotiate with him (Patterson 1996). In each of these instances, General MacArthur used the press to build support for his desire to escalate the war in Korea and roll back Communism to the Chinese border. President Truman, who favored the reduction of American commitment in Korea to thus avoid a wide-scale war, was angered by the public nature of the debate.

MacArthur's lobbying for his policies, his personality conflict with civilian and military leadership, and his goals that clashed with those of the Truman administration all led to the general's removal on April 11, 1951. It would have been a difficult decision for any president, but MacArthur's removal was exacerbated by the fears generated by the Cold War, divided government, the media, and public opinion. Nevertheless, General MacArthur—hero of the war in the Pacific, rebuilder of postmilitaristic Japan, and commander of American forces engaged in a hot war on the Korean peninsula—was called home.

By late May 1951, after his removal and his replacement by General Matthew Ridgeway, MacArthur returned home to a victory parade, public support, and congressional approval. President Truman, despite general support among his policy makers and from major American newspapers, saw his public support decline (Weintraub 2000). This dichotomy was punctuated on April 19, 1951, when MacArthur spoke to a joint session of Congress and continued to press his point for victory. In the speech MacArthur again stated his case for escalating the war and fighting a battle against Communism not only in Europe but also in Asia. "The issues are global," MacArthur said, "and so interlocked that to consider the problems of one sector oblivious to those of another is to court disaster for the whole. While Asia is commonly referred to as the gateway to Europe, it is no less true that Europe is the gateway to Asia, and the broad influence of the one cannot fail to have its impact upon the other" (1951). The general faded into the sunset, but not without having what he felt to be the last and most visible word on the correct policy in Korea.

As MacArthur moved into retirement, the military situation in Korea ground to a stalemate. The positions held by United Nations, South Korean, and American troops against the Chinese and North Korean forces in June 1952 were the same as those agreed upon at the armistice of 1953. Military success on the battlefield was replaced with negotiations. The limited war desired by President Truman resulted in stalemate, negotiation, and frustration. It wasn't until President Eisenhower used the overt threat of nuclear weapons in Korea that a negotiated settlement was reached even though a formal peace treaty on the peninsula was never realized.

Can students confront the political, military, diplomatic, and interpersonal realities that faced President Truman in midwinter of 1950? Let's see!

The Investigation

To initiate the lesson, students brainstorm a list of factors that might affect public support for a war. Important at this juncture is to focus them on how unpredictable wars are and how managing public opinion is an especially important factor for modern American presidents to consider when employing troops in military engagements. To substantiate the importance of public opinion, they analyze a series of public opinion polls taken during the first eight months of the Korean War (Figure 8.2).

As a full class we discuss the changes over time revealed in the public opinion poll, what these changes might indicate about the public's support for the efforts in Korea, and what events in Korea may have been the impetus for these changes in public opinion. The definitive shift in public opinion as expressed in the polls serves as the platform upon which I try to elicit empathy for President Truman as decision maker. Like most presidents, Truman had to consider public sentiment. Unlike his predecessor, though, Truman led the nation during the dawn of opinion polling. The public's views on issues could now be quantified, published, and debated—thus increasing their influence on political decision making. The data within the polls clearly present the realities on the ground in Korea. It is through the polls that students begin considering the war through the eyes of President Truman.

The subtext of the data is an important consideration. Students usually accept polling as a scientific absolute and without a perspective. Realization that the formation of the questions, stratification of the sample,

Figure 8.2

The Korean War: Public Opinion

Examine the following public opinion polls taken in the United States during the Korean War and summarize what each one describes. Next, describe any trends or changes demonstrated by the data. Be specific, and be ready to discuss.

Public Opinion Polls

July 1950: Some people state that we should pull our troops out of Korea and stop fighting there. Other people say we should go on fighting in Korea. With which point do you agree?

Stop fighting and pull out	12%
Continue fighting	77%
No opinion	11%

October 13, 1950: Should the fighting stop when we have succeeded in pushing the North Koreans back over the line from where they started—or do you think we should continue to fight in their territory until they have surrendered?

Stop fighting	27%
Continue fighting	64%
No opinion	9%

January 22, 1951: Now that Communist China has entered the fighting in Korea with forces far outnumbering the United Nations troops there, which one of these two courses would you prefer that we follow: pull our troops out of Korea as fast as possible, or keep the troops there to fight these larger forces?

Pull out	66%
Stay there	25%
No opinion	9%

April 2, 1951: Do you think the United States made a mistake in going to war in Korea, or not?

Mistake	51%
Not a mistake	35%
No opinion	14%

April 2, 1952: Suppose a truce settlement is reached in Korea. As matters stand today, which side—ours or the enemy's—do you think will have won the bigger victory?

Our side	30%
Enemy	33%
Neither	23%
No opinion	14%

Summary of the trends or changes shown in the polls:

Source: *The Gallup Poll: Public Opinion, 1935–1971,* as it appeared in Mueller (1973).

and sample size all affect the material found within the text is eye-opening for students. We see a particular manifestation of the influence of subtext in the lack of consistency in the poll questions. It is important at this juncture to help students understand the subtext within polling data and to help them arrive at this realization.

To fully appreciate the issues facing Truman, especially after the entrance of Communist China into the war early in the winter of 1950, I debrief a reading on the early phases of the war. We've examined the causes of the war the previous day, and this reading focuses solely on the battlefield and the domestic politics within the United States. Depending on students' reading abilities, this selection could be read in class or be delivered via another pedagogical approach. The reading I use is teacher generated so that I can ensure greater focus on setting as complete a context as possible for the student investigation. The early ebb and flow of the war, the Pusan Perimeter, landing at Inchon, the push past the 38th parallel, and the Chinese invasion highlight the military aspect of the reading. Domestically, inter- and intraparty tensions as well as electoral politics take center stage. The intention of the reading is to establish a context for the decision President Truman faced in the winter of 1951.

Student attention gravitates to the connections between the trends and changes in the public opinion polls and the changing nature of the American involvement in Korea. I have students focus on the invasion of Chinese troops in 1950 and ask them to consider whether the president should base his policy on public opinion. Next, students learn that in light of the difficulties in the Korean War, President Truman was faced with a decision: Should he escalate the war as recommended by his field commander General Douglas MacArthur, or should he return to the original goal of containing Communism at the 38th parallel?

Other Options

This phase of the lesson could easily be facilitated through a series of documents that outline the thoughts and opinions of the president, his advisers, his political opponents and supporters, the media, General MacArthur, and other indicators of the thinking endemic to the time frame being analyzed. That said, I want to share investigations formatted in several different ways so that readers can see the flexibility the approach provides. In this instance I offer another avenue to conducting a historical investigation that diverges from the more traditional approach. Dividing students into groups

Figure 8.3

The Korean War: A Lesson in Presidential Decision Making

On a separate sheet of paper, create a T-chart of reasons for keeping General Douglas MacArthur and reasons for firing him. Be specific in your notes, and be prepared to decide what to do with General MacArthur.

Pre–July 1950
- General Douglas MacArthur serves as commander of the Pacific forces in World War II and the head of the American forces occupying Japan after the war.

July 1950
- MacArthur flies to Taiwan to meet with Chiang Kai-shek, leader of the Chinese Nationalists. Chiang's forces lost the civil war in China to the Chinese Communists led by Mao Tse-tung, and retreated to the island of Formosa (Taiwan). Their presence places pressure on the United States to protect them from the Communists on Mainland China. MacArthur wants to use Chiang's troops to fight in Korea and makes it known that the United States will defend Taiwan if necessary.

August 1950
- President Harry Truman issues a statement saying that he is the commander in chief and as such will determine how to use the American military. He also warns against any actions by others, implying MacArthur, that would lead to a war beyond the Korean peninsula.
- General MacArthur tells the Veterans of Foreign Wars that the United States should defend the Chinese Nationalists on Taiwan against the Chinese Communists.
- Truman orders MacArthur to withdraw his statement.

September 1950
- General MacArthur executes a daring and dangerous landing at the South Korean port of Inchon and breaks the trapped American troops out of the Pusan Perimeter. The risky plan, opposed by many of the president's military advisers, allows the U.S./U.N. troops to go on the offensive and push the North Koreans back over the 38th parallel, dividing North and South Korea.
- American policy makers approve the move from containing Communism at the 38th parallel to rolling it back to the Chinese border and defeating the North Koreans. The decision to roll back Communism is unanimously agreed upon by the Joint Chiefs of Staff and supported by the president.

October 1950
- President Truman and General MacArthur meet on Wake Island. While discussing the war, the general provides assurances that the Chinese will not invade. President Truman accepts MacArthur's apology for his statements and actions about Taiwan.
- American troops capture the capital of North Korea and push to the Chinese border.
- 250,000 Chinese troops invade North Korea.

November 1950
- General MacArthur directly violates the order not to enter the provinces adjacent to China and the Soviet Union when he pushes north toward the Chinese border. Despite this violation, he issues a communiqué denying mobilizing an offensive to reach the Yalu River dividing China from North Korea.
- MacArthur grants an interview to *U.S. News and World Report* in which he argues that the problems in dealing with Communist China were caused by the restrictions Washington placed on the military. He follows this interview with press releases criticizing the Pentagon, the State Department, and the CIA for faulty intelligence on China.
- U.N. and U.S. forces are pushed back into South Korea by advancing Chinese and North Korean troops.
- The National Security Council and President Truman agree that Korea cannot be allowed to blossom into a global conflagration. As Truman says in his diary, "We should not allow the action in Korea to extend to a general war. All-out military action must be avoided." Truman, the Pentagon, and the Joint Chiefs of Staff

(continued)

Figure 8.3 *(continued)*

agree that the war in Korea cannot escalate. "What we are doing in Korea is this," Truman says, "We are trying to prevent a third world war." The view of the majority of Truman's foreign policy establishment is that the real war to contain or destroy Communism will take place in Europe, not Asia. This will require the United States and its Western European allies to fight the Soviets, and Truman does not want to fight the "second team" in Asia and endanger the ability to fight the decisive battles of the Cold War in Europe.

December 1950
- As a direct result of General MacArthur's interviews with the press, President Truman issues Order 157. The order says that any speech, press release, or public statement cannot be made without clearance.

March 1951
- When the Chinese offensive stalls just south of the 38th parallel, President Truman begins work on a peace proposal. The plan would reestablish the original border between North and South Korea and remove all foreign troops from both countries.
- A few days after MacArthur receives notice of President Truman's peace proposal, he announces his own terms for ending the fighting. Next, he grants interviews in Tokyo in which he discusses the need to avoid limited war and how Truman's cabinet is blocking his ability to effectively defeat the Chinese because of the obsession with fighting Communism in Europe.
- MacArthur begins a series of meetings with the press in which he advocates for his views on the war. Again, in direct violation of the president's gag order, the general argues that the Communists' "insatiable" desire for power is focused on "world conquest." According to MacArthur, "they see in Asia the gateway to their nefarious purpose. They must be stopped."
- General MacArthur inquires about the atomic capability of the United States to take out Manchurian airfields.
- MacArthur offers the Chinese the opportunity to negotiate with him. In each of these instances, he uses the press to build support for his desire to escalate the war in Korea and roll back Communist forces to the Chinese border.
- President Truman, who favors reducing the American commitment in Korea with the intent of avoiding a wide-scale war, is angered by the public nature of the debate.
- In a public statement, again without getting any clearance from Washington, MacArthur taunts the Chinese for failing to conquer South Korea. He threatens to attack China unless the Chinese surrender. He even says he will meet with the enemy military commander to arrange how to end the war.
- When informed of President Truman's desire to negotiate for peace, MacArthur, without clearance from Washington officials, issues a message telling the Chinese to quit or be destroyed. He asks for China's unconditional surrender, and asks the Joint Chiefs of Staff for permission to bomb Chinese industrial sites, blockade the Chinese coast, unleash the forces of Chiang Kai-shek, if not allowed, and then the United States should withdraw. MacArthur's announcement is an ultimatum to China. It torpedoes Truman's diplomatic efforts to negotiate a cease-fire. America's allies wonder who is really in charge of U.S. foreign and defense policy.
- President Truman is stunned. "By this act," he later wrote, "I could no longer tolerate his insubordination."

April 1951
- In the midst of the debate over peace in Korea, MacArthur's Republican supporters in Congress release a letter in which the general declares, "There is no substitute for victory." MacArthur's letter to Joseph Martin, Speaker of the House, criticizes the "Euro-centrism" of U.S. foreign policy, and argues that there could be "no substitute for victory." Martin reads the letter on the floor of the House.
- Responses are immediate and volatile. Senator Robert Taft and other Republicans defend the general and argue that his progress is being limited by the Truman administration.

to analyze volumes of evidence can become repetitive. Historical investigations need diversity just as much as any other instructional approach. Believe me, students are quick to let me know when what was once exciting and different has taken a turn toward the mundane and predictable. As long as there is a historical disciplinary concept at the heart of the investigation—in this case, empathy—and source work within the procedures, then the lesson can promote investigation of the past without having a number of historical sources at its core.

In this instance, the lack of numerous pieces of historical evidence does not mean that the Truman-MacArthur investigation is devoid of serious devotion to the historical investigations model or the attendant source work. Nor does it dilute students' efforts to draw empathetic ties to President Truman. The public opinion polls that frame the beginning of the investigation will be contrasted with other polling data and political cartoons. This analysis is done so that students can examine the effect of Truman's decision. In addition, students must analyze the text, context, and subtext of each piece of evidence so that the sources are approached in a manner parallel to any other historical investigation. This constitutes the source work element of the investigation and allows the Truman-MacArthur lesson to be investigatory in its implementation without having historical sources at the center of the process.

It is important to understand that a historical investigation can and should be flexible enough to adjust to student needs, and is not required to be administered in the same format every time. I have conducted investigations structured as trials, congressional hearings, debates/discussions, presentations, and most other instructional formats you can think of. The point is to focus instruction on a historical question, examine evidence, and use that evidence to evoke responses to the question. Don't get caught up in format; just keep an eye on the overarching goals, and you will be okay.

For this lesson I have students consult a time line of events and create a T-chart to record information for and against the removal of General MacArthur (Figure 8.3). Working individually and then in pairs, they list the actions and thoughts of the two protagonists. As they gather information, they decide whether President Truman should follow General MacArthur's advice or relieve him of command.

Organized into groups of four, students discuss and debate the choices available to President Truman. One way I try to engender an empathetic understanding of the president's thought process is by prompting discussion with questions that reflect those being discussed at the time. In this instance they include the following:

- ⊕ If the United States does not fight this war to win, will it be perceived as a weakness by the Soviet Union and China?
- ⊕ Our goal in Korea is to contain Communism. If we expand the war as General MacArthur suggests, could it not lead to a larger war, possibly a third world war?
- ⊕ Since the president is constitutionally the commander in chief, hasn't General MacArthur violated the Constitution with his actions and words?
- ⊕ Although the president is constitutionally the commander in chief, shouldn't he listen to his generals, whose job it is to give military advice?

During this portion of the lesson, students are drawn to the potential consequences of General MacArthur's actions. Unfortunately, they often use clichés and modern analogies to support their opinions. This past year I heard, "All is fair," and "Go hard or go home." Cognitively, students use these clichés to associate new material with something they already know. Interestingly, though, they attach historical content to them, so the discussion is not fully divorced from its historical context.

After their small-group discussions, students divide themselves into one of three groups. The first are those who believe President Truman should fire General MacArthur and negotiate peace with North Korea. The second group consists of those who think Truman should fire MacArthur but follow his advice to escalate the war on the Korean peninsula. The final group aggregates students who think Truman should look past MacArthur's behavior and adopt his policies regarding the war. In an effort to continue students' empathetic understanding of the issues from the perspective of President Truman, I facilitate a discussion between the three groups and require them to reference historical evidence. The discussion is interspersed with comments about "violating orders," "overstepping boundaries," and the need to "respect General MacArthur's opinion."

Halftime

Because I teach a forty-five-minute class, this point in the lesson provides a natural opportunity to check my students' mental progress. To determine how well they have been able to consider the historical context that defined President Truman's decision, I ask them to make a quick list of the factors that they think occupy his thoughts in the winter of 1950–1951. Almost 90 percent of my students identify the potential reactions to, or effectiveness of, following General MacArthur's advice as the number one factor on Truman's mental radar. Following closely behind is MacArthur's disobedience and public opinion.

When asked to explain her thinking at the midpoint of the investigation, Miranda identified the sources of her initial thoughts as the public opinion polls and MacArthur's actions. When MacArthur threatened to attack China," she said, it took her back to the public opinion polls. Since China invading was the exact reason why public opinion changed," Miranda argued, "the importance of public opinion and MacArthur's disobedience were directly connected. Public opinion was extremely low already and MacArthur's actions put fuel to the fire, making it worse, and Truman needs someone to support him not oppose him." Thus, Miranda expresses some degree of empathy with President Truman's geopolitical reality by March 1951. Full empathy, no. Tempered empathy, yes—tempered by the evidence pool she can swim in, the time spent investigating the question, and the limits of the teenage brain to encounter and process multiple issues at one time.

Another student, Nick, also mentioned the "general public's opinion" and "MacArthur's disregard of [Truman's] authority." His evidence trail was also from the time line and public opinion polls, but for different reasons. His emphasis on the importance of MacArthur's disregard for presidential authority stems from the actions President Truman had already taken. From Truman's meeting with the general on Wake Island, to his ordering MacArthur to withdraw his comments, Nick gave more weight to the president's concrete actions. Of great import to Nick was Order 157. In his mind, this clearly demonstrated the connection between MacArthur's actions and the realities of public opinion. Public opinion is something that the president needs to "keep in the back of his mind."

Selecting the implications of General MacArthur's actions as their key focal point indicates that students have considered the information presented in the time line. Absent a series of letters, telegrams, diary entries, newspaper stories, or the like, the time line is the key source of historical evidence available. In light of my self-imposed limitations in the evidence trail, students tend to fall back on either the public opinion polls, facts from the time line, or a political cartoon I display in the process of discussing MacArthur's feelings about the war. A deeper well of evidence from which to draw would aid students' ability to connect their arguments to the residue of the past. I have consciously chosen to limit this reservoir for this lesson. Nevertheless, students have made use of the evidence afforded them. As Miranda and Nick's comments indicate, students can articulate how their intermediate conclusions about Truman's perspective emanate from the evidence. Does this mean that they are now empathetic to President Truman's view of the Korean War? I highly doubt it. But that does not discount trying to have students engage in historical empathy. Unlike the slave auctions mentioned earlier, this empathetic experience is based on historical evidence, not a tenuous emotional connection to the past via handcuffs.

Back to Work

The second day of the lesson allows students to revisit the evidence from the previous day and render a final decision. First, I conduct a quick review of the pertinent historical content. Then I ask, "Given the realities President Truman faced in 1951, what should he decide?" I survey the students' decisions, count up totals, and announce the class decision.

To finish the investigation, students examine the reactions to President Truman's decision to fire General MacArthur and pursue peace negotiations. The reason I have them examine and present these sources is twofold.

Figure 8.4

Figure 8.5

First I want to bring the implications of Truman's decision to light. In addition, I want to see whether my students will decontextualize his decision in light of its contemporary public reception. I want to focus their analysis by having them concentrate on what the resource indicates about public support for President Truman's decision to remove General MacArthur. Student groups examine either political cartoons (see Figures 8.4 and 8.5) or public opinion polling data from 1951 and then share their analysis with the class.

Assessing Student Empathy

To assess this lesson I ask students to assume the role of President Truman's press secretary and write a press release that responds to the following prompt:

> You have been hired as President Truman's press secretary and asked to write a press release describing the outcome of the debate on the Korean War. Your press release should address the situation in Korea and the outcome of the decision to remove General MacArthur from the perspective of President Truman. A press release is very formal, very concise, and very precise in its writing. When crafting your press release be sure to address these elements:
> - Causes of the Korean War
> - Events that altered the course of the war
> - General MacArthur's demands and actions regarding the war in Korea
> - Why President Truman made his decision
>
> **Dateline: Washington, April 11, 1951**
> *The White House announces today that . . .*

The test of my students' empathetic understanding is if they can compose a justification to the public that reflects the Truman administration's viewpoint of the issue as they saw it in April 1951. As the responses below indicate, some students can shift to viewing the past on its own terms:

> "His [MacArthur's] disregard for higher authority and poor decision making has led to this decision. He has spoken out a number of times while leaking information to the media. This led to the Order 157 prohibiting any public statements without clearance."

"But the answer is not, as MacArthur believes, to demolish it through a third World War. Instead, we must continue to focus on containing it [Communism?] as peaceably as we can, simultaneously keeping alive countless American troops . . . MacArthur has repeatedly complained to the press about Truman's administration. That is not only disrespectful, but also against policy."

"The Korean War was a conflict based on America's duty to contain the spread of Communism in Asia. The U.S. joined the fight when Communist Northern Korea invaded Southern Korea. [President] Truman felt that [General MacArthur's actions] would just exacerbate tensions of the war and begin WWIII. President Truman in result [*sic*] fired MacArthur for disobeying his orders and criticizing his administration."

"General MacArthur is being recalled from the Korean battlefield. The fight to contain Communism will only be blown out of proportion and may turn into an even bigger war if General MacArthur's insubordinance [*sic*] continues. He has repeatedly violated orders . . . and he has continued to leak information to the press while criticizing my administration."

In each instance above, students draw on General MacArthur's behaviors and President Truman's stated concern about escalating the conflict into a broader world war. These decisions can be traced directly to the historical evidence used in the investigation. Although the responses are too vague for my tastes, they nonetheless show students' ability to consider a historical decision from the perspective of the time period—in a nutshell, historical empathy.

What, you may ask, is the measure we can use to evaluate how closely students are coming to empathizing with a historical figure on his or her own terms? Honestly, that rubric would be so complicated that making it would neutralize my desire to even approach this concept in the classroom. Unlike causality or chronology, where a student's ability to implement and articulate these skills is clear, empathy is not easy to measure. What I do is compare the students' press releases to the speech President Truman gives on April 11, 1951. There is a startling parallel between his national radio address and their writing. In particular they both emphasize avoiding a third world war, General MacArthur's counterproductive actions, and containment. These parallels are pronounced when one examines Rachel's letter (Figure 8.6) next to the transcript of President Truman's address (Figure 8.7).

Although my student lacks the polish of a trained press secretary, she does get to the heart of the issue. Just as President Truman did when

Figure 8.6

The White House announces today that... after fighting in the korean war, General MacArthur will be returning to the United States. The korean war started because of the attack on South Korea. As defenders of democracy, we had to step in and contain the Comunism. MacArthur was trying to demolish Communism and refused to follow our polocy of containment so President Truman was forced to releive him of his position. MacArthur was set on using the atomic bomb and Truman was set on stopping another world war. Since he has been removed korea has been able to set up the Armestice agreement and we have held them to their border.

Figure 8.7

My fellow Americans:

I want to talk to you plainly tonight about what we are doing in Korea and about our policy in the Far East.

In the simplest terms, what we are doing in Korea is this: We are trying to prevent a third world war.

I think most people in this country recognized that fact last June. And they warmly supported the decision of the Government to help the Republic of Korea against the Communist aggressors. Now, many persons, even some who applauded our decision to defend Korea, have forgotten the basic reason for our action. . . . . .

I believe that we must try to limit the war to Korea for these vital reasons: to make sure that the precious lives of our fighting men are not wasted; to see that the security of our country and the free world is not needlessly jeopardized; and to prevent a third world war.

A number of events have made it evident that General MacArthur did not agree with that policy. I have therefore considered it essential to relieve General MacArthur so that there would be no doubt or confusion as to the real purpose and aim of our policy.

It was with the deepest personal regret that I found myself compelled to take this action. General MacArthur is one of our greatest military commanders. But the cause of world peace is much more important than any individual. (Truman 1951) addressing the nation, Rachel emphasizes the three major factors concerning Truman and does not get caught in the public opinion trap. With three exceptions, my student also does not allow public reaction to the decision to influence her explanation. This is a strong indicator that Rachel empathizes with the decision in light of the facts known before its implementation and while ignoring the reactions to the decision.

Other Examples

An interesting aside is a similar lesson on Lincoln and slavery. After meeting with his presidential advisers, my student Lincolns render a decision regarding how to deal with the questions surrounding emancipation and the war. The advisers have discussed constitutional, military, diplomatic, emotional, and political aspects of the decision about slavery. My Lincolns have gained insight into issues of contraband and self-emancipation, the decisions of General John Frémont, issues with the border states of Maryland, Kentucky, Missouri, and Delaware, Lincoln's own persistent beliefs in colonization, and the pressures from Northern abolitionists such as Frederick Douglass. The advisers present student Lincolns with the options of gradual compensated emancipation, freeing only those enslaved within the confederacy, immediate emancipation, or leaving the issue alone and concentrating on winning the war.

Deeply immersed in the historical context and seemingly empathizing with President Lincoln's decision in the summer and fall of 1862, my students without fail have never selected the freeing of those enslaved within areas of rebellion. Never, in more than ten years. When asked why, they say they did not see it as a real option because "the North did not control these areas." Others say that this seemed like "a pointless choice" since it essentially "did nothing." The dissonance between their thoughts and Lincoln's provides a wonderful window to discuss the Emancipation Proclamation and its impact. Although on the surface this may seem like a failure of empathy, I see it instead as testament to how difficult this disciplinary concept is to engender.

Conclusions

Without fail, students respond to my efforts to foster historical empathy through exercises in presidential decision making with a wide range of responses. Some see the context within the realities of the time period.

Others cannot shed any of their current notions, and examine the decision and the decision-making process from the present. Still, when I get them into the best position I can to empathize with a president, many become aware of the difficulties such a decision maker has to face. They realize they have to consider such variables as public opinion, congressional or judicial opposition, electoral pressures, age, memory, technology, and the myriad of other factors. I will be the first to admit that students are not fully immersed in the past, devoid of their present beliefs, attitudes, and judgments. That is impossible. The ever-present clichés and counterfactuals students offer during discussion are a testament to the sheer difficulty of stripping them of the present and immersing them in the past. I also feel less confident about my ability to measure whether they are empathizing with whatever presidential decision they are investigating. But I feel strongly that in the words of Nick, the opportunity to employ historical evidence to see the ultimate decision to fire General MacArthur through the eyes of President Truman was and is "more interesting that you just telling us or reading it from the book."

Historical empathy brings us full circle. To maximize students' ability to think with historical empathy, we return to the historical investigations model introduced in Chapter 1 (see Figure 8.8). The historical investigations model's ultimate goal is to employ students in the service of a historical question. To develop an evidence-based answer to a guiding problem, students must conduct source work, compare, contrast, and synthesize the ideas extracted from the evidence, and defend their answer to the overarching historical question. Empathy is the ultimate by-product of the historical investigations model. Students cannot understand how people in the past "saw things" and use this knowledge to "make sense of what was done" unless they can contrast various interpretations of the past and ask questions about the following:

Causality
Chronology
Multiple perspectives
Contingency
Change and continuity over time
Influence/significance/impact
Intent/motivations

My efforts to promote historical empathy—just like causality, multiple perspectives, chronology, and change and continuity over time—continue to

Figure 8.8 Conducting a Historical Investigation

I. Establish a focus question to guide students' investigation
- Question should be provocative and encourage investigation and discussion.
- Question should be central to the curriculum needs of the teacher.
- Question should help deepen students' understanding of history as an interpretive discipline.
- Focus questions should emphasize disciplinary concepts such as the following:
  - Causality
  - Chronology
  - Multiple perspectives
  - Contingency
  - Empathy
  - Change and continuity over time
  - Influence/significance/effect
  - Contrasting interpretations
  - Intent/motivation

II. Initiate the investigation
- Access prior knowledge by reading from a narrative, poem, or journal entry, or by examining a map, broadside, political cartoon, or other historical source.
- Hook students' attention and set the context for the event or person being investigated.

III. Conduct the investigation
Teacher: Collect relevant and conflicting historical sources that allow students to investigate all aspects of the event or person being investigated. Be sure to identify relevant vocabulary and edit for readability.

- Analyze one document individually. Instruct students to take notes on the information they can glean from their source in addition to determining the who, what, when, where, and why information.
- Determine the answers about context and subtext and how these answers affect the central question.
- Group students so that all documents are represented in a group, and have them generate an interpretation of the documents based on the focus question.
  1. As students share their interpretations, they must cite information from documents as evidence.
  2. Multiple interpretations can emerge and may or may not be accepted by everyone, but that is okay at this point.

IV. Report interpretations and class discussion
- Share group interpretations and discuss the sources that most influenced their decisions and why.
- Discuss the various interpretations presented, looking for commonalities and differences.

V. Debrief student investigations
- Teacher-driven discussion of the event or person being investigated. The teacher should solidify the basic historical facts and clarify the reasons for varying interpretations.

IV. Assess student comprehension of the content of the past and historical thinking
- Assess students' understanding of the historical content and the process used by historians.

Adapted and modified from Bruce VanSledright (2002), Stuart J. Foster (2001), and the University of California, Davis, History Project (2006).

generate teacher-student dialogue about the past. Confronted with historical questions and forced to analyze evidence, my students are engaging with the past just as a historian approaches a historical problem. This is the essence of promoting historical thinking. Facts are inert unless they are employed in the pursuit of a question. As a very insightful student once told me, "Yes, I remember eighth-grade U.S. history, but why would I remember the information? It is not like I have used it since." True. One hundred years of testing in American history proves it. The engagement of my students is what sold me on the history lab/historical thinking/historical investigations approach I have outlined. Engaging with and using historical content is an integral part of my teaching. But, by investigating the past and using historical thinking skills, my students are going beyond simply memorizing the facts and are enjoying it.

The seven concrete examples of historical investigations I have shared cannot serve as a student's only occasions for thinking historically. For teachers to offer an instructional program that melds content and historical investigation, they must consider a number of factors. From here, I will discuss some programmatic decisions teachers should consider before implementing this approach in their classrooms.

CHAPTER 9

"How Am I Supposed to Do This Every Day?"

Historical Investigations Versus Sleep

If the subject [of history] loses all its charms by our handling, the fault is ours, and we should not blame the child.

—Thomas Wentworth Higginson (1885)

Asked for a single word to define their experience with history in school, [the respondents in the survey] most frequently answered with "boring" and "irrelevant."

—Roy Rosenzweig and David Thelen (1998)

Having presented lessons about historical thinking to hundreds of teachers across the country for Teaching American History grant programs and as part of districtwide professional development workshops, I am often met with a response similar to the one that forms the title for this chapter. "But," query some audience members, "lectures, movies, crossword puzzles, and textbooks worked for me; why can't it work for my kids?" My response is simple: Because the record clearly indicates what we are doing isn't working as well as it could. I am not saying that history teachers are not hard working, well intended, and knowledgeable about their subject matter. Almost one hundred years separate Higginson's quote from Rosenzweig and Thelen's survey results, and yet the results have not changed.

Many teachers see the inherent benefits of investigating the past but are faced with the demands of local or state assessment tools that they perceive as contradictory to the goals of these accountability measures. In addition, time, the need for instructional diversity to maintain student interest, the confines of coverage, the immediacy of gaining and maintaining classroom control, and the numerous other demands on instruction (parent phone calls, grading papers, meetings, paperwork, and on and on) mean teachers have to make difficult choices about what to prioritize. Teachers face a broad spectrum of pressures, not the least of which is the continual unveiling of initiatives, programs, and political agendas dressed up as educational policy, and the onslaught of acronyms. It would be dishonest to say that I have not stood as an "impediment to reform" or "pushed back" against a bureaucratic initiative or graded papers during a presentation of the newest fad. I completely understand the resistance that teachers bring to instructional change.

Effective teachers spend countless hours combining their passion for a subject, their personality, and their knowledge of students into a package that effectively educates all of their students. Many times they undertake these efforts well outside the hours for which they are paid. As a result, the imposition of the newest acronym-driven reform inherently comes across as an insult. "You are not doing a good job, so if you simply do this and this, then student achievement will improve" is what the internal voice in many teachers' heads says during numerous professional development activities. What makes the emphasis on historical thinking and investigating the past different from any other proposal for reforming educational practice? Moving from memory-history to a discipline-based approach allows professional educators to link their love of the content and the desire to open it up for students to a methodology that engages students and teachers simultaneously. In addition, this instructional approach is based on teacher choice rather than a top-down dictate. What has maintained my enthusiasm for this approach are the more positive feelings my students have about studying the past, the increased effort they put into their work, and the fact that teaching the past has become more of an informed conversation between myself and them. If teachers do buy into the idea of transforming their instructional approach, I have several suggestions that can ease them through the process. Many of these ideas are inherent in the examples illustrated in the previous chapters, but I want to make some of the assumptions behind my decisions apparent.

Advice #1: Follow the KISS Principle

My first piece of advice for teachers considering shifting their instructional program to one centered on historical investigations is to not try to do it all at once. As the old saying goes, keep it simple. Trying to develop the questions; locate, read, and adapt a series of historical sources; develop confidence in the elements of the investigations model; and in turn inculcate students with the same confidence is an absolutely overwhelming task to accomplish in one year. As any teacher will tell you, your first year is an experience that someone should have to survive only once. Taking on a transformation from being a proponent of memorization to historical investigator can make even the most experienced classroom instructor feel like a first-year teacher all over again.

To avoid burnout, I recommend during the first year of implementing this approach that teachers consider developing an initial unit that introduces the language of historical investigations, particularly the concepts of text, context, and subtext. Establishing this introductory unit enables teachers to recast their students' perceptions of what it means to study history. Bob Bain recommends that we "construct a different, more complex view of the structure of the discipline [history]," and that's exactly why I teach the Nat Turner lesson so early in the year (Bain 2000, 337; Shemilt 1980). The Turner lesson, combined with others that teach about historical sources, provides an opportunity to practice reading sources. It also introduces the historical investigations model and the vocabulary that structures its approach. Teaching about Nat Turner enables me to immerse students quickly into a new paradigm for examining the past. If the intent is to have them consider history differently, then a structure must be introduced early.

Sam Wineburg again blazes the way in this regard. As part of the Stanford History Education group, he and his colleagues have designed, put into practice, and made available materials from their "Reading Like a Historian" project (http://sheg.stanford.edu/?q=node/45). Relevant here are the lesson plans and materials that structure their introductory unit. The project provides posters and worksheets that embody the common approach and language that enable students and teachers to think like historians. These lesson plans also make it possible for teachers to design and teach a first unit that sets the stage for a yearlong exploration of historical questions through the residue of the past. Regardless of the materials used, teachers who are truly going to facilitate a course of study that emphasizes the interrogation of historical evidence to tackle historical problems must challenge their students' conceptions of what history is and how it is studied right out of the gate.

In addition to developing an initial unit, teachers should ensure that the conceptual framework and common vocabulary that define this approach continue to constitute the architecture that structures the entire year and not simply the introductory unit. Introducing students to the vocabulary and design of historical investigations is a waste of time if using them does not become a habitual practice. Imagine a science teacher running one laboratory experience a year. Why do it? The kids would forget the lab safety requirements and the expectations of a lab report. Instead of developing and refining their scientific skills, they would see the laboratory experience as not central to the learning of science. It is essential that students continually approach their study of the past by interrogating historical evidence to address questions in an effort to develop their evidence-based interpretations.

Advice #2: Slow and Steady Wins the Race

My second piece of advice is that teachers consider developing one investigation per unit. Most high school and middle school curricula consist of ten to fourteen units per year. Developing one investigation per unit enables teachers to continually hit on the important concepts related to a discipline-based approach without overwhelming both their students and themselves. Designing an investigation gets easier once you can anticipate how your students will react to the question posed and you know their comfort level with interrogating historical sources. In order for instructors to develop this classroom sense of anticipation, they need time to reflect on how the investigation fared with their students. Focusing on one in-depth experience per unit allows for downtime to reflect on the organization, implementation, and assessment results generated by the history lab just put into action. Translating the lessons learned from one investigation into the next, and then into the next, creates a cumulative repository of instructional wisdom that will make the second and third years of a teacher's transition from memory-history to a disciplinary approach much easier. Classroom veterans will be the first to tell you that being able to access the wisdom of your own mistakes and successes is the most useful teaching tool when it comes to changing classroom instruction.

Traditionally, the key organizational decision in a history classroom has been choosing which topics, names, dates, events, ideas, and personalities need to be covered. Content, despite such off-base charges that social studies has destroyed what was once a history-centered curriculum that inspired laudatory levels of knowledge retention (Ravitch and Finn 1987; Gagnon 1989), has always been central to the teaching and assessment of historical knowledge. Instead of simply teaching the list of topics required to be covered, I argue that the terms found in Step 1 of the historical investigations model (See Figure 1.2 in Chapter 1) enable teachers to structure their lessons so that content and process can be married while simultaneously reinforcing the key elements of historical thinking. The following concepts form the core of my recommendation:

- Causality
- Chronology
- Multiple perspectives
- Contingency
- Empathy
- Change and continuity over time
- Influence/significance/impact
- Contrasting interpretations
- Intent/motivation

Between the "once a unit" investigations that will define the initial year of this approach—and the multiple investigations per unit in future years—are other lessons on refining students' confidence with understanding and applying these concepts to the study of the past. A lesson that emphasizes chronology or causality or multiple perspectives but is not developed into a full-blown investigation nevertheless enables students to practice the approach in microcosm.

Source work does not have to include multiple contradictory historical sources to establish the idea that history can be investigated. In fact, for students to experience ever-widening degrees of facility with the sheer variety of historical sources, limiting them to one or two lessons and focusing on the application of the questions of text, context, and subtext can actually pay huge dividends when they are engaged in a full-scale investigation. Thus, I propose that teachers make historical sources the centerpiece of every lesson. Using one or two sources can help students understand the strengths and weaknesses of a type of source (diary versus newspaper article, advertisement versus photograph, and so on). In turn, when students confront these sources as part of a larger historical investigation, they will enter the activity with familiarity at minimum and perhaps a significant level of confidence.

Even the much-maligned textbook can become a vehicle for student appreciation for the sheer variety of materials that can illuminate questions about the past. It is essential to ensure that students are questioning the sources and the evidence they provide. If the historical sources are simply treated as repositories of information devoid of context and subtext, then the notion of investigating the past through the pursuit of evidence to interpret historical questions is rendered neutral.

Advice #3: It All Starts with Questions

Approaching every topic through the lens of a question will also help students and teachers through this transition. The false dichotomy between history-as-fact versus history-as-investigation can be mitigated by showing students that questions are at the heart of the discipline and factual information is key to making reasoned arguments about the past. Instead of simply showing a film or having students copy notes or read the textbook for the purpose of answering the review questions, teachers should keep the notion of questions at the forefront of their planning, instruction, and assessment.

Advice #4: You Will Still Be in Charge!

As teachers progress along a continuum from anxious to confident about engaging students in historical investigations, they will have the opportunity to confront the two impediments that make most instructional alterations stillborn: the effect on coverage and control. The rewards structure within schools, and among internal peer systems, provides positive feedback for teachers who can exert positive control over student behavior and cover the content required (McNeil 1988; Onosko 1991; Thornton 2005). At first, the idea of historical investigations as a model for promoting student understanding of history both as a discipline and a body of substantive knowledge necessary to successfully master whatever assessment tool is required presents clear challenges to coverage and control (Barton and Levstik 2003, 2004). What I have discovered is that historical investigations and coverage are not necessarily diametrically opposed. Yes, the inch-deep, mile-wide demands of the Advanced Placement (AP) United States History course do not make a good bedfellow for this approach. This does not mean that students in an AP course could not use this method. It does mean that its implementation would need to be more precisely calibrated so that whatever investigations take place complement the coverage demands and the assessment format that drives the AP examination. Outside of such a highly visible assessment vehicle as AP, historical investigations and coverage are not sworn enemies. In my experience, anything that increases student interest in and enthusiasm for history ultimately makes my job easier when it comes to measurements of student understanding.

The county in which I am employed requires that all students taking eleventh-grade U.S. History sit for a countywide final examination. Examining the American past through the lens of historical investigations has not in any way been detrimental to my students' success on the exam. I deal more specifically with how reforming our discipline's obsession with coverage can aid an investigative approach in Chapter 10; suffice it to say at this point that I firmly believe that by scaffolding the implementation of historical investigations into instruction, teachers will no doubt find that it does not mean the evisceration of coverage, nor will it destroy control of student behavior.

Will students listen to me? What if they don't? How long will it take for one of them to challenge my authority? These and scores of other questions flood teachers' minds before they enter the classroom. Controlling student behavior is the most essential element of the instructional package teachers must master. A classroom without control will never be able to promote learning. Most teachers will tell you that no matter how long you practice your craft, the question of managing student behaviors will always be in the forefront of your mind. One student can alter the brittle calculus that is classroom management and skew the equation for an entire class for an entire year. Just like all of my colleagues, I have clear expectations for my students in the classroom and harbor great trepidation for the slightest factor that could alter a highly functioning classroom atmosphere.

When I first considered having my students investigate historical questions, gather and interrogate historical sources, and finally develop and defend historical interpretations, I was panic stricken at the effect it might have on student behavior. In all honesty, sometimes the demands of the approach and my students' behavior do not coincide in a positive manner. That said, I have learned to make adjustments so that I can still promote student investigation of historical questions, source work, and the development and defense of evidence-based historical interpretations and maintain the order necessary for a safe and on-task learning environment. Reducing the number, length, and types of historical sources, full-group activities versus small groups, periodic quick-writes to assess students' comprehension at the moment—all facilitate my implementation of the core elements of the historical investigation approach without sacrificing classroom management. With most of my classes, I spend much less time on active management during investigations than I do during lessons that do not take this approach. Of course this reality changes from group to group and year to year. Nevertheless, the approach and management need not be antagonistic, but can be harmonious if clear expectations are set, consistently reinforced, and rewarded.

Advice #5: Before and After Are as Important as During

Trying to sustain student connection to the historical investigations approach for an entire year is still a significant challenge for me. Thoughtful investigations take time. Teachers must consider the relationship between the numerous benefits of investigating the past with the "tyranny of coverage" mandated by standards documents, curricula, school organization of contact time with students, and assessment (Loewen 2009, 19). Thus my final recommendation is for teachers to consider carefully what they do with the topics that are addressed before and after an investigation. Deciding how to balance the coverage constraints with the joys of investigations is often predicated more on how you approach other topics than on the time you spend on an investigation. If you cover the topics before and afterward via lecture, video, textbook reading, or other techniques more affiliated with a memory approach to the past, then you end up defeating the purpose of having students examine the past in a manner consistent with historians. On the other hand, if you try to run investigation after investigation, you will end the year well short of what you are required to cover. My counsel is to plan your year by starting at the end and working your way backward and, while doing so, to consider the following (Wiggins and McTighe 2005):

1. Lay out where you need to be by the last day of school.
2. Determine the units that will define the division of the course content.
3. Identify within each unit one historical investigation that will be conducted. (This will change each year as you add more investigations to each unit.)
4. Within each unit, examine the remaining content that needs to be covered to meet state or local demands.
5. Aggregate the remaining content in a manner that enables you to reinforce the key elements of the historical investigations approach (key questions, source work, disciplinary concepts) and organize the lessons with the remaining content that are broader than most investigations.
6. Remember that you cannot cover it all.

Between historical investigations, not getting lost in the list of content to be covered frees up time for teachers to conduct the more rewarding experiences that better replicate the work done in the discipline of history.

Nevertheless, underneath the thin veneer of idealism I espouse to the world lies a realist. The demands of coverage, even more than those of control), are the most significant impediments to this approach (Barton and Levstik 2004). I draw out in the next chapter more systemic changes that might ease these demands on history educators.

As teacher confidence crescendos, the reservoir of materials available to promote effective investigations grows, and teachers realize that the technique effectively engages students and promotes greater levels of achievement, they will find this approach the new normal and wonder why they were initially resistant to the change. In lieu of major changes to curricular scope and sequence, I advise teachers to go slowly with any adjustments to their approach to history instruction. Attempting to have students engage in an investigatory process every day will cause them—and you—to burn out quickly. The first year you attempt to recast your instruction toward historical investigations, you should shoot for incorporating one historical investigation into each unit. The next year, revise the investigations developed the first year and incorporate a second one into each unit. The third year, assuming someone does not see fit to change your schedule, revise the first two years' worth of investigations and develop a third round. By your fourth year you will have a cabinetful of historical investigations, the confidence to implement them with students, and the evidence that the approach is doable.

CHAPTER 10

Overcoming the Barrier to Change

I dislike how AP classes . . . have become nothing more than learning the maximum amount of content in order to pass the exam . . . I spent all of my junior year taking my U.S. History textbook with me everywhere and in class we only reinforced what we had read previously . . . It is incredibly unfortunate that the range of information on the AP exam is so broad because having to learn 300+ years of history in class of 180 days is almost impossible.

—Student reflection on Advanced Placement history versus a more focused approach to investigating the past

During the year I was completing this book, Janelle, quoted above, was assigned to me as a student aide. A senior, Janelle had completed AP U.S. history under the guidance of a fantastic teacher. She was well prepared for the exam and earned a score of five. Then, as a senior, she sat through my class, often becoming a participant, and experienced firsthand an alternative method to the sprint through American history represented by the AP syllabus.

After watching investigations in my eleventh-grade U.S. history class, Janelle would make comments such as, "I remember hearing about that event/person, but I never really understood it." Or that she had written "numerous DBQs [Document-Based Questions]" but did not "understand about historical evidence." Janelle, like most students, is more interested in deep learning than in exposure to multiple topics. This difference is key. Exposure means fact-based, one-word answers that prepare students for a random Jay Leno interview. Deep learning allows a student to apply content in a manner that gives it meaning and illustrates the purpose for knowing the information. My conversations with Janelle throughout the year crystallized my feelings that coverage is the fundamental obstacle in the way of promoting a deeper, richer understanding of the past.

At the 2010 National Council for History Education (NCHE) annual conference in San Diego, Sam Wineburg told a story about his son that sheds light on this distinction. While reviewing for the AP U.S. History exam, he asked his dad if the Korean War happened before or after World War II. Wineburg used this anecdote to explain why broad coverage is actually an impediment to learning. What his son was expressing through his question was what Wineburg calls "a fundamental misunderstanding of the impact of World War Two on power relationships in the world." For Wineburg, his son's error was "not an issue of chronology but of understanding." In my estimation, the younger Wineburg and Janelle are victims of the crime of coverage. Forced to digest reams of information, the younger Wineburg exposed not his lack of knowledge—his proud father was quick to indicate his high score on the AP exam—but his inability to utilize this information to make sense of the past. It is this trade-off, between coverage of volumes of information and understanding, that causes me to cast coverage as a criminal in the study of history.

And Then . . . and Then . . . and Then . . .

The story of Sidney Shea opens a chapter of the 1982 report *Making History Come Alive: The Place of History in the Schools*:

He was a tiger among teachers. Feared by the faint, respected by all, Sidney Morgan Shea pressed his students as hard as he chewed the end of his pipe.

But they liked it, and they learned. Shea was never undone, but if anything came close to undoing him, it was the accumulation of history. Every year there was more, "and," he was often heard to growl when final exams came in sight, "I haven't even reached the election of 1932!" There was a lot of history when Sidney Shea taught school in the 1940s, and there has been more since. There will always be more than history teachers can cover. (Howard and Mendenhall 1982, 51)

There is a little of Sidney Shea in all history teachers. We love history. It is the subject matter that leads us to choose to teach what we teach. Ending a school year without investigating our favorite dead friends, debating the most thought-provoking moments, or allowing students to analyze a favorite historical source, is disappointing yet perennial. Every history teacher can empathize with Sidney Shea's frustration. But Shea's difficulties remind me of the apocryphal definition of insanity: doing the same thing over and over again and expecting different results. Not that Shea, or any other history teacher, is a candidate for the asylum, but we continue to end each year frustrated that there is too much to cover or having our enthusiasm tempered by the results of standardized tests. Yes, telling the story from soup to nuts has its appeal. Ultimately, though, wouldn't it be better for both teacher and student if the maddening drive to teach it all, which Shea correctly acknowledges will never get easier but simply worsen, were replaced with a deeper, more meaningful experience with the past akin to those exposed by Janelle's comments at the outset of the chapter? I believe it would.

Janelle's words, Sam Wineburg's tale, and Shea's conundrum speak clearly to the fact that history education often confuses understanding with knowledge. In turn, the educational reforms represented by the push for state and national standards that delineate what students need to know actually retard intellectual growth rather than promote it (Perkins 1992; Stearns 1993; Hampel 1985; Loewen 2009; Gagnon 2003). Because the ultimate goal of any education is for students to learn, "to sacrifice comprehension for coverage is a deadly sin" (Howard and Mendenhall 1982, 52). Battling the negative permutations of coverage is a challenge that cries out loudly to the leaders in history education to address the central impediment to promoting evidence-based historical thinking.

What Does the Brain Tell Us?

Research in cognitive psychology clearly illustrates that student learning is optimized when depth replaces breadth. Learning for understanding implies that students use factual information within a conceptual framework organized so that they can retrieve and apply that information (Donovan and Bransford 2005). The ability to use thinking skills is dependent on the amount of deep knowledge, also called background knowledge, that students have established in a particular area. The higher the cognitive task required of a student, the more depth of knowledge that student must have, or the ability to relate a new concept to another area of deep knowledge. A student can't know something unless it is related to something he or she already knows. There is minimal cognitive benefit to breadth of content, because it creates cognitive clutter that students cannot wade through in order to focus deeply on something. Because we fail to assist students in creating a neural network to support the breadth of knowledge being imparted, it is quickly forgotten.

Research into cognition also shows that coverage is not consonant with how the brain learns. For students to think deeply, they must have something to think about. Students cannot use deeper cognitive processes, usually referred to as critical thinking skills, unless they have background knowledge. For our purposes, historical thinking skills and the investigation of the past are the deeper skills that are best employed when they are intertwined with content. Thus, coverage by its very definition provides exposure to a wide array of facts. But because the majority of instructional time is spent ensuring that these facts are covered, there is no time to use them to think deeply about the past. Coverage ensures neither understanding nor the ability to foster a deep cognitive process such as those promoted through historical investigations (Willingham 2009).

For students to think historically, then, they must understand the context of a topic. Once this background is established, they can evaluate evidence and apply it to a historical question. In addition, practicing the implementation of the historical investigations model ensures the cognitive practice that can further strengthen learning, make retention of information more long lasting, and increase the chances that the skills embedded in the model will transfer to new situations (Willingham 2009; Jensen 2005; Marzano, Pickering, and Pollock 2001). Cognitive psychology is consonant with historical thinking, and the lessons shared within these pages are intended to provide practical links between cognitive research and historical thinking.

Why Coverage?

Coverage is a political—not an educational—decision. History, more than any other subject matter, has its content dictated by political considerations. Yes, the diversification of the canon in literature has generated argument. The battles between evolution and creationism—now given the moniker "intelligent design"—periodically rage in science. But it is in the discipline of history where what and who is covered in the curriculum is hotly contested.

One need only revisit the fight over the National Standards for History to see how divisive it can be to determine what history is to be taught to students (Nash, Crabtree, and Dunn 1997; Symcox 2002; Evans 2004). A process that initially involved K–12 classroom teachers, historians, and curriculum specialists culminated with the U.S. Congress voting 99–1 to reject the document. Lynne Cheney, head of the National Endowment for the Humanities at the time, led the critics. For her, the National Standards for History spent too much time on the negative aspects of the American past, to the detriment of famous individuals. To the mind of the standards' critics, the document was anti-American in its tone, its selection of exemplars to be studied, and in the teaching suggestions provided for educators. Most critics compared the number of times George Washington appeared in the standards (zero) to the number of times the Ku Klux Klan appeared (seventeen). A mathematical evaluation of figures from the American past fed the debate over whose stories were being told and who was being left out. The document was championed by, among others, Gary Nash and Charlotte Crabtree, the co-directors of the National History Standards Project. From their perspective, national standards for American history needed to include "the study of previously ignored groups in our history" (Nash 1997). The clash between a triumphalist view of the American past and a more critical view ultimately destroyed the National Standards influence.

The scars left behind from the debate over the National Standards kept history as a testable subject out of the design of the landmark No Child Left Behind Act. The current debate over revisions to the Texas standards shows that the combustibility of history standards is still part of the debate within the history education community and the public at large (Robelen 2010).

Part of the politicization of what is taught in history classrooms stems from its origins in the curriculum of American public schools. Since 1827, when the study of history was made a legal requirement for schoolchildren in Massachusetts and Vermont, the goal of history instruction has been to promote "patriotism and good citizenship," "truth, honesty, and patriotism," "a true comprehension of the rights, duties, and dignity of American citizenship," and "truth, justice, and patriotism" (Pierce 1926, 6–7). This continues today. Coverage of historical content, goes this argument, facilitates an attempt to inculcate citizens with what they need to know about their nation. To understand the story of the nation, students must study the nation's past from its birth to the present day. Only this way can they truly appreciate America in its relationship to the world.

My animus toward coverage should not be interpreted as a lack of appreciation for the relationship between historical knowledge and an informed citizenry. I in no way devalue the importance of educating students to be effective citizens in a participatory democracy. It is essential for students to understand how their nation's collective historical experiences illustrate its core principles. It is also imperative that students understand that current problems always have a historical component. But, as Sidney Shea's conundrum illustrates, what needs to be covered always increases, so it is incumbent upon history educators to stop adding to the list and make some hard choices. Yet what all these debates forget is that we are fast approaching the one hundredth anniversary of one of the first attempts to measure what it means to understand history (Bell and McCollum 1917). For one hundred years, students taking survey courses have neither retained specific facts nor shown increased interest in the discipline of history (NCES 1998, 2002, 2006; Neal and Martin 2000; Rosenweig and Thelen 1998; Gagnon 1989; Ravitch and Finn 1987; Whittington 1991; Schick 1991). Students' lack of either the big picture or the small details makes it incumbent upon the policy makers who develop the structure within which we must teach to change the way we approach instruction. Revelations in cognitive psychology have opened a door that links historical thinking to effective classroom practice. Since that inaugural measurement, we have spent the century documenting that we do not understand the past. In addition to these dismal measurements, two factors remain constant that contribute to this lack of knowledge of and interest in history: coverage, and the attendant pedagogical methods that promote that goal—that is, lecture, textbook reading, recitation, and multiple-choice assessment questions. Perhaps the hardest realization history educators must make is that a more influential factor on student achievement may be *how* history is taught rather than *what* is taught.

My Modest Proposal

Because students are overwhelmed by the sheer volume of information they must digest, the most significant reform to history education would be to design courses that focus on student learning and measure the depth of their understanding rather than surface coverage (VanSledright 1997; Brophy 1990; Rothstein 2004; Wineburg 2004; Grant 2006). Imagine an instructional program focused on deep learning, the utilization of evidence, and knowledge of the content from an abridged part of time, all measured not by multiple-choice questions but by student work. That is change all teachers can believe in.

My overarching goal with this book is to persuade history educators to consider a different and potentially more effective method for engaging students in the study of the past. To fully facilitate this transformation, I recommend that school districts, testing companies, textbook producers, and other elements of the education establishment consider one key change that would unleash good teachers to motivate and engage students and promote higher degrees of student learning: stop trying to cover it all!

Clear in my mind is also the tendency of students and often teachers to prefer teaching either a narrow topic in great depth or current events rather than history. Divining the causes of America's current military engagements rather than the multiple causes for the fall of the Roman Empire has a certain cachet for students and teachers alike. Six weeks on the American Civil War as interpreted by Ken Burns is more attractive to some educators than balancing their analysis of the war with other periods in American history. Reducing coverage demands would potentially free up teachers to teach the present and neglect the past. I do not advocate coverage reduction to those ends.

My intention is to narrow coverage only to the degree to which it allows instruction to promote the acquisition and refinement of historical thinking skills. In fact, if the requirement of having to cover it all were replaced with the demand that students show facility with doing source work and evaluating historical evidence to generate answers to historical questions, one could still teach the full length of American history. What would be sacrificed are the lists of names and dates and events that populate almost every United States history standards document in the nation with the exception of Colorado. Instead of embracing the checklist approach to history instruction, Colorado's new state standards embrace historical thinking as the organizational approach to teaching the past.

Yes, given the demands placed upon students from other subjects, more time for the study of history would seem like a policy pipedream. Yet, there is an emerging consensus when it comes to educational reform that the educational system must be able to demonstrate that classroom instruction leads to student learning. Input—output: this makes sense. By altering the delivery of the discipline to be one not based on the digestion and regurgitation of volumes of information, but one that is instead focused on the analysis of evidence to develop answers to historical questions, we deepen the study of history. If we drop the obsession with coverage that is a mile wide and an inch deep and replace it with inputs related to historical thinking about content, doesn't it make sense that we will substantially deepen the outputs we can measure?

Stop Complaining and Do Something About It!

As the popular aphorism goes, don't complain unless you are going to do something. What could a United States history curriculum look like if it was not driven by coverage and instead was organized to promote historical thinking and an understanding of historical content? In some ways we already have functioning models at the university level and at some high schools: the elective. Electives in history narrow the content to be examined and provide teachers the latitude to be creative in their approach to the topic. History majors can testify to the fact that after the 100-level surveys came the courses they loved. Courses on the Civil War, the Renaissance, Antebellum America, and so on were designed to look at a period of time in greater depth and sometimes organized around an investigatory approach to understanding the past. It was here, after anyone not interested in history had moved on to science, math, accounting, or other courses that historians actually pulled back the curtains and allowed students to gain an understanding of how the past is investigated and the debates that define our understanding.

What might an eighth- or eleventh-grade United States history course look like if it were organized in such a manner? The pathbreaking work of Lendol Calder at Augustana College in Illinois provides guidance. Frustrated with the bored look on his students' faces and the general societal dislike of history, Calder embarked on an effort to design and implement a course driven not by coverage but by what Grant Wiggins and Jay McTighe cleverly call "uncoverage." In *Understanding by Design* (2005), Wiggins and McTighe call for the promotion not of the retention of facts but the employment of these facts to generate a deeper understanding of the past. Coverage, the sprint through time that exposes students to the major events, personalities, and ideas of the past, is replaced with uncoverage. Taking these ideas, Calder redesigned his introductory survey course in American history.

Calder's altered introductory survey course asks students to develop acumen with questioning, connecting, sourcing, and making inferences, to consider alternate perspectives, and to recognize the limits of knowledge. These skills are developed, refined, and applied to the examination of a defined period of American history: World War II to the present. Calder divides his course into several segments, starting with an introduction to historical study. That is followed by weeklong examinations of the following topics: "The Origins of the Cold War," "Society and Culture in the 1950s," "The Civil Rights Movement," "Kennedy/Johnson Liberalism," "Vietnam," "Sixties Cultural Rebellion," "1980s Culture Wars," and "The End of the Cold War." Each three-session mini-unit has students develop questions about the topic, conduct a history workshop that examines primary evidence to develop interpretations about it, and finally, contrast interpretations of the topic as reflected through comparative synthesis. Calder's efforts to promote uncoverage are laid out in a fascinating Web site that serves as a companion to his 2006 article in the *Journal of American History*.

If coverage can be reenvisioned as a melding of skills, depth of content, and increased student engagement posited by Wiggins and McTighe and Calder, the question is how? Central to this model is the identification of the key questions that should structure students' investigation of the American past. These questions are derived from the historiography of the time period, the historical sources available, and student interests. They will inform the content to be examined in the course. The purpose of the course is to explore the past and to gain an understanding of the important ideas, events, and personalities that defined a particular period of time. After identifying the content to be examined and how it relates to the broader themes within United States history that students should understand, curriculum designers should identify the language that will delineate the historical investigations and the historical thinking skills to be emphasized in the course.

One way to assuage the fears of those who will argue for breadth rather than depth is to tie the defined time period to be studied into broader themes that link the entire span of the American experience. Economic change, growth of democracy, engagement with the world, and alterations in the role of government can provide the scaffolding that will link the in-depth examination of the time period to the events preceding and following it. This would necessitate placing the time period to be studied in the context of American history and upon completing its study to link the events, personalities, and ideas to the current time. Using the aforementioned themes or others in their stead allows a teacher to ensure that the material investigated is not divorced from its broader historical context or significance to change and continuity throughout American history. If the time period to be investigated spans Reconstruction to World War II, students would need to have a broad understanding of the political, economic, social, and governmental changes of those times to make any sense of their investigations.

The History Lab Model

Central to the reenvisioned approach to school history is the idea of the history lab. The goal of the history lab is to have students engage in explorations of the past modeled after the historical investigations model outlined in Chapter 1. These laboratory experiences find students unleashed on historical sources to generate answers to historical questions that frame the organization of the overall course. The difference between the science approach and the history approach is that in science labs students attempt to replicate a previously conducted experiment in order to reinforce a theory already learned. History, despite the arguments of some, does not pivot on the provability of theories. Instead, history is about the debate between competing interpretations of events, individuals, and ideas of the past based on historical sources. The laboratory work conducted in the reenvisioned history class is exactly that: interrogating historical sources to develop and defend a source-based interpretation that responds to a question about the past. Key to the model is that content does not take a backseat to process but the two work hand in hand. The content that students are immersed in to set up the investigation and that they examine during the actual lab is all fair game for assessments. Designed and implemented by New Jersey high school teachers Mike Walsh and Phil Nicolosi, the history lab serves as an important model for embracing historical thinking in the classroom.

My school district is implementing a Teaching American History Grant program that places a version of the history lab model at the center of classroom instruction. The program's goal is to empower teachers to make many of the changes discussed within these pages in their own classrooms. Teacher-participants are asked to design instruction that encourages students to replicate the work of historians. By developing questions that drive student investigation of the past, promoting the analysis of historical evidence, and assisting in the construction of competing narrative explanations for the guiding questions, teachers and students can change the way they think about history. To meet these goals, participants are exposed to the literature on history education and historical investigations, and they explore a series of topics with a historian and master classroom teacher. The two demonstrate how to design and execute historical investigations with students in grades five, eight, or eleven. Teacher and student growth is measured through an external evaluation and classroom observation for teachers and a series of exams for students. Success is measured by growth in both the general content knowledge of students and teachers and, more important, the growth in students' and teachers' facility with evaluating historical sources and applying these sources to a historical question. Over the lifetime of the project my district will train ninety elementary, middle, and high school teachers in the approach delineated in the historical investigations model. It will be intriguing to participate in and witness the efficacy of this program with such a wide range of educators.

Assessment and Accountability

Finally, my proposed model does not dodge issues of accountability (Rothstein 2004). In fact, I say bring it on! Measure students' abilities to examine historical sources, to use their acumen with subtext and context, and to address questions about causality, significance, and other residue of historical thinking, and ask them questions about the basic content of the time period examined. I firmly believe that accountability should be one measure of the success of teaching and learning and that the ideas embodied in this proposal are not aimed at avoiding the current rage in education. The measures used to assess the learning and teaching cannot be the simplistic multiple-choice questions that dominate measurements such as the National Assessment of Educational Progress (NAEP). In addition, they are not the massive writing experiences that have come to populate the Advanced Placement Examinations in history. Instead, effective assessment for historical investigation must determine whether students have acquired the following skills:

- Identify text, subtext, and context for a historical source
- Use these sources to develop an interpretation to a historical question
- Present their evidence-based interpretation in some format
- Demonstrate an understanding of the basic content of the time period examined

⊕ Make connections between the people, events, and ideas of the time period and the broader American historical experience.

This means that the measure must be designed in a way that allows students time to sit for the exam, and that scoring must move from NAEP-esque multiple-choice questions to much more time-intensive evaluative devices (Rothstein 2004).

I have been progressively moving away from multiple-choice questions and toward assessments that attempt to isolate students' understanding of source work and various disciplinary concepts. My unit exams consist of ten to fifteen multiple-choice items that get at the key content, two historical thinking questions that assess their abilities with source work and disciplinary concepts, and an essay question that asks them to craft a historical argument using evidence from the time period. What have been rewarding thus far are the student responses to the historical thinking questions. For example, on a recent end-of-unit exam on World War I, I posed this document question:

> Jacob Lawrence completed The Migration Series in 1941 at the age of 23. (See Figures 10.1 and 10.2.) His parents were part of the first wave of the migration, having moved from South Carolina to Philadelphia. He later settled in Harlem, New York, a location crowded with migrants from all parts of the South. Lawrence once said that "teachers, friends, even actors on the street corners helped me to understand how my own experiences fit into a much larger story—the history of African Americans in this country. It seems inevitable that I would tell this story in my art. I spent many hours at the Schomberg Library in Harlem reading books about the great migration and I took notes."
>
> What information is presented in the text of the images?
>
> What does the author's background tell us about how the subtext affects the information provided by the images?

The question is derived from our investigation of the migration of African Americans out of the South that began during the Great War. Student responses indicate that they are able to apply the concepts of context and subtext to their analysis of this historical evidence:

> "The text of the images [*sic*] shows all the people from the south who are migrating north and to western cities for a better life. The author's

Figure 10.1

Figure 10.2

background tells us that he knows what it [migration] was like. The
paragraph underneath the pictures tells us how his own experiences fit
into a much larger story."

"The Great Migration was an era in which African Americans were brought
together by their common goals for finding work and improving the lives
of their family. The author's background helped to give a more positive
outlook."

Both students' responses contain some errors about content. In addition,
neither nails down that the subtext is the artist's reflection of both his own
family's history and that of the larger African American community.
Nevertheless, both are associating the author's background (subtext) with
his artistic interpretation of the migration northward (text). I can walk
away from this assessment feeling that my students can carry the concepts
and apply them to historical documents. In essence, I can measure their
facility with historical thinking.

Here are some other assessment examples that focus on measuring students' abilities with source work and disciplinary concepts such as causality, chronology, or multiple perspectives:

During this unit we encountered two new types of historical sources
(autobiographies and newspapers). Pick one and describe (without using
the word *bias*) the challenges it presented when you attempted to
interpret past events.

During this unit we dealt with a number of testimonies (Triangle
Shirtwaist Fire testimonies, Haymarket Riot court testimonies, Pullman
congressional testimonies, the Homestead Steel Strike, and so on)
Without using the word *bias*, describe the following:

- How the various subtexts of the testimonies made it challenging to
  use the documents
- How you/we were able to address these problems and still develop
  an interpretation of the event(s)

In 1868 Thomas Nast, one of the most famous political cartoonists in
American history, turned his attention to the corrupt New York City
administration of Tammany Hall Democrats led by William "Boss" Tweed
(Figure 10.3). For the next three years *Harper's Weekly* and the *New York
Times* campaigned against Tweed. Nast's cartoons were so effective in

depicting Tweed as a sleazy criminal that legend has it that the Boss dispatched his minions with the command, "Stop them damn pictures. I don't care what the papers write about me. My constituents can't read. But, damn it, they can see the pictures." Voters ousted Tweed and his compatriots in November 1871.

Figure 10.3

"THAT'S WHATS THE MATTER."

Boss Tweed. "As long as I count the Votes, what are you going to do about it? say?"

1. What is the argument made by the text (visual)? (One sentence)
2. What challenges are presented to a historian who might be using this source to discuss the role of political machines during the industrial period of American history? (Two–three sentences)

It has been only over the past three years that I have attempted to align my instructional changes with assessment. Even given this small window, I am happy with the changes I have made thus far. Over the course of the year, students exhibit greater dexterity in applying historical thinking skills. In addition, I think my assessments are a better mirror of my instruction. When I first initiated the use of a disciplinary approach to teaching the past, my assessments never quite matched. Students were tested on reams of substantive historical content and not on any of the skills required to investigate the past. Now I think I have struck a balance between assessing core content and historical thinking skills. My students also seem more confident about summative assessments because they more closely reflect what we do on a daily basis in the classroom. Providing tools for teachers so they can both teach and assess historical thinking in their classrooms would be an important next step in promoting historical thinking.

Materials of Instruction

Access to materials of instruction that put into the hands of teachers intelligently designed, classroom-tested, and kid-approved resources is an essential next step in the movement toward history instruction that places disciplinary skills at the focal point of instruction. One of the greatest impediments to instructional change is the lack of time to devote to securing resources to promote a particular methodology. The market is flooded with primary sources, Document-Based Questions, and materials claiming to make history come alive. Yet there is a noticeable dearth of materials that promote a true disciplinary approach to studying the past.

Three factors are central to the development of materials of instruction that promote the approach delineated within these pages. One, materials must focus instruction on historical questions that call on students to interrogate historical sources in order to develop and defend evidence-based interpretations. Second, there must be a common vocabulary that drives the development of the questions. Causality, chronology, multiple perspectives, contingency, empathy, change and continuity over time, influence/significance/impact, contrasting interpretations, and intent/motivation or other historical concepts should form the structure of the questions the materials pose to students. Just as important is the common vocabulary that defines how students undergo the source work element of their investigation. Approaching the examination of sources and applying the evidence derived should be done consistently throughout the program. With resources and models readily available, greater numbers of teachers can choose to approach the teaching of history in a manner parallel to that of historians.

Other barriers to promoting historical investigations in the classroom include the training of preservice teachers, the dysfunctional relationship between history and education departments in universities, and licensure requirements set forth by state departments of education, among others (Frankel and Stearns 2004; VanSledright 2011; Mayer 2006; Bain and Mirel 2006; McDiarmid and Vinten-Johansen 2000; Warren and Cantu 2008; Fragnoli 2005; Van Hover, Hicks, and Irwin 2007). Although each barrier is important, they fall outside the scope of this book. Addressing the coverage issue and promoting the approach with solid materials will go a long way toward empowering more teachers to embrace historical thinking in the classroom.

Investigating the past by using the same skills historians use is a more engaging approach to teaching history. If desired, we can measure student learning resulting from this approach just as we measure students' content knowledge. Perhaps the results will be different from the dismal one-hundred-year record of student performance in history we now face. Perhaps. But if we keep doing what we do in the classroom, I am less than sanguine that the results will ever change.

Afterword

The End or Just the Beginning?

Are my methods perfect? Not even close. Are they always successful? No. Am I offering the magic formula for all that ails history teachers everywhere? Again, no.

As any good teacher will tell you, working with kids is a humbling experience. The best lesson one year can fall flat the next. Students' interests and abilities fluctuate yearly. Administrative dictates shift resources, priorities, and educational outcomes frequently. Given all these realities it would be foolish for me to offer up a classroom that promotes historical thinking as the panacea for all that ails history education. But I would not have taken the time to shift my instructional focus from memory-history to skills related to the discipline of history, and to write this book, if I did not feel strongly about its efficacy with students. Simply put, students can be more engaged in their study of the past when they are actively generating evidence-based answers to historical questions.

On the off day that I might lecture to make up for a series of snow days, students always ask why I am doing it. They still may not be history's greatest fans, but they prefer investigating the past to simply being told what I believe happened. Their comments and thoughts push me further and further into my unabashed support for historical thinking. In their own words, they've told me how they've benefited from this approach:

- "Before I entered this class I did not like history, in fact I wasn't looking forward to it in the slightest. But that changed the first day when we discussed interpretations and how that's all history is. I got interested and stayed interested through the rest of the course."
- "I was able to step into the shoes of all parties and understand their justifications for their views."
- "You made it enjoyable to learn new topics and stayed away from the overused way of just lecturing."
- "I liked how you would try and get us to think about situations from other perspectives."
- "I really enjoyed the class and liked the way you made us think and get into discussion. I liked your use of slides and journals to put us in the past."
- "You made people think deeply and then support their opinions."
- "You challenged us to think. And we need to be challenged to think and not just memorize."

Education is about students, and mine seem to benefit from a disciplinary approach to investigating and learning about the past.

If I stay in the classroom for the remainder of my career, my goal is to build momentum for this approach to history instruction, fine-tune its delivery to my students, and promote its benefits with other history educators. Putting to paper what I have done over eighteen years of teaching has recharged my enthusiasm for using the method I have described. As all teachers know, we are inspired when our love of subject matter and the needs of our students intersect. The moments when students understand a key concept, pose a contemplative question, write an evidence-supported essay, or in any other manner show they understand the discipline of history are what keep us in the classroom.

My advocacy for historical thinking and historical investigations in the classroom stems directly from the fact that they benefit both teachers and students. Having students confront the past through the lens of an interpretive question, interrogate historical evidence, and apply that evidence to the development of an evidence-based answer is a model that increases the opportunities for students and love of subject matter to intersect. Doing science is the core of the discipline of science and is what interests students. Solving math problems is the core of the discipline and is what interests students. Doing history is the core of our discipline. Lessons about Nat Turner, the Rail Strike of 1877, the Bonus March, Little Bighorn, Truman and MacArthur, and the civil rights movement illustrate that this approach can be taken with students. It works. Give it a try. Be patient. And please, let me know how it goes.

Bibliography

Achugar, Mariana, and Mary J. Schleppegrell. 2005. "Beyond Connectors: The Construction of Cause in History Textbooks." *Linguistics and Education* 16 (3): 298–318.

Andrews, Thomas, and Flannery Burke. 2007. "What Does It Mean to Think Historically?" *AHA Perspectives* 45: 32–35.

Anti-Defamation League. 2006. "Teaching About the Holocaust: Why Simulation Activities Should Not Be Used." http://www.adl.org/education/Simulationinteachinghol.pdf.

Arnesen, Eric. 2009. "Reconsidering the 'Long Civil Rights Movement.'" *Historically Speaking* 10 (2): 31–34.

Bain, Bob. 2000. "Into the Breach: Using Research and Theory to Shape History Instruction." In *Knowing, Teaching, and Learning History*, ed. Peter Stearns, Peter Sexias, and Sam Wineburg. New York: New York University Press.

Bain, Robert B. 2005. "'They Thought the World Was Flat?': Applying the Principles of *How People Learn* in Teaching High School History." In *How Students Learn: History, in the Classroom*, ed. M. S. Donovan and J. D. Bransford. Washington, DC: The National Academies Press.

———. 2006. "Rounding Up Unusual Suspects: Facing the Authority Hidden in History Classrooms." *Teacher College Record* 108 (10): 2080–2114.

Bain, Robert, and Jeffrey Mirel. 1982. "Re-enacting the Past: Using R. G. Collingwood at the Secondary Level." *The History Teacher* 15 (3): 329–345.

———. 2006. "Setting Up Camp at the Great Instructional Divide: Educating Beginning History Teachers." *Journal of Teacher Education* 57 (3): 212–219.

Baker, James T. 1998. *Nat Turner: Cry Freedom in America*. Fort Worth, TX: Harcourt Brace.

Barton, Keith. 1997a. "I Just Kinda Know": Elementary Students' Ideas About Historical Evidence. *Theory and Research in Social Education* 25 (4): 407–430.

211

————. 1997b. "History—It Can Be Elementary: An Overview of Elementary Students' Understanding of History." *Social Education* 61 (January): 13–16.

————. 2004. "Research on Students' Historical Thinking and Learning." *AHA Perspectives Magazine* (October): 19–21.

————. 2005. "Primary Sources in History: Breaking Through the Myths." *Phi Delta Kappan* (June): 745–753.

Barton, Keith C., and Linda Levstik. 1988. "'It Wasn't a Good Part of History': National Identity and Ambiguity in Students' Explanations of Historical Significance." *Teachers College Record* 99 (3): 478–513.

————. 2003. "Why Don't More History Teachers Engage Students in Interpretation?" *Social Education* 67 (6): 358–361.

————. 2004. *Teaching History for the Common Good*. Mahwah, NJ: Lawrence Erlbaum.

Baxter, Maurice, Robert Ferrell, and John Wiltz. 1965. *The Teaching of American History in High Schools*. Bloomington: Indiana University Press.

Bell, J. Carelton, and David F. McCollum. 1917. "A Study of the Attainments of Pupils in United States History." *Journal of Educational Psychology* 8 (5): 257–274.

Bracey, Gerald. 1991. "Why Can't They Be Like We Were?" *Phi Delta Kappan* 73 (2): 104–117.

————. 1997. "What Happened to America's Public Schools?" *American Heritage* 48 (7): 38–52.

Branson, Margaret Stimmann. 1971. "Using Inquiry Methods in the Teaching of American History." *Social Education* 35 (7): 776–782.

Brophy, Jere. 1990. "Teaching Social Studies for Understanding and Higher Order Applications." *The Elementary School Journal* 90 (4): 351–417.

Brugger, Robert J. 1988. *Maryland: A Middle Temperament, 1634–1980*. Baltimore: Johns Hopkins University Press.

Bruner, Jerome S. 1961. "The Act of Discovery." *Harvard Educational Review* 31 (1): 21–32.

Calder, Lendol. 2000. "Uncoverage: Toward a Signature Pedagogy for the History Survey." *Journal of American History* 92 (4): 1358–1369.

Caron, Edward. 2005. "What Leads to the Fall of a Great Empire? Using Central Questions to Design Issues-Based History Units." *The Social Studies* 96 (2): 51–60.

Cuban, Larry. 1982. "Persistent Instruction: The High School Classroom, 1900–1980." *Phi Delta Kappan* 64 (2): 113–118.

————. 1984. *How Teachers Taught: Constancy and Change in American Classrooms, 1890–1980*. New York: Longman.

————. 1991. "History of Teaching in Social Studies." In *Handbook of Research on Social Studies Teaching and Learning*, ed. J. Schaver. New York: Macmillan.

Curry, Andrew. 2002. "The Better Angels: Why We Are Still Fighting Over Who Was Right and Who Was Wrong in the Civil War." *U.S. News and World Report*, September 30.

Daniels, Roger. 1971. *The Bonus March: An Episode of the Great Depression*. Westport, CT: Greenwood.

Danzer, Gerald, and Mark Newman. 1991. "Tuning In: Primary Sources in the Teaching of History." In *Bring History Alive: A Source Book for Teaching United States History*, ed. Kirk Ankeney, Richard Del Rio, Gary B. Nash, and David Vigilante. Los Angeles: National Center for History in the Schools.

D'Este, Carlo. 2002. *Eisenhower: A Soldier's Life*. New York: Henry Holt.

Dickson, Paul, and Thomas B. Allen. 2004. *The Bonus Army: An American Epic*. New York: Walker and Company.

Donovan, M. Suzanne, and John D. Bransford, eds. 2005. *How Students Learn: History in the Classroom*. Washington, DC: The National Academies Press.

Drake, Frederick, and Sarah Drake Brown. 2003. "A Systemic Approach to Improve Students' Historical Thinking." *The History Teacher* 36 (4): 465–489.

Drake, Frederick, and Lynn Nelson. 2005. *Engagement in Teaching History: Theory and Practices for Middle and Secondary Teachers*. Upper Saddle River, NJ: Pearson.

Eisenhower, Dwight D. 1967. *At Ease: Stories I Tell to Friends*. Garden City, NY: Doubleday.

Ellis, Richard. 2007. *To the Flag: The Unlikely History of the Pledge of Allegiance*. Lawrence: University Press of Kansas.

Evans, Ronald. 2004. *The Social Studies Wars: What Shall We Teach the Children?* New York: Teachers College Press.

Farkas, Steve, and Jean Johnson. 1998. *A Lot to Be Thankful For: What Parents Want Children to Learn About America*. Washington, DC: Public Agenda.

Fertig, Gary. 2005. "Teaching Elementary Students How to Interpret the Past." *The Social Studies* 96 (1): 2–8.

FitzGerald, Frances. 1980. *America Revised: What History Textbooks Have Taught Our Children About Their Country and How and Why Those Textbooks Have Changed in Different Decades*. New York: Vintage Books.

Foner, Eric. 1988. *Reconstruction: America's Unfinished Revolution, 1863–1877*. New York: HarperCollins.

Foner, Philip. 1977. *The Great Labor Uprising of 1877*. New York: Monad.

Foster, Stuart. 2001. "Historical Empathy in Theory and Practice: Some Final Thoughts." In *Historical Empathy and Perspective Taking in the Social Studies*, ed. O. L. Davis, Elizabeth Ann Yeager, and Stuart J. Foster. Lanham, MD: Rowman & Littlefield.

Fragnoli, Kristi. 2005. "Historical Inquiry in a Methods Classroom: Examining Our Beliefs and Shedding Our Old Ways." *The Social Studies* 96 (6): 6247–6251.

Frankel, Noralee, and Peter Stearns. 2004. "The Development of Benchmarks for Professional Development in the Teaching of History as a Discipline." *AHA Perspectives* (April): 41–47.

French, Scot. 2004. *The Rebellious Slave: Nat Turner in American Memory*. New York: Houghton Mifflin.

Gabella, Marcy. 1994. "Beyond the Looking Glass: Bringing Students into the Conversation of Historical Inquiry." *Theory and Research in Social Education* 22 (3): 340–363.

Gaddis, John Lewis. 1997. *We Now Know: Rethinking Cold War History*. Oxford: Clarendon Press.

Gagnon, Paul, ed. 1989. *Historical Literacy: The Case for History in American Education*. Boston: Houghton Mifflin.

———. 2003. *Educating Democracy: State Standards to Ensure a Civic Core*. Washington, DC: The Albert Shanker Institute.

Gardner, William, Robert Beery, James R. Olson, and Kenneth Rood. 1970. *Selected Case Studies in American History,* Vol. 2. Boston: Allyn and Bacon.

Gerwin, David, and Jack Zevin. 2003. Teaching United States History as Mystery. Portsmouth, NH: Heinemann.

Gillett, Sylvia. 1991. "Camden Yards and the Strike of 1877." In *The Baltimore Book: New Views of Local History*, ed. Elizabeth Fee, Linda Shopes, and Linda Zeidman. Philadelphia: Temple University Press.

Goodland, John. 1984. *A Place Called School: Prospects for the Future*. New York: McGraw-Hill.

Gough, Robert. 2004. "What We Should Know About Precollegiate Learning." *AHA Perspectives* (January): 37–39.

Grant, S. G. 2003. *History Lessons: Teaching, Learning, and Testing in U.S. High School Classrooms*. Mahwah, NJ: Lawrence Erlbaum.

———, ed. 2006. *Measuring History: Cases of State-Level Testing Across the United States*. Greenwich, CT: Information Age.

Green, S. 1994. "The Problems of Learning to Think Like a Historian: Writing History in the Culture of the Classroom." *Educational Psychologist* 29: 89–96.

Greenberg, Kenneth. 2003. "Name, Face, Body." In *Nat Turner: A Slave Rebellion in History and Memory*, ed. Kenneth Greenberg. New York: Oxford University Press.

Grossman, Pamela. 1991. "What Are We Talking About Anyway? Content Knowledge of Secondary English Teachers." *Advances in Research on Teaching* 2: 245–264.

Hall, Jacquelyn Dowd. 2005. "The Long Civil Rights Movement and the Political Uses of the Past." *Journal of American History* 91 (4): 1233–1263.

Hall, Stanley G. 1989. *Methods of Teaching and Studying History*. Boston: DC Heath.

Hampel, Robert. 1985. "Too Much Is Too Little." *Social Education* 49 (5): 563–565.

Hartzler-Miller, Cindy. 2001. "Making Sense of the 'Best Practice' in Teaching History." *Theory and Research in Social Education* 2 (4): 672–695.

Hertzberg, Hazel. 1985. "Students, Methods, and Materials of Instruction." In *History in the Schools*, ed. Matthew Downey. National Council for the Social Studies (Bulletin 74): 25–40.

Hicks, David, Jeff Carroll, and Peter Doolittle. 2004. "Teaching the Mystery of History." *Social Studies and the Young Learner* 16 (3): 14–16.

Hicks, David, Peter Doolittle, and Thomas Ewing. 2004. "The SCIM-C Strategy: Expert Historians, Historical Inquiry, and Multimedia." *Social Education* 68 (3): 221–225.

Higginson, Thomas Wentworth. 1885. "Why Do Children Dislike History?" In *Methods of Teaching History*, ed. G. Stanley Hall. Boston: Ginn, Heath, and Company.

Historical Inquiry: Scaffolding Wise Practices in the History Classroom. www.historicalinquiry.com/inquiry/index.cfm.

Historical Thinking Matters. www.historicalthinkingmatters.org.

The History Project. 2006. University of California, Davis. http://historyproject.ucdavis.edu/pdfs/Process_of_Historical_Investigation.pdf.

Holt, Thomas. 1990. *Thinking Historically: Narrative, Imagination, and Understanding*. New York: College Entrance Examination Board.

Hoover, Herbert. 1932. The President's News Conference, July 29, 1932. The American Presidency Project. http://www.presidency.ucsb.edu/ws/index.php?pid=23187.

———. 1952. *The Memoirs of Herbert Hoover: The Cabinet and Presidency, 1920–1933*. New York: Macmillan.

Horton, Paul. 2000. "A Model for Teaching Secondary History: The Case of Fort Pillow." *The History Teacher* 33 (2): 175–182.

Howard, James, and Thomas Mendenhall. 1982. *Making History Come Alive: The Place of History in the Schools. Report of the History Commission of the Council for Basic Education*. Washington, DC: The Council for Basic Education.

Howe, Irving, and Lewis Coser. 1974. *The American Communist Party: A Critical History*. New York: Da Capo Press.

Hughes, John. 1986. *Ferris Bueller's Day Off*. DVD. Hollywood, CA: Paramount Pictures.

Hunt, Martin. 2000. "Teaching Historical Significance." In *Issues in History Teaching*, ed. James Arthur and Robert Phillips. London: Routledge.

Husbands, Chris. 1996. *What Is History Teaching? Language, Ideas and Meaning in Learning About the Past*. Buckingham, England: Open University Press.

Hynd, Cynthia 1999. "Teaching Students to Think Critically Using Multiple Texts in History," *Journal of Adolescent & Adult Literacy* 42 (6): 428–436.

Inman, Mason. 2006. "Pluto Not a Planet, Astronomers Rule." *National Geographic News*. http://news.nationalgeographic.com/news/2006/08/060824-pluto-planet.html.

Jensen, Eric. 2005. *Teaching with the Brain in Mind*. 2nd ed. Alexandria, VA: Association for Supervision and Curriculum Development.

Kaufman, Burton. 1999. *The Korean Conflict*. Westport, CT: Greenwood Press.

Kennedy, David. 1999. *Freedom from Fear: The American People in Depression and War, 1929–1945*. New York: Oxford University Press.

Klehr, Harvey, and John Earl Haynes. 1992. *The American Communist Movement: Storming Heaven Itself*. New York: Twayne.

Klehr, Harvey, John Earl Haynes, and Fridrikh Lorevich Firsov. 1995. *The Secret World of American Communism*. New Haven, CT: Yale University Press.

Kobrin, David. 1996. *Beyond the Textbook: Teaching History Using Documents and Primary Sources*. Portsmouth, NH: Heinemann.

Lattimer, Heather. 2008. "Challenging History: Essential Questions in the Social Studies Classroom." *Social Education* 72 (6): 326–329.

Lee, Peter J. 2005. "Putting Principles into Practice: Understanding History." In *How Students Learn: History in the Classroom*, ed. M. Suzanne Donovan and John D. Bransford. Washington, DC: The National Academies Press.

Lesh, Bruce. 1999. "Using Primary Sources to Teach the Rail Strike of 1877." *OAH Magazine of History* 13 (4): 38–47.

———. 2002. *Primary Sources in United States History: Reconstruction, 1865–1877*. Villa Maria, PA: The Center for Learning.

———. 2004. *Primary Sources in United States History: Jacksonian America, 1820–1840*. Villa Maria, PA: The Center for Learning.

———. 2005. *Primary Sources in United States History: America and the Age of Imperialism, 1898–1920*. Villa Maria, PA: The Center for Learning.

———. 2008. "Limited War or a Rollback of Communism? Truman, MacArthur, and the Korean Conflict." *OAH Magazine of History* 22 (4): 47–53.

Lévesque, Stéphane. 2008. *Thinking Historically: Educating Students for the Twenty-First Century*. Toronto: University of Toronto Press.

Levstik, Linda. 1997. "'Any History Is Someone's History': Listening to Multiple Voices from the Past." *Social Education* 61 (1): 48–51.

Levstik, Linda S., and Keith C. Barton. 2001. *Doing History: Investigating History in Elementary and Middle Schools*. Mahwah, NJ: Lawrence Erlbaum.

Liebovich, Louis. 1990. *Press Reactions the Bonus Army of 1932: A Re-evaluation of the Impact of an American Tragedy*. Columbia, SC: Association for Education in Journalism and Mass Media.

Linden, Glen. 1972. "Teaching History Through Inquiry: The S.M.U. Experiment." *The History Teacher* 5 (2): 28–33.

Linenthal, Edward, and Tom Engelhardt. 1996. *History Wars: The* Enola Gay *and Other Battles for the American Past*. New York: Owl Books.

Lisio, Donald J. 1974. *The President and Protest: Hoover, Conspiracy, and the Bonus Riot*. Columbia: University of Missouri Press.

Loewen, James. 1995. *Lies My Teacher Told Me: Everything Your American History Textbook Got Wrong*. New York: Touchstone.

———. 2009. *Teaching What Really Happened: How to Avoid the Tyranny of Textbooks and Get Students Excited About Doing History*. New York: Teachers College Press.

Lortie, Daniel. 1975. *School Teacher: A Sociological Study*. Chicago: University of Chicago Press.

Lowenthal, David. 1985. *The Past Is a Foreign Country*. Cambridge, England: Cambridge University Press.

———. 1996. *The Heritage Crusade and the Spoils of History*. New York: Viking.

MacArthur, Douglas. 1951. "Farewell Address to Congress." http://www.americanrhetoric.com/speeches/douglasmacarthurfarewelladdress.htm.

———. 1964. *Reminiscences*. New York: McGraw-Hill.

Mandell, Nikki. 2008. "Thinking Like a Historian: A Framework for Teaching and Learning." *OAH Magazine of History* 22 (2): 55–59.

Mandell, Nikki, and Bobbie Malone. 2007. *Thinking Like a Historian: Rethinking History Instruction—A Framework to Enhance and Improve Teaching and Learning*. Madison: Wisconsin Historical Society Press.

Marchand, Roland. 1999. "Further Comment on Daniel D. Trifan's 'Active Learning a Critical Examination.'" In *Perspectives on Teaching Innovations: Teaching to Think Historically: A Collection of Essays from Perspectives, the Newsletter of the American Historical Association*, ed. Susan Gillespie. Washington, DC: American Historical Association.

Martin, Daisy. 2008. "From Lecture to Lesson Through 'Opening Up the Textbook.'" *OAH Newsletter* 36 (4): 9–11.

Martin, Daisy, and Chauncey Monte-Sano. 2008. "Inquiry, Controversy, and Ambiguous Texts: Learning to Teach Historical Thinking." In *History Education 101: The Past, Present, and Future of Teacher Preparation*, ed. Wilson J. Warren and D. Antonia Cantu. Charlotte, NC: Information Age.

Martin, Daisy, and Sam Wineburg. 2008. "Seeing Thinking on the Web." *The History Teacher* 41 (3): 305–319.

Marzano, Robert, Debra J. Pickering, and Jane Pollock. 2001. *Classroom Instruction That Works: Research-Based Strategies for Increasing Student Achievement*. Alexandria, VA: Association for Supervision and Curriculum Development.

Mayer, Robert. 1998. "Connecting Narrative and Historical Thinking: A Research-Based Approach to Teaching History." *Social Education* 62 (2):97–100.

———. 1999. "Use the Story of Anne Hutchinson to Teach Historical Thinking." *The Social Studies* 90 (3): 105–110.

———. 2006. "Learning to Teach Young People How to Think Historically: A Case Study of One Student Teacher's Experience." *The Social Studies* 97 (2): 69–76.

McCullough, David. 1992. *Truman*. New York: Simon and Schuster.

McDiarmid, G. Williamson, and Peter Vinten-Johansen. 2000. "A Catwalk Across the Great Divide: Redesigning the History Teaching Methods Course." In *Knowing, Teaching, and Learning History: National and International*

Perspectives, ed. P. Stearns, Peter Sexias, and Sam Wineburg. New York: New York University Press.

McKeown, Margaret, Isabel Beck, and Jo Worthy. 1993. "Grappling with Text Ideas: Questioning the Author." *The Reading Teacher* 46: 560–566.

McNeil, Linda M. 1988. *Contradictions of Control: School Structure and School Knowledge.* New York: Routledge.

Miller, James R., and James Hart. 1973. "History as Inquiry." *The History Teacher* 6 (3): 353–364.

Moreau, Joseph. 2003. *School Book Nation: Conflicts over American History Textbooks from the Civil War to the Present.* Ann Arbor: University of Michigan Press.

Mueller, John. 1973. *War, Presidents and Public Opinion.* New York: John Wiley.

Nash, Gary. 1997. "Reflections on the National History Standards." *National Forum* 77: 14–18.

Nash, Gary, Charlotte Crabtree, and Ross E. Dunn. 1997. *History on Trial: Culture Wars and the Teaching of the Past.* New York: Vintage Books.

National Center for Education Statistics. 1998. *1994 NAEP U.S. History Group Assessment.* Washington, DC: National Center for Education Statistics, United States Department of Education.

———. 2002. *The Nation's Report Card: U.S. History 2001.* Washington, DC: National Center for Education Statistics, United States Department of Education.

———. 2006. *The Nation's Report Card: U.S. History 2006. National Assessment of Educational Progress at Grades 4, 8, and 12.* Washington, DC: National Center for Education Statistics, United States Department of Education.

National Center for History in the Schools. 1996. *National Standards for History, Revised Edition.* Los Angeles: NCHS.

nbcnewyork.com. 2008. "Black Students Bound, Humiliated in Slavery Lesson: White Teacher Selects Black Students to Act Like Slaves for a Class Lesson." http://www.nbcnewyork.com/news/local-beat/Black-Students-Bound-Humiliated-in-Classroom-Slavery-Lesson.html.

Neal, Anne, and Jerry Martin. 2000. *Losing America's Memory: Historical Illiteracy in the 21st Century.* A Report of the American Council of Trustees and Alumni Washington, DC.

Nishi, Dennis, ed. 2003. *Korean War: Interpreting Primary Documents Series.* San Diego: Greenhaven.

Nokes, Jeffrey, Janice Dole, and Douglas Hacker. 2007. "Teaching High School Students to Use Heuristics While Reading Historical Texts." *Journal of Educational Psychology* 99 (3): 492–504.

Novick, Peter. 1988. *That Noble Dream: The "Objectivity Question" and the American Historical Profession.* Cambridge: Cambridge University Press.

Oberly, James. 1997. "Comment on Daniel D. Trifan's 'Active Learning: a Critical Examination.'" In *Perspectives on Teaching Innovations: Teaching to Think Historically. A Collection of Essays from Perspectives, the Newsletter of the American Historical Association*, ed. Susan Gillespie. Washington, DC: American Historical Association.

Ogden, Nancy, Catherine Perkins, and David Donahue. 2008. "Not a Peculiar Institution: Challenging Students' Assumptions About Slavery in U.S. History." *The History Teacher* 41 (4): 470–488.

Onosko, Joseph. 1991. "Barriers to the Promotion of Higher Order Thinking Skills in Social Studies." *Theory and Research in Social Education* 19 (Fall): 341–366.

Painter, Nell Irvin. 1987. *Standing at Armageddon: The United States, 1877–1919.* New York: W. W. Norton.

Patrick, John J., and Sharryl Davis Hawke. 1982. "Social Studies Curriculum Materials." In *The Current State of Social Studies: A Report of Project SPAN,* ed. Project SPAN Staff. Boulder, CO: Social Science Education Consortium.

Patterson, James. 1996. *Grand Expectations: The United States, 1945–1974.* New York: Oxford University Press.

Paxton, Richard. 1997. "Someone with Like a Life Wrote It": The Effects of a Visible Author on High School History Students." *Journal of Educational Psychology* 89: 235–250.

———. 1999. "A Deafening Silence: History Textbooks and the Students Who Read Them." *Review of Educational Research* 69: 315–337.

Percoco, James. 1998. *A Passion for the Past: Creative Teaching of U.S. History.* Portsmouth, NH: Heinemann.

Perkins, David. 1992. *Smart Schools: From Training Memories to Educating Minds.* New York: The Free Press.

Perret, Geoffrey. 1996. *Old Soldiers Never Die: The Life of Douglas MacArthur.* New York: Random House.

Pierce, Bessie L. 1926. *Public Opinion and the Teaching of History in the United States.* New York: Alfred A. Knopf.

Ragland, Rachel, and Kelly A. Woestman, eds. 2009. *The Teaching American History Project: Lessons for History Educators and Historians.* New York: Routledge.

Ravitch, Diane, and Chester E. Finn, Jr. 1987. *"What Do Our 17-Year-Olds Know?" A Report on the First National Assessment of History and Literature.* New York: Harper and Row.

Reisman, Avishag, and Sam Wineburg. 2008. "Teaching the Skill of Contextualizing in History." *The Social Studies* 99 (5): 202–207.

Robelen, Erik. 2010. "History a Flash Point as States Debate Standards." *Education Week*, March 25.

Roosevelt, Theodore. 1985. *Theodore Roosevelt: An Autobiography.* [Reprint.] New York: Da Capo Press.

Rosenzweig, Linda, and Thomas P. Weinland. 1986. "New Directions for the History Curriculum: A Challenge for the 1980s." *The History Teacher* 19 (2): 262–277.

Rosenzweig, Roy, and David Thelen. 1998. *The Presence of the Past: Popular Uses of History in American Life.* New York: Columbia University Press.

Rothstein, Richard. 2004. "We Are Not Ready to Assess History Performance." *The Journal of American History* 90 (4): 1381–1391.

Sanchez, Tony. 2006. "The Triangle Fire: A Simulation-Based Lesson." *The Social Studies* (March/April): 62–68.

Sandler, Stanley. 1999. *The Korean War: No Victors, No Vanquished.* Lexington: The University Press of Kentucky.

Sandwell, Ruth W. 2003. "Reading Beyond Bias: Using Historical Documents in the Secondary Classroom." *McGill Journal of Education* 38 (1): 168–186.

———. 2005. "School History Versus the Historians." *International Journal of Social Education* 20 (1): 9–15.

Schaller, Michael. 1989. *Douglas MacArthur: The Far Eastern General.* New York: Oxford University Press.

Schick, James B. 1991. "What Do Students Really Think of History?" *The History Teacher* 24 (3): 331–342.

Schur, Brodsky Joan. 2007. *Eyewitness to the Past: Strategies for Teaching American History in Grades 5–12.* Portland, ME: Stenhouse.

Sellers, Charles. 1969. "Is History on the Way Out of the Schools and Do Historians Care?" *Social Education* (May): 509–569.

Sevareid, Eric. 1963. "The Man Who Invented Panama." *American Heritage* 14 (5). Available online at http://www.americanheritage.com/articles/magazine/ah/1963/5/1963_5_106_print.shtml.

Sexias, Peter. 1993. "The Community of Inquiry as a Basis for Knowledge and Learning: The Case of History." *American Educational Research Journal* 30 (2): 305–324.

———. 1997. "Mapping the Terrain of Historical Significance." *Social Education* 61 (1): 22–27.

Shanahan, Cynthia. 2003. *Using Multiple Texts to Teach Content*. Naperville, IL: Learning Point.

Shaver, James P., O. L. Davis, Jr., and Suzanne Helburn. 1979. "The Status of Social Studies Education: Impressions from Three NSF Studies." *Social Education* (February): 150–153.

Shemilt, Dennis. 1980. *History 13–16: Evaluation Study*. New York: HarperCollins.

———. 1984. "Beauty and the Philosopher: Empathy in History and the Classroom." In *Learning History*, ed. A. K. Dickinson, P. J. Lee, and P. J. Rogers. London: Heinemann.

Shermis, Samuel. 1967. "Six Myths Which Delude History Teachers." *Phi Delta Kappan* (September): 9–12.

Sipress, Joel. 2008. "Why Students Don't Get Evidence and What We Can Do About It." *History Teacher* 37 (3): 351–364.

Smith, Robert. 1982. *MacArthur in Korea: The Naked Emperor*. New York: Simon and Schuster.

Spoehr, Kathryn, and Luther W. Spoehr. 1994. "Learning to Think Historically." *Educational Psychologist* 29: 71–77.

Stacy, Jason. 2009. "The Guide on the Stage: In Defense of Good Lecturing in the History Classroom." *Social Education* 73 (6): 275–278.

Stahl, Stephen, Cynthia Hynd, Bruce Britton, Mary McNish, and Dennis Bosquet. 1996. "What Happens When Students Read Multiple Source Documents in History?" *Reading Research Quarterly* 31 (4): 430–456.

Stahl, Stephen A., Cynthia R. Hynd, Shawn M. Glynn, and Martha Carr. 1995. "Beyond Reading to Learn: Developing Content and Disciplinary Knowledge Through Texts." In *Developing Engaged Readers in Home and School Communities*, ed. P. Afflerbach, L. Baker, and D. Reinking. Hillsdale, NJ: Erlbaum.

Stahl, Stephen, and Cynthia Shanahan. 2004. "Learning to Think Like a Historian: Disciplinary Knowledge Through Critical Analysis of Multiple Source Documents. In *Adolescent Literacy Research and Practice*, ed. T. L. Jetton and J. A. Dole. New York: Guilford Press.

The Stanford History Education Group. 2010. www.sheg.stanford.edu.

Stearns, Peter. 1993. *Meaning over Memory: Recasting the Teaching of Culture and History*. Chapel Hill: University of North Carolina Press.

———. 1996. "A Cease-fire for History." *The History Teacher* 30 (1): 65–81.

Stockley, David. 1983. "Empathetic Reconstruction in History and History Teaching." *History and Theory* 22 (4): 50–65.

Symcox, Linda. 2002. *Whose History: The Struggle for National Standards in American Classrooms*. New York: Teachers College Press.

Thornton, Stephen. 2005. *Teaching Social Studies that Matters: Curriculum for Active Learning*. New York: Teachers College Press.

Trifan, Daniel. 1999. "Active Learning: A Critical Examination." In *Perspectives on Teaching Innovations: Teaching to Think Historically. A Collection of Essays from Perspectives, the Newsletter of the American Historical Association*, ed. Susan Gillespie. Washington, DC: American Historical Association.

Truman, Harry. 1951. "Radio Report to the American People on Korea and U.S. Policy." April 11. http://www.trumanlibrary.org/whistlestop/ study_collections/koreanwar/index.php?action=sss.

U.S. Department of Education. 2010. "Teaching American History." http://www2.ed.gov/programs/teachinghistory/index.html.

van Hover, Stephanie, and Walter F. Heinecke. 2005. "The Impact of Accountability Reform on the 'Wise Practice' of Secondary History Teachers: The Virginia Experience." In *Wise Social Studies Teaching in an Age of High Stakes Testing: Essays on Classroom Practices and Possibilities,* ed. Elizabeth Anne Yeager and O. L. Davis. Greenwich, CT: Information Age.

van Hover, Stephanie, David Hicks, and William Irwin. 2007. "Beginning Teachers Thinking Historically? Negotiating Between the Context of Virginia's High Stakes Tests." *International Journal of Social Education* 22 (1): 85–114.

VanSledright, Bruce. 1997. "Can More Be Less? The Depth-Breadth Dilemma in Teaching American History." *Social Education* 61 (1): 38–41.

———. 2002. *In Search of America's Past: Learning to Read History in Elementary School.* New York: Teachers College Press.

———. 2004. "What Does It Mean to Think Historically . . . and How Do You Teach It?" *Social Education* 68 (3): 230–233.

———. 2008. "Narratives of Nation-State, Historical Knowledge, and School History Education." *Review of Research in Education* 32 (February): 1–39, 109–146.

———. 2011. *The Challenge of Rethinking History Education: On Practices, Theories, and Policy.* New York: Routledge.

Voss, James. 1998. "Issues in the Learning of History." *Issues in Education* 4 (2): 163–210.

Warren, Wilson, and D. Antonia Cantu, eds. 2008. *History Education 101: The Past, Present, and Future of Teacher Preparation.* Charlotte, NC: Information Age.

Weintraub, Stanley. 2000. *MacArthur's War: Korea and the Undoing of an American Hero.* New York: The Free Press.

Weiss, Iris. 1978. *Report of the 1977 National Survey of Science, Mathematics, and Social Studies Education.* Research Triangle Park: North Carolina Center for Educational Research and Evaluation.

Westoff, Laura M. 2009. "Lost in Translation: The Use of Primary Sources in Teaching History." In *The Teaching American History Project: Lessons for History Educators and Historians*, ed. Rachel Ragland and Kelly Woestman. New York: Routledge.

Whittington, Dale. 1991. "What Have 17-Year-Olds Known in the Past?" *American Educational Research Journal* 28 (4): 759–780.

Wiggins, Grant, and Jay McTighe. 2005. *Understanding by Design.* Expanded 2nd ed. Upper Saddle River, NJ: Pearson.

Wiley, Jennifer, and James F. Voss. 1999. "Constructing Arguments from Multiple Sources: Tasks That Promote Understanding and Not Just Memory for Text." *Journal of Educational Psychology* 91 (2): 301–311.

Willingham, Daniel T. 2009. *Why Don't Students Like School? A Cognitive Scientist Answers Questions About How the Mind Works and What It Means for the Classroom.* New York: Jossey-Bass.

Wilson, Suzanne. 2001. "Research on History Teaching." *Handbook on Teaching.* 4th ed., ed. Virginia Richardson. Washington, DC: American Educational Research Association.

Wilson, Suzanne, and Sam Wineburg. 1988. "Peering at History Through Different Lenses: The Role of Disciplinary Perspectives in Teaching History." *Teachers College Record* 89 (4): 525–539.

Wineburg, Sam. 1991a. "Historical Problem Solving: A Study of the Cognitive Processes Used in the Evaluation of Documentary and Pictorial Evidence." *Journal of Educational Psychology* 83: 73–87.

———. 1991b. "On the Reading of Historical Texts: Notes on the Breach Between School and Academy." *American Educational Research Journal* 28: 495–519.

———. 2001. *Historical Thinking and Other Unnatural Acts: Charting the Future of Teaching the Past.* Philadelphia: Temple University Press.

———. 2004. "Crazy for History." *The Journal of American History* 90 (4): 1401–1414.

Wineburg, Sam, and Daisy Martin. 2009. "Tampering with History: Adapting Primary Sources for Struggling Readers." *Social Education* 73 (5): 212–216.

Wineburg, Sam, Susan Mosberg, Dan Porat, and Ariel Duncan. 2007. "Forrest Gump and the Future of Teaching the Past." *Phi Delta Kappan* (November): 168–177.

Winks, Robin, ed. 1968. *The Historian as Detective: Essays on Evidence.* New York: Harper and Row.

Wyoming Tails and Trails. 2010. Custer and the Battle of the Little Bighorn. www.wyomingtalesandtrails.com/custer6.html.

Yeager, Elizabeth, and Stuart J. Foster. 2001. "The Role of Empathy in the Development of Historical Understanding." In *Historical Empathy and Perspective Taking in the Social Studies*, ed. O. L. Davis, Elizabeth Ann Yeager, and Stuart J. Foster. Lanham, MD: Rowman & Littlefield.

Yearley, Clifton K., Jr. 1956. "The Baltimore and Ohio Railroad Strike of 1877." *Maryland Historical Magazine* 61 (3): 188–211.

Index

Page numbers followed by *f* indicate figures.

Page 17: Figure 1.1—Historical Thinking Skills used with permission of National Center for History in the Schools, UCLA. http://nchs.ucla.edu.

Page 29: Figure 2.1—"With Bible and Sword," *The Nat Turner Slave Insurrection* by Roy F. Johnson, Johnson Publishing Company, 1966.

Page 31: Figure 2.2—*Nat Turner's Slave Rebellion* © 2006 by Capstone Press. All rights reserved.

Page 32: Figure 2.3—NAT TURNER (1800–1831). American slave leader. Wood engraving, 19th century. Image # 0003742. © The Granger Collection, New York. Used with permission.

Page 55: Figure 3.1—PANAMA CANAL CARTOON, 1903. The Man Behind the Egg. American cartoon, 1903, giving Philippe-Jean Bunau-Varilla (left) credit for the negotiations by which President Theodore Roosevelt acquired the Panama Canal Zone for the United States. Image # 0058863. © The Granger Collection, New York. Used with permission.

Page 60: Figure 3.2—[Theodore Roosevelt, head-and-shoulders portrait, facing front] courtesy of the Library of Congress, LC-USZ62-13026.

Page 81: Figure 4.1—"Sixth Regiment Fighting Its Way Through Baltimore" (August 11, 1877) cover courtesy of HarpWeek.

Page 83: Figure 4.2—Rail strike battle image courtesy of the Ohio Historical Society.

Page 84: Figure 4.3—"The Frenzy, and What Came of It" (August 18, 1877) cover courtesy of HarpWeek.

Page 85: Figure 4.4—Gatling Gun Company letter from the Collection of the B&O Railroad Museum.

Page 86: Figure 4.5—Hayes letter from the Collection of the B&O Railroad Museum.

Page 89: Figure 4.7—"Statement of Losses and Damages during Strike in July 1877" from *Encountering Maryland's Past* Primary Source Kit. Courtesy of the Maryland Historical Society.

Page 97: Figure 5.1—[Encampment of shanties built by Brooklyn veterans in the Bonus Expeditionary Forces in Washington, D.C.] courtesy of the Library of Congress, Theodor Horydczak Collection, LC-DIG-ppmsca-05576.

Page 99: Figure 5.2—[Encampment built by veterans in the Bonus Expeditionary Forces in Washington, D.C.] courtesy of the Library of Congress, Theodor Horydczak Collection, LC-DIG-ppmsca-05577.

Page 102: Figure 5.3—[Bonus veterans battle with Washington police officers] courtesy of the Library of Congress, New York World-Telegram and the Sun Newspaper Photograph Collection, LC-USZ62-115570.

Page 118: Figure 6.2—[Southington, Connecticut. School children pledging their allegiance to the flag] courtesy of the Library of Congress, LC-USW3-041733-E.

Page 119: Figure 6.3—Pledge of Allegiance illustration courtesy of the Pacific Grove Museum of Natural History (www.pgmuseum.org).

Page 121: Figure 6.4—LITTLE BIGHORN, 1876. Custer's Last Fight: lithograph, 1895, after the painting by Cassilly Adams. Image # 0026004. © The Granger Collection, New York. Used with permission.

Page 122: Figure 6.5—"Battle of the Little Big Horn" by Kicking Bear. Muslin painting, courtesy Braun Research Library, Southwest Museum, Los Angeles, CA. Image ID number: 1026.G.1.

Page 142: Figure 7.1a—[Rev. Martin Luther King, head-and-shoulders portrait, facing right, speaking at a rally in Crawfordville, Georgia] courtesy of the Library of Congress, LC-USZ62-122992.

Page 142: Figure 7.1b—[Rosa Parks mug shot] courtesy of Montgomery, AL, Sheriff's Department.

Page 143: Figure 7.1c—[Civil rights march on Washington, D.C.] courtesy of the Library of Congress, LC-DIG-ppmsca-03128.

Page 144: Figure 7.2—"Shelley House," photograph by Geralf L. Gilleard. Courtesy of the U.S. National Park Service.

Page 158: Figure 8.1—[Stowage of the British slave ship Brookes under the regulated slave trade act of 1788] courtesy of the Library of Congress, LC-USZ62-44000 and LC-USZ62-34160.

Page 172: Figure 8.4—[President Truman Wearing General MacArthur's Hat] courtesy of the Library of Congress, LC-USZ62-69946.

Page 172: Figure 8.5—FIRING OF MACARTHUR. American cartoon by L. J. Roche, 1951, showing President Harry S. Truman, Secretary of State Dean Acheson, and the Pentagon in the proverbial frying pan over Truman's decision to remove General Douglas MacArthur from his post as supreme commander of U.N. forces in Korea. Image # 0033645. © The Granger Collection, New York. Used with permission.

Page 203: Figure 10.1—The Migration Series, Panel #1 © 2011 The Jacob and Gwendolyn Lawrence Foundation, Seattle / Artists Rights Society (ARS), New York.

Page 203: Figure 10.2—The Migration Series, Panel #45 © 2011 The Jacob and Gwendolyn Lawrence Foundation, Seattle / Artists Rights Society (ARS), New York.

Page 205: Figure 10.3—*Thomas Nast, His Period and His Pictures* (1904) by Albert Bigelow Paine. Chelsea House, New York.